Fiona Horne has been a practising Witch for 34 years. She is also a commercial pilot, best-selling author, rockstar and radio and television personality, world record sky diver, sailor, yoga instructor, spin instructor, humanitarian aid worker … Yes, she is living more than one dream! Fiona owns nothing except her freedom and her happiness, and is now a nomad and considers planet Earth her home.

Teen Witch *was originally published in 2004 as* Life's A Witch *in Australia and* Witchin': A Handbook for Teen Witches *in the UK/USA and was Fiona's third book. This extensively reworked and rewritten edition is now Fiona's 14th book.*

Also by Fiona Horne

The Art of Witch

The Naked Witch

The Magick of You Oracle Deck

Witch: A Personal Journey (The original! Still available through Penguin
Random House Australiain Kindle format)

Witch: A Magickal Year 20th Anniversary Edition (Harper Collins
International; available internationally in Kindle and also in paperback.
This book was originally written at 'Penrith', Mount Macedon, Victoria,
Australia and reworked, rewritten and re-edited 17 years later at 'Pelican
Heaven', St Thomas, US Virgin Islands, Malibu, California
and Melbourne, Australia.)

TEEN
MAGICK

WITCHCRAFT FOR A NEW
GENERATION

FIONA HORNE

ROCKPOOL

Some Wise Witchy Words

◇◇

The Craft of the Witch is creative and borne of wild places in
nature and inside the soul. Like any Craft that involves flames and sharp
objects, Witchcraft poses some inherent risk.

Always place a fireproof dish beneath candles and incense. Leave
clearance above and around flames. Do not place flammable objects
near flames and never leave flames or burning incense unattended.
Users of this book take full responsibility when using fire.

The author and publisher are not liable or responsible for any
outcome of magickal spells performed from this book or otherwise.
Readers agree to cast spells, work with fire, ingest herbs, soak in bath
salts, light candles and incense, channel deities and perform any and all
other magickal practices at their own risk.

Readers accept full personal risk and responsibility for the outcome,
consequence and magick of any spells they cast.

Blessings to you as you forge your own unique magickal journey …

THANK YOU!

Lots of love and gratitude to my Rockpool Publishing family, Lisa Hanrahan, Paul Dennett, Andrés Engracia, Dana Brown and Emily Van Arendonk … and my divine editor, Katie Day.

Heartfelt thanks to Michael and Sue Gudinski and David Smith for their generosity and friendship from the original writing sessions of this book. And deep gratitude always to Liam Cyfrin, who supplied his advice, wisdom and insight so generously twenty years ago! Blessed be!

Thank you also to Jessica of the Nightstar Teen Pagan Network, who agreed to be interviewed for the original version of this book and whose interview stands the test of time. And much love and gratitude to all the teens who contributed emails, questions and comments for this edition.

Finally thank you to all the real life Goddesses I am so blessed to know, including: Sarah, Dannii, Emily, Jessica, Beki, Shari, Lydia, Linda, Tania, Susan, Ginger, Pam, Denise, Kiki, Carlotta, Jet'aime and Shelleylyn.

A Rockpool book
PO Box 252
Summer Hill, NSW 2130
Australia
rockpoolpublishing.co
Follow us! f 🅾 rockpoolpublishing
Tag your images with #rockpoolpublishing

First published in 2000 as *Life's a Witch! A Handbook for Teen Witches*
by Random House Australia ISBN 9781740510226

Copyright text © Fiona Horne 2021
Copyright design © Rockpool Publishing 2021
Published in 2021 by Rockpool Publishing

ISBN 978-1-925924-41-1

Design by Dana Brown, Rockpool Publishing
Cover Cocept by Jessica Le
Edited by Katie Evans

Printed and bound in China
10 9 8 7 6 5 4 3 2

Contents

Spell Index

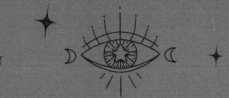

For my father, Kevin Horne

Dad, I know I was a handful as a teenager and you were tough on me.
But because of you I learned to work hard and not give up . . .
and I achieved extraordinary life experiences.
Thank you for everything — and may you rest in beautiful peace.
– F. H.

introduction

Twenty years ago, Teen Witches and would-be Witches seemed to be everywhere … and they were. But 20 years ago there was also no social media, no #WitchesofInstagram … no reality TV. Now Teen Witches meet after school in groups or get online for full moon rituals in different towns or countries via Zoom. Or they find time alone to cast spells to help them pass tests, to attract boyfriends or girlfriends, or to help them get along with their parents. Modern Teen Witches are taking selfies of their magickal work and of them looking 'Witchy', or taking photos of their favourite oracle-card spreads and hashtagging them to attract more followers on Instagram (where the biggest wave of online Witches currently congregates). Or they may tune into their favourite magickal podcast, like Tonya Brown's 'The Witch Daily Show' and Lucy Cavendish's 'The WitchCast'. Or they might make a Witchy playlist on Spotify and promote it to get followers (check out my current fave 'The Season of the Witch'). And then there are the Moon Children – not all are avowed Witches but all are making magick with moon worship, checking esoteric moon reports daily and arranging their social calendars and school commitments according to the phases of the moon.

But there is one other thing that has massively changed for the modern Teen Witch: they are no longer occult (meaning 'secret' or hidden). The modern Teen Witch is OUT LOUD and PROUD. And EVERYWHERE. However, this also puts more pressure on them to keep up with everyone else, to have the most followers on Instagram or Snapchat, the most influence amongst their peers and the pressure to have everything perfect – because they know they have the power. Never have Witches been so surrounded by like-souled individuals, yet often feel so alone and stressed.

Maybe that is the symptom of our hectic modern life – 20 years ago the human population of the world was 6.042 billion; as of writing in 2021 it is now 7.8 billion.

Six of the seven continents in the world are heavily and permanently inhabited by humans. We are all over everything – and not to great effect in a lot of cases.

Teen Witches are now evolving in a world of concerns of climate, race, religion and politics. During the editing of this book the extraordinary events of COVID19 shut and locked down the world with no end in sight, and held individuals and communities accountable for each other in a way never before seen. On a global scale we became aware that the actions of one truly impact everyone … for better and for worse. During the lockdown we also witnessed nature taking a deep breath, as humans' heavy impact lessened. We saw dolphins returning to the canals of Venice, the peaks of the Himalayas visible for the first time in 30 years and the oceans blossom with fish.

The blessings of the extraordinary times of COVID19 are there if we are prepared to witness them, through the dust and veils of confusion and corruption. The brave Teen Witch questions everything ... which is how they become magickal in the first place.

The mainstream media, with its emphasis on everything wrong in the world and its attempts to garner more ratings by inciting intoxicating fear and drama into people's lives, would have the Teen Witch believe their future is doomed, but they are actually poised to make the most positive and far-reaching change in the way humans exist on the planet, and in the history of our species. At night, when other teens are out getting drunk or stoned, switching off from life, Teen Witches are out under the starry sky, turning on to the magick of Life.

Mass Media Madness

In all my books I have advised to not watch mainstream news and to not engage with advertising. Once a noble institution serving the community, mainstream media is now predominately driven by hidden corporate and political agendas fuelled by advertising revenue and aimed at making money and filling the pockets of a few, without caring about the trail of destruction in its wake. This is rapidly leading to decimation of the planet and all its inhabitants.

Teen Witches need to be aware of this insidious evil, educate themselves about it and not blindly accept and consume what is fed to them. I mean, isn't independence, spiritual and physical freedom, reverence for our sacred world and all its inhabitants what draws you to the path of the Witch?

You have already chosen the path less trod – don't be afraid to stand up, trust your gut and think and do what you know in your heart is right. The Teen Witch questions everything and then determines their own authentic truth; they know that, no matter what is going on in the crazy world of humans, moments spent in quiet reverence with nature allow them to know their true selves without question.

◇◇

When this book was originally written, a lot of Teen Witches were the children of those who got into the Craft back in the 80s when the Wiccan population of the world skyrocketed. It's now likely that most of today's Teen Witches are born of the 90s wave of Wiccan and spiritually identifying witches. Others come from more conventional families and have been inspired to explore Witchcraft by watching movies like *Practical Magic* and *The Craft*, or TV shows like *Charmed* (the 90s original version and now the rebooted version). The entertainment industry still deems the Witch as eminently entertaining and the remakes are even more popular than the originals. And whilst the majority of the characters in these shows are girls (Hollywood often misses the mark by a long shot in depicting Witchcraft as a girls-only club), people identifying as all genders know that they have an important place to fill in the Craft. Witchcraft is uniquely welcoming to the LGBTQIA communities because it encourages all individuals to explore their innate potential beyond gender, race and creed, for that matter. The great thing about Teen Witchcraft is that it's inclusive, empowering and positive, encourages confidence and boosts self-esteem. Teen Witchcraft strengthens an individual's respect and relationship with the earth, and their friends and family.

GENDER IDENTITY AND WITCHCRAFT

◇◇◇

Throughout this book the terms 'girl' and 'boy', 'her' and 'his' are used. As we evolve we are embracing the fact that many people don't necessarily identify as a binary male-female gender, irrespective of the physical reproductive system they were born with. Witchcraft, however, in its core principles, is a nature-worshipping spiritual path, which includes recognising the dualistic principle of divinity as it relates to human procreation. Sperm/egg, blade/chalice, Lord/Lady are all gender-specific interactive terms. Individual Teen Witches who are experiencing alternative gender identity understand that – as people who may identify as 'non-gender' or 'between gender' or 'non-physically determined gender' – Witches still recognise and venerate these foundational processes of creation literally and figuratively in our rituals and spells.

The LGBTQIA community finds acceptance and authentic spiritual self-expression in Witchcraft because it is an ever-evolving, inclusive spiritual path that reflects the experience of all who walk it. This is what makes it one of the most beautiful and relevant spiritual expressions of the human race.

All Witches, irrespective of the gender they identify as, and who they fall in love or bond physically with, can experience and work with the qualities and energies of feminine, masculine and everything and anything in between ... and even beyond! For more information see page 199.

◇◇◇

Some adults, including some older Witches, dismiss teens practising Witchcraft and put it all down to them going through a phase.

There's probably some truth in this – after all, some of the most strait-laced adults around today used to be hippies in the 60s or punks in the 70s, or grunge rockers in the 90s!

One theory of the derivation of the words 'Witch' and 'Wicca' is that they come from an old Anglo-Saxon word 'wicce', meaning wise, which raises the issue: 'Can a teen be wise?' Looking back at *my* teen years, I am sometimes horrified at the risks I took and the dangerous situations I put myself in; but somehow I escaped from harm. But if I had been practising Witchcraft I know for a fact that I wouldn't have found myself in those situations in the first place. You can't practise the Craft without picking up at least some of its wisdom, and so most Teen Witches are in a much stronger position than I was at their age. This is because Teen Witches respect the sacredness not only of all life, but particularly their own. They know that their lives, bodies, thoughts – the totality of their being – is sacred and powerful. They don't need to prove anything to anyone. Teen Witches trust their intuition and work to develop it and their personal power to be the best that they can be.

The Sacred Pentagram and its Symbolism

The five-pointed star is a sacred symbol of Witchcraft. After decades of contemplation and meditation on it I have come to experience it as a profound tool of wisdom in understanding the Witch's place in her magickal world. The four base points of the star relate to the sacred four elements: earth, air, fire and water. The fifth point at the top is 'Spirit' i.e. the human element. Whilst the fifth point is not superior to the other four elements, in our experience of this physical life it is powerful in that it determines how we experience the four elements weaving together and creating the world through which we walk our path. Another way of looking at it is to consider the following: 'The world answers according to the questions we ask of it.' When we work ritual and magickal spells we are 'visualising with Spirit' the way the world will reflect the efforts of our spells. This is wonderful and empowering to contemplate because it proves that when things are really tough, the challenge isn't a chance to show us how weak we are but instead how strong we can be. We can shape our world with our thoughts and dreams using the element of Spirit, and then apply ourselves to the other four physical elements by taking action. By 'acting practically and thinking magickally', the Teen Witch is empowered to experience their best life.

◇◇◇

For many of today's teens, their fascination with the Craft isn't going to be 'just a phase'; rather, it is the beginning of a lifelong spiritual and magickal adventure. The teenage years are an ideal time to begin the study of Witchcraft. Young minds are loaded with passion and wonder about the world. Channelled well, these energies are perfect for the experience of magick. All these are things older Witches also need to work on. In fact, developing a deeper understanding of yourself and developing your personal power are never-ending experiences along the magickal path of a Witch's life. It's a journey of progress, not perfection. There are many, many books about Witchcraft available now, but still not a lot for Teen Witches. One of the reasons for this is the perception that teens are too young to handle the responsibility of guiding themselves along their own spiritual path. People think that the energies that can be conjured up during ritual and spell-working are too much for teens to handle. These days teens are more sophisticated and have more responsibilities than ever before – they also have the power of the consumer dollar more than ever before … and then there is the internet and social media. So, the reality is that teens can pick up any book about Witchcraft and start trying it, and type in any Witchcraft-related hashtag into Instagram to see images and information.

This is great, but also sometimes overwhelming! You might find the information too much to absorb, the ideas not specifically geared to the things going on in your own life, or the images and standards intimidating and competitive – so much so that you have to 'keep up with' those standards. The other problem, of course, is the temptation to try certain forms of magick without having first learnt their dangers. The classic example would be to try a hexing spell without having assimilated the knowledge that, whilst hexing people sounds powerful, it's actually very disempowering and brings more trouble than it's worth.

In my opinion, the bottom line is that when treated responsibly and respectfully, Witchcraft is great for teenagers. If you're lucky enough to be in a Witchy family, it's an ideal way to share and communicate with your relations. And if not, you're discovering your spirituality and power for yourself, which can strengthen you in so many other aspects of life as well. I know that every teen who sends me an email says they feel better about themselves as a Teen Witch. They feel they have a unique identity and are special, loved and at home in the

Universe. And when the Teen Witches who read this original edition of this book 16 years ago write to me or come to my spoken word events, they say that being an avowed Teen Witch strengthened their inner self and facilitated a profound journey of life as a Witch.

Well, Fiona, Why Weren't You a Teen Witch?

◇◇

Beats me! No, seriously – I tangibly knew I was a Witch at about age 17, but I had a very magickal vibe early in my life that saw me communing with nature spirits in my bushland home, casting spells with my intuition as my only guide and tapping into some innate inherited Witchy wisdom (my blood is German/Hungarian after all!) as young as seven years of age. I also played mad Witchy games with my girlfriends. One of my favourite memories is of a sleepover with friends where we were all tucked away in bed with the lights out, and one girl was lying on the floor with the rest of us kneeled around her – one at her head, one at her feet and two either side at her waist. We each placed just our two index fingers under her and then my best friend at the time, Linda, instructed us to repeat what she said and did. In grim unison, we chanted 'She is dead, let her rise from her coffin.' To our astonishment, as we raised our arms, rise she did, as light as a feather until she was stretched out on the total of eight fingers, well over our heads. My distinct memory is of a choking presence, so that my eventual gasp of surprise got stuck in my throat and came out as a loud gurgle, at which point we promptly dropped her. It was the most surreal experience

I'd ever had at that young point in my life, though at the time I didn't equate it with anything magickal.

I didn't pursue any other kind of magickal processes until I was about 12 and feeling very isolated and disillusioned. To rebel against my Catholic upbringing, I began to explore Satanic ideas and started lighting black candles whilst saying the Lord's Prayer backwards and reading scary horror novels. In retrospect, that phase was a total detour and really didn't have anything to do with my later discovery of real Witchcraft. It was just one of the 'so extra' things you do to prove you're independent from your parents. I found my little foray into Satanism disempowering, and … boring. Its emphasis on fear and oppression reminded me too much of what I didn't like in my Christian religious education.

Right at the end of my teens, I was drawn to Witchcraft and entered society's acknowledged age of adult life. However, it wasn't until I was 18 and dealing with life after a particularly dark period that I really discovered my inner magick and a sense of wonder and excitement woke inside me. Over the next several years, I went through lots of ups and downs but never lost my sense of self again, and whenever things were hard I knew I had the tools to work through it and learn. For a long time I lived by the edict: 'The more sorrow carved out of you, the more joy you can contain.' I started to understand the cyclical nature of life and stopped feeling the overwhelming sense of futility and angst that had shadowed so many of my early years. Having said that, growing as an adult I have still experienced lots of self-doubt; but somewhere I know that eventually the dust will settle and I will see the glowing green 'Exit' sign and move on to happier times, grateful for the lessons (especially the hardest ones, because that's where most of the personal growth can happen). My favourite saying at the time of this rewrite is 'progress, not perfection'. And this affirms the statement I coined 16 years ago even more deeply: 'When I gave up being a perfectionist ... suddenly everything was perfect.' Your teen years are possibly the most challenging of any, but they are the gateway to the rest of your life: what you make of them will form the foundation of how you launch yourself into the future. But try not to feel pressured by it – the Universe always has something bigger and better than you can imagine just around the corner... if you just stay out of your own way.

Before We Get Started

Since I originally wrote this book my practice has evolved and changed a lot, as has the world and its Witches. In recent times I have gone so far as to recommend not casting spells and trying to micro-manage the world to be what we think it should be. Instead I suggest modern Witches do rituals of gratitude for what is and allow the path to be revealed to them, with their main goal being the gentle erasing of ego and their most powerful achievement being able to stay out of their own way. However, it's beneficial for young Witches – specifically Teen Witches – to master the art of spell-casting, and understand its workings and ramifications in order to explore the world magickally on a daily basis. In my recent manifesto *The Art of Witch*, which explains concepts I've collated after 30 years of practice, I talk about how the ego is useful in the early, linear years of life, but that by the mid-thirties, ego becomes a destructive force. The goal of the Witch is to gradually erase its increasingly limiting role.

This book contains many spells and ego-oriented tasks and goals. That is because, in our early years, it is important and relevant to explore parameters, set boundaries and come to know 'ourselves' and how we forge our individual colourful creative identities and offer them to the world. In *Teen Magick*, I also offer traditional methods for circle casting/directions and correspondences. Over the years, my practice now has become more intuitive and innate, which reflects my experience. I do a lot of spontaneous ritual and do not stick rigidly to physical method and discipline other than purely energetic. By this I mean I use the parameters of method, morals and discipline in what I conjure and move in energetic realms – the long-term effects of these filtering to the physical plane. I find that it's important to have this structure and understanding of the formal way of doing things. The more you experience the more you can trust your personal methods.

A Note On Tools For Spells

The ingredients, coloured candles, crystals and so on recommended to use in the various spells and rituals offered in this book are chosen to align energetically and enhance the success of the goals of the various spells and rituals. I have kept the things needed to a tight list and there are substitutions suggested along the way too. The main thing is for you to feel confident and ready to just practise your Craft. Don't get hung up on not being able to find the right ingredient. Back when this book was first written 16 years ago, Amazon didn't exist and online ordering was minimal and expensive. These days if you don't have a Witchy supply store in town, it is super easy to order anything and everything online. Be wary of getting seduced into excessive consumerism ideals and the ideas 'I consume therefore I exist – I can buy anything online so I don't have to put that much effort in' or 'I buy cool Witchy stuff therefore I am a Witch'. Remember all these magickal and healing modalities that modern Witches embrace evolved from when people lived close to the earth and the seasons and in harmony with our planet. We were aligned energetically with the moon and the stars and the turning of the seasons – we sensed and knew the inherent magick of existence itself. It is our interpretation of the items used and their potential that unlocks their greatest magickal impact in our lives. Real magickal power in the individual must be earned through lessons and effort – not just bought. So it's totally okay to buy something quickly online, but balance this with sincere research on the qualities of the item. Use the internet to research the magickal and medicinal qualities of the different herbs and oils suggested. If you buy something online consider doing something in your local natural world to balance the energies. Maybe you will plant a tree, clean up some trash from a natural space or spend some time in meditation to align your energies with the exotic thing you have just purchased. Let your intuition guide you. Feel and be connected and grateful – and then your magickal powers will truly blossom in a exciting and uniquely 'you' way.

Tips On Getting the Most Out of This Book

✕✕✕

This book is just the beginning. In it you will find rituals and spells that are written just for you as a teenager finding your way in the Craft. The same subjects in other books written for an older perspective have been recast, here, just for you. Some things will be harder because they will be encouraging you, as a Teen Witch, to dig deep inside and learn about all the magick that is inside of you. Since I originally wrote this book, my own practice has evolved significantly. I no longer practise spells to manifest things; instead I perform rituals of gratitude for what I have. And I'm not talking about possessions – I'm talking about wisdom, life experience and the opportunity to be of service in the world as an evolved Witch. You will benefit from doing rituals of gratitude as well as casting spells. You are exploring powers, setting boundaries and growing the survival and adaptability skills that will serve you and others in your adult years. So spellcasting is useful and appropriate. Here are some of the best skills to hone as you embark on the path of Teen Witchcraft.

USE YOUR INTUITION: at times you won't be able to follow everything to the letter, and this is when you need to stop, listen to and trust your instinct. A lot of the spells and guidelines in this book are quite in-depth and demanding. I am confident that you have a greater ability to grasp magickal concepts and work with magickal energies at this time of human evolution than some would give you credit for. At the same time, I have included lots of quick-fix, instant spells that will work immediately and reliably when fuelled with an honest heart and honest intent. The more demanding spells are just as achievable as the 'easy'

14

ones, and they're also often ultimately more rewarding because the more effort you put in and the more focused you are the better the results will be. Don't worry! You can't do anything absolutely, irrevocably and horribly wrong (as long as you don't break the Witches' Laws, which are established to liberate you to explore magickal powers in a way that is sustainable and the best expression of your growing capabilities). You'll almost certainly make a lot of small mistakes – but that's good, and they will help you learn. If you're inspired to do something in particular – maybe a particular spell or ritual – and it resonates beautifully and strongly within you (and again doesn't break any Witches' Laws), then go ahead and try it!

RESEARCH AND LEARN: use this book as a map to lead you further along your path. Not all the answers are here, but a lot of the questions that you need to ask are. Again, this book is a starting point to hopefully encourage you to continue exploring the wonderful world of the Craft.

THE WITCHES' LAWS: the original Witches' Laws were as follows:

1. Do what you want to do as long as you don't hurt anyone.
2. Do what you want to do as long as you don't interfere with another's free will.
3. That which you send out returns upon you threefold – minimum!

A note on the third law: it's not quite as simple as 'I'll do nice things so three times as nice things will come back to me' or 'I won't do bad things because I don't want three times as bad things to happen to me', though this obviously makes for a better case for blessings than curses!

The third (or threefold) law exists to keep Witches responsible and aware of the ramifications of all their acts. Real Witches don't seek to harm others however bad the individual's behaviour might be, because the act of healing wrongdoers, or binding them, to prevent them doing further harmful things is far more powerful and effective, and it won't bounce back on the Witch. Witches also don't do things to achieve a selfish goal. As mentioned in my earlier books, most Witches discover that they work better magick for a friend than they do for themselves, so once again, on a purely practical level, selfish magick is not a true display of a Witch's power. Real Witches are aware that everything is interconnected, and they value collective balance well ahead of short-term personal gain. After over 30 years of practice and interacting with other Witches, I have an additional law for you to consider, which is Moral Law: allow others to be as you would be. The Witch is responsible for the upholding of spiritual, transformative law – that good will always triumph, and what is good and evil should not be decided by the Witch but will reveal itself as relevant and appropriate to the time. The consummate Witch cultivates the Moral Law and mindfully adheres to method and discipline; thus, it is in the Witch's power to witness success.

If you don't understand a word or description, just flip to the glossary (Witchy Words) at the end of the book, where I have put together a list of explanations for unusual terms. If at any point you are reading a spell you want to try and you don't understand why something is being done, or what the Goddess or god mentioned represents, research it straight away (you can start with Chapter 16 'Magickal Meanings') and make some notes in your magickal journal or Book of Shadows. My book *Witch – A Magickal Journey (20th Anniversary Edition)* has comprehensive lists of the magickal qualities of herbs, planets, numbers; anything that you can't find in this book is listed there. In this book I have also tried to narrow the majority of herbs, crystals and other objects suggested to a choice of easily accessible and obtainable items. If you are searching online consider the messenger, and if the site is well composed, not preachy or makes extreme claims and doesn't charge exorbitant fees then it's very likely to be a good one for you.

Something to remember: there is so much Witchy information around – so many Goddesses and Gods, herbs, crystals, spells, paths and traditions to understand and remember – it may seem bewildering. If you identify yourself strongly as a Teen Witch, the Craft is likely to be something you will explore for the rest of your life. So take your time; allow your personal magickal world to weave itself within and around you. It will ebb and flow in varying intensity over the years so don't feel that you need to know everything at once, and don't be afraid to make mistakes. As long as the Craft is meaningful to you, and as long as you feel magickal, then you are on the path. Enjoy the journey!

To Me From Me

by Fiona Horne (age 17)

◇◇

Here's an insight from a young girl I once knew!

This is something I wrote when I was 17. I recorded it in my first Book of Shadows (though I didn't call it that at the time – it was just a notebook. But I can see now it was the start of something magickal …)

Reading about the Craft is a valid pursuit and use of time, because as I read, it exists in my mind. This is just as valid as a physical ritual to express and reaffirm my beliefs.

A healthy body will make me a more efficient Witch!

Adults use ten per cent of their brains – the key to the other ninety per cent is myth and ritual. When a child is born I think they use one hundred per cent of their brain before becoming adult-erated. Imagination, games, ritual and 'make believe' are the keys to opening up to magickal powers and the other ninety per cent of our brains.

The key to practising the Craft (which I feel instinctively is my heritage) is meditation – stilling and focusing my mind.

When I am feeling unconfident in ritual, all I need to do is stop and meditate. If I take it slow I will eventually evolve as I'm meant to – 'You are on the path, you don't need to know where it goes, just follow it'. One small step at a time will gradually integrate the Craft into my everyday life.

Magick and beliefs aren't about how many rituals you do, how complicated they are, or if you did them correctly. It's about feeling it deep inside and integrating it plus connecting with the timeless knowledge of ourselves that we are born with and forget as we 'grow up'. Just do what feels right, relax and there will be time for everything. Belief in yourself and your methods is all you need.

◇◇◇

CHAPTER ONE

WHAT IS A REAL WITCH?

◇◇◇

The following email was sent to me because it addresses one of the most common questions asked by Teen Witches. It was originally sent in 2004 but is still relevant now.

> Hiya Fiona,
>
> Just an idea for the book. A question too I guess. Watching films such as The Craft and TV shows such as (The Chilling Adventures of) Sabrina, (rebooted) Charmed and reruns of Buffy, magick is glorified so easily. It comes up as being the answer to all of life's problems and looks awesome. I guess in a way it is. Not strictly speaking though. These shows have some of the ideas and 'morals' of witchcraft correct, but many things they promote just

don't happen in true magick. I see these shows as promoting witchcraft as the answer to anything and everything and also helping teens to think they are witches when they really aren't.

These days it is all too easy for teenagers to open a magazine, find a 'spell', do it and call themselves witches. They have no idea what magick really is though.

They don't know where it really comes from or what it really means.

Do you have any advice for true teen witches on how to stand apart from all the rest? This may sound a little crazy as all of the true teen witches I know don't boast about it and generally don't tell anyone. It's just very hard to be accepted as a true witch, especially by older, more experienced witches when there are so many 'try hards' running around today. Maybe you could write a little section on the true meaning of being a witch. You could explain that just because you do a spell from a magazine, own a witchcraft book or buy a Spellbox set and do what the instructions say (or you take a picture of your crystals on a full moon and tag it #witchesofinstagram and it gets 12K likes) ... that that doesn't make you a witch. I think it is important and needs to be said in a book such as yours that is being aimed and promoted towards teenagers.

Thanks

Jackie (aged 17)

Jackie raises an important point – then and now. Back then it did seem that anyone could, for example, buy a copy of (the wonderful) *Witchcraft* magazine, try a spell and say 'I am a Witch.' These days they can download the fantastic e-zine 'WitchWay' and tag themselves on Instagram and get 100K followers for having the best Witchy manicure whilst they shuffle oracle cards and say they are a Witch. But this doesn't need to put a sincere Teen Witch's nose out of joint! Everyone finds their way along the path of the Wise … and if they are not growing in wisdom they ultimately wander away from it. So if there are kids at your school who you think are Witch wannabees and who go around waving their wands, banging their chests for attention and threatening to cast (not very nice) spells on all and sundry, just ignore them. Don't give them any of your energy. There's room in the Universe for everyone, so just go about your own business. However, if someone is really driving you nuts carrying on about being a Witch but it seems like a lot of hot air, just start talking to them about the Craft or offer to do some basic ritual work with them. This will quickly sort out whether they're pretenders or whether they know what they're talking about!

And again, if they really bug you ignore them. Hang out with the Witches who make you smile, not frown.

My friend and long-time Witch, Liam Cyfrin, shares his wisdom here: *in many respects, the word 'Witch' has more in common with terms like 'artist' or 'magician' than 'Buddhist' or 'Hindu'.*

Whilst various types of self-dedications and initiation are commonly used in the Craft, they are better understood as being primarily rituals of recognition than as admissions to a club. One 'becomes' a Witch gradually through attempting to be one, just as artists or musicians earn the right to their titles.

Of course, anyone who can hold a paint brush can claim to be an artist and anyone who knows how to bang out two chords on a guitar can profess to be a musician. But whether they – or anyone else – truly believes these claims is another matter.

We judge musicians by their performances and artists by their art, and we can generally sense when we're in the presence of talent regardless of whether the precise form of the artistry is our cup of tea. The same thing precisely applies to Witchcraft.

Real Witches stand out by moving far beyond the dabbling try-a-spell-or-two stage to going the long haul. Quoting one of the Witches' Laws is appropriate here: 'That which you send out returns upon you threefold' … if you're lucky! It may hit a whole lot harder than that. This is why it's very unlikely that you or anyone you know will ever encounter a real curse. Those who know their Craft are too smart to use it, and those who might consider a hex are generally total newbies without the skills or experience to control the spell. (See page 29 for the Four Magickal Principles, especially 'to know' and 'to be silent'.) Sure, you can be initially attracted to Witchcraft's exotic and rebellious face. Now more than ever, Witchcraft is being packaged commercially as a form of entertainment instead of a genuine spiritual path. More and more spell kits, articles and magazines pop up everywhere. But real Witches get past that dabbling stage pretty quickly and find that the glamour and mystique are still there, but in a more subtle and profoundly empowering way that goes far beyond shock value and trendy fashion appeal.

As for older Witches not taking Teen Witches seriously – well, ignore 'em! Every Witch is an individual and some are more intolerant and crabby than others: no one is perfect! Some Witches out there seem to have forgotten that they were new to the Craft themselves once, and had to learn as they went. Some of them also seem to have very little sympathy or respect for any young would-be Witch following a different path from the one they took themselves.

Strangely enough, many of those same people are big on the notion that a Witch shouldn't have any authority higher than his or her own conscience and intuition.

On the bright side, though, there are plenty of older Witches who, when they consider their own first steps, are very supportive of the new Witchy wave, and are happy to admit that they're envious of the resources around for today's new Witches. So be assured there are plenty of older Witches you can learn from and be inspired by, and who won't be so quick to judge you. If you are genuine and on 'the path', they will sense this in your presence and hear it in your words. If a potential teacher or older Witchy person rejects you when you know you're genuinely a seeker, then you don't want their approval anyway. I meet heaps of Teen Witches and wannabees in my travels and, believe me, I can tell the difference! But I don't shun the wannabees; I just try to give them some constructive advice.

Real Witches worship nature and always work to recognise and connect with the cycles of the seasons and see them reflected in all facets of their lives. We honour the concept of the Goddess and god (or Lady and Lord), and we recognise that this divinity exists within us as well as without and has many faces and forms. We work magick by harnessing the elemental forces of nature – air, earth, fire and water – and focus and direct these energies with our will, fuelling them with our emotions. We seek to help and heal rather than harm and destroy. We understand that a full life is not only about the good and easy times but also the difficult and dangerous.

Hexing: You're Being Paranoid

Some Teen Witches write to tell me they are worried about someone casting a bad spell on them. Let me assure you that 99 per cent of hexes work only if you are susceptible to them. Nearly all cultures have traditions of hexing or cursing, and most of these practices work on a single principle: the spell isn't what does the work. It's the victim's belief that he or she is just that – a victim – that gives them trouble. So, step one in keeping hex-free is to remember you're not a victim.

You can open yourself up to certain energies, and by the same token if you don't allow things to attack you they won't. You can diffuse negativity – it's like blowing smoke away or pouring water on a fire. If you feel like you've got a lot of negativity around you and you want to clear the air, try the following spell.

⊕ Blow It Away Spell

YOU WILL NEED:

- salt
- four sticks of incense (rosemary, sandalwood or nag champa are good, or any magickal store-made blend for banishing) or four charcoal blocks in dishes of sand with incense sprinkled on top
- a glass of water

DIRECTIONS

Sprinkle the salt around you in a deosil (anti-clockwise/sunwise direction in the southern hemisphere and clockwise in the north – you are casting in the direction the sun appears to move across the sky). Stand a stick of incense at the north, south, east and west quarters. Light them, and as they burn take some time to focus on who you think has hexed you or the situation you feel negatively trapped in. Then go to the first stick of incense with the water and say:

> Smoke within this space,
>
> Capture the trap that's placed.
>
> One, two, three – I blow away its hold on me.

Gently blow the incense smoke so that it leaves the salt circle. Then put out the incense in the glass of water (pour water on the discs). Now do this to each incense quarter.

When you have finished, push the salt circle open in a widdershins direction (clockwise against the sun in the southern hemisphere, anti-clockwise in the northern hemisphere) as you say:

I release any sadness bound to me, for the good of all. So mote it be. Remember! Doing any hexing yourself is not recommended.

Real Witches know that to really get in touch with their abilities they need to respect the existence of hexing but also be aware that it actually weakens and ultimately destroys a Witch's power.

Dear Fiona,

I'm having a bit of trouble. I'd like to be a witch, and I consider myself a witch. But it's just that the books I've read say that I must search for the Lady, and that I must be initiated. I'm a lone witch, though wouldn't mind finding a Coven. It's just that I'm keeping this a secret. I can't keep an altar because my parents don't know and I don't want to tell them. I was wondering, what does it take to be a witch, and can you be one even though you aren't initiated?

Also, I wear a necklace with a pentacle, it has a little tear drop hanging off it. Is it still a pentacle, and is it wrong for me to wear it when I'm not a 'real' witch?

Rainbow Love (aged 14)

As far as having to hide your Witchy interests from your parents, I address this at length in the chapter 'Doing What You Will'. Right here, though, I can say that if you are scared your family won't understand your interest, it's probably because you fear them judging you as silly or perhaps even worrying that they'll think that it's something evil and to do with Satanism.

This is an old misconception about Witchcraft that is rapidly shifting, so why not try sharing with them a bit of information about what Witchcraft really is? Perhaps show them this book. Really, there's so much literature and online newspaper articles around now debunking any connection between the Craft and Satanism that you can share educational information relatively easily. Hopefully this will open a positive discussion.

Real Witchcraft isn't about wearing a pentacle (though heaps of Witches do, either as jewellery, often beautifully styled and embellished, on clothing, or as tattoos). It is about taking the first steps, and if this means buying a spell kit and trying it or reading a book and identifying with the word 'Witch', then that's okay.

As far as needing to be initiated into a Coven in order to be considered a real Witch – well, like thousands of Witches the world over, I have never been initiated into a Coven. I have been mostly solitary for over 30 years, though I certainly have had a lot of contact with other Witches. In 2005 I formed a Coven whilst living in Los Angeles and it was a rewarding and potent magickal experience. Ultimately we dispersed as we were unable to gather regularly. And since then my life has been so nomadic, virtually and IRL, that to regularly work with a group of people continues to not be feasible.

People project energy, and real Witches, as solitary as so many of us are, are eventually drawn together. Many Witches find group rituals very rewarding and appropriate for the way they choose to experience their Craft. But that doesn't mean you have to be part of a Coven.

On page 33 there is a self-dedication ritual that you can do to formally declare to the Universe you are a budding Witch. Further along the Witchy path of your life you will have other opportunities to make formal declarations of your path and Craft, and you may end up being initiated into a Coven or other particular Wiccan tradition.

You are a real Witch as long as you are genuine and honest. It's between you and the Universe. Some Witches are obviously more adept than others, but every super-together and powerful Witch had to start somewhere!

The final word on 'am I a real witch?' is this: if you are asking the question, then you are.

Teen Covens

◇◇◇

A teen Coven does not have the hierarchical structure of some adult Witch Covens. The adult Coven structure reflects the levels of knowledge and experience of individuals within the group.

A teen Coven is more like a working group of equally experienced people exploring their Craft together. You can celebrate sabbats and esbats, do spells together and share your problems and successes. I know a group that regularly organises trips to interesting magickal places and group shopathons for Witchy clothes and tools. Another has a garden plot at a communal garden and grows magickal herbs there.

A teen Coven can be a fantastic support group as you inspire and help each other to keep going with your Craft and use it to make the most of your life. There should be no leader in the bossy sense of the word – everyone should share tasks and knowledge. Having said that, if everyone is happy for one person to organise and co-ordinate things, that's fine too. It's important to remember that everyone is equal, and that ego trips are for idiots and not Witches.

The Four Magickal Principles:

To Know, To Dare, To Will, To Be Silent

The principles speak for themselves, really, but I'll spell them out for you in more detail!

TO KNOW: Witches are seekers of knowledge. We know we can never stop learning: about ourselves, others, the world, magick, life – everything! We are also strong in our identity as Witches and trust and believe in our methods.

TO DARE: Witches do not live life with blinkers on: we face the onslaught of existence, good and bad, head on, and take full responsibility for our actions.

We are not afraid to make mistakes in our quest for knowledge and personal development, and we do not shy away from the 'dark side' – not in the sense of valuing evil but in accepting that pain, loss, hardship and death are all necessary and unavoidable parts of life. We confront and explore our fears and subconscious, and we embrace the light and dark of life, all shades of grey and all the dazzling colours in between.

TO WILL: Witches work magick by focusing their will.

The cornerstone of our spell-casting is our will, and understanding the precept that magick is the 'art of changing consciousness at will'. In other words, the world will answer according to the questions you ask of it. Witches understand that they can change their life, that they have a say in it and that they can use their will to work to assist others. Will is also part of the word 'willing' – a Witch knows that her greatest power will shine when she is willing to contribute, serve, grow and also stay out of her own way and allow the

Universe to guide her – even when the path is dark and difficult or the complete opposite of what she wants to do in that moment.

TO BE SILENT: perhaps because Witches were persecuted for so long – and even now we still cop a lot of flak – to be silent can be seen as a protective statement. But it also means that we don't need approval or gratuitous attention, and we don't attempt to preach and convert. We also know that to talk (let alone brag) about our magickal undertakings will dilute their potency. So when spells are in progress we don't talk about them (that would be like digging up a seed you just planted to see how it's growing).

Over the years I have spent as a public Witch, the 'to be silent' edict is an interesting one for me. I have a few basic ways I relate to it and practise it. For a start, in social situations I never announce that I am a Witch. However, if someone asks me if I am I will answer honestly. I consider one of my roles as a Witch is to provide information for those who choose to read, listen to and perhaps absorb it in some way.

Even though I have now written 14 books and appeared on countless TV and radio shows, done public rituals and written songs about the Craft, and have a significant digital and social media footprint, there is still a part of my practice that I keep just between me and the Universe. Witchcraft is an occult tradition and always will be – there will always be a hidden element that is fuelled by every individual Witch.

We come into this life alone and we go out alone, and it's in our deepest, deepest sense of self that the roots of our individual Craft anchor.

BLOOD SPELLS

Once blood was used by witches as their individual 'stamp' to seal their intention/life force to the spell or ritual they were working. A common practice was to prick their index (power) finger with a pin and extract a few drops of blood to anoint an object or consecrate a parchment upon which a charm was written. In modern times Teen Witches are aware of the positive responsibility to treat themselves and others kindly and respectfully with regard to personal and shared hygiene and health, so using a charmed red vegetable dye fingerprint stamp instead of blood is conscious, creative and empowering.

⊕ BLOODPRINT INK

YOU WILL NEED:

- 1 large beetroot
- saucepan
- 2 cups of hand-collected rain or fresh river water

Note: if you cannot collect pure water by hand, use bottled spring water.

DIRECTIONS:

Chop the beetroot into quarters and place in the saucepan with the water. Bring to a rolling boil for five minutes and then reduce to a very slow simmer for at least one hour (two to three hours is better, as long as you don't leave it unattended).

Remove the beetroot quarters with a fork and place on a plate.

When the liquid has cooled, pour into a flat bowl with a lid. There should be ¾–1 cup remaining after your long, slow simmer.

Light a candle and, by its light, eat the beetroot quarters as a healthy snack. Doing this also links you energetically to the dye, which you will use magickally.

When you have completed this bonding ritual, place your bloodprint dye in the fridge.

Note: any red organic vegetable dye can be used, but I recommend creating your own in a sacred ritual as described above to ensure maximum power and effectiveness.

⊕ Self-dedication Ritual

The following ritual is something you can do to formally announce to the Universe that you are a budding Witch. It's not a substitute for the years of knowledge and practice that you need to accumulate to become an adept Witch, but it will align your energies and can give you a sense of credibility and focus as you embark on the path. Before you do this ritual, though, you should read the next chapter Circle Casting and the Tools of Witchcraft (as well as the rest of the book!), which explains all the things you need to know and understand about doing rituals and spell work.

Often when I am on television or a radio show I will be called a 'white Witch'. I always politely correct this by saying I'm 'just a Witch'. To call myself a white Witch is reinforcing the stereotype that some Witches are inherently bad and evil.

Life is never white or black, only both and all shades of colour in between.

Witchcraft is about the totality of life – all experiences good, bad and indifferent. Witchcraft is not a lightweight philosophy that runs away from darkness and danger or seeks to convert everything into 'white light'; rather, it's gutsy and potent, honouring the balance of creation and destruction.

Best time: a full moon.

YOU WILL NEED:

- three leaves – use your instinct to guide you to which plant or tree
- a piece of white cord that is exactly your height
- a white candle
- a black candle
- a lock of your hair
- a medium-sized cloth bag, preferably decorated with a pentagram
- a garland of ivy or other green, leafy vine woven with seasonal white flowers (whatever is blooming at the time)
- a special garment never worn before (if you choose not to be skyclad/naked)

- special anointing oil 1/4 cup of almond or olive oil, 4 teaspoons of sandalwood powder mixed with half a teaspoon of crushed sea salt and three drops of lavender oil mixed together to form a paste **Note:** if you cannot get sandalwood powder (for purity) use another powder. Nutmeg can work to enhance intuition and is easily obtained.

DIRECTIONS

You first need to gather the leaves from a living tree. Originally I recommended oak because it is a direct link to the Celtic origins of Wicca. Its presence denotes wisdom, which is what you are seeking as a Witch. So consider a tree in your environment that is large and old and carries the wise qualities of the oak.

Kneel at the base of the tree and ask its permission for three leaves:

Great tree, I ask thee

For your leaves of three.

Your blessing bestow on me,

Oh mighty tree.

If three leaves flutter down, fantastic! Gratefully accept these. Otherwise, carefully pluck three from a single branch, bow three times in thanks and then walk away for at least 20 paces without turning your back.

Place all your objects on your altar, and prepare yourself for the ritual by bathing. If you can jump in a freshwater lake or the ocean, great! Otherwise, have a bath with a cup of strained rosemary tea added, or perhaps a bath bomb (the salt is purifying). Either stay skyclad or dress in your special garment and place the ivy and flower garland on your head.

Cast Circle (see Chapter 2) with the full ritual, using frankincense incense or another incense that you love – the scented smoke is purifying and sacred to the element of air. Anoint yourself with the paste at your third eye and heart and the tops of your feet as you say:

Lord and Lady, bless me

As I undertake a journey

With no beginning and no ending.

Sit and meditate for a moment on how you feel about being a Witch – the things you hope to learn and achieve, both physical and mystical.

Now light the white and black candles from the same flame as you say:

As above, so below,

Light and dark,

So my journey goes.

My heart is true,

My intention pure,

The Craft of the wise I seek to pursue.

Meditate on the candle flames and contemplate the fact that being a Witch involves challenge and risk. You will be called upon by the Universe to prove your worthiness of the title. Absolutely every Witch I know has had to confront some of life's toughest issues – it seems to come with the territory – but every challenge makes us stronger, better, more accomplished. In walking the path of Witchcraft, you are not hiding away from the realities of life but facing them head on – good and bad.

Hold the leaves in your hands and say:

The wisdom of those gone before I seek to honour.

The wisdom of those to come I seek to inspire.

Place the index finger of your power hand (the hand you write with) gently into your bloodprint ink and mark your print on each of the leaves. Wipe your finger dry with the cloth. Place them back on the altar. Now take up the cord (the same length as your height) at each end. Raise it in offer and say:

Lady and Lord, accept this measure

Of my commitment to Witchcraft. I present myself to all creation

And ask to be acknowledged as Witch.

Now cut a lock of your hair and place it, the cord and the leaves into the bag; then close Circle (see Chapter 2).

This bag needs to be kept somewhere safe where it will not be disturbed.

You may like to repeat this ritual further down the track and embellish it at your own discretion as your experience and knowledge grow. Each time you do it take a new measure of your height, and instead of the leaves you may choose another natural object that represents qualities you are seeking to develop as you grow as a Witch.

Note: the anointing paste that you created can be used again in private rituals to help focus your psychic abilities. Just apply some to your third eye before casting Circle.

Remember that when it comes to Witchcraft we work on Goddess time — that is, time can be experienced as a straight line of past/present/future (linear) as well as 'round', with all things happening at all times. So don't worry that you're casting a Witch's Circle and practising magick before you've even formally declared you are a budding Witch. If you are drawn to the Craft to the point of making the self-dedication above, then the ability to do the ritual is within you. Just trust and work with your intuition and desire.

HEREDITARY WITCHCRAFT

I am adopted and it was quite a revelation to find out at the age of 27 that I was half Hungarian and half German. On my father's side I'm Jewish (though of course I can't inherit this as it is a matrilineal culture, but I have the genetic memory of my ancestors), and on my mother's side I'm Lutheran. I have sometimes wondered why I have such a strong calling to Witchcraft, but on finding out my ancestry I stopped questioning why Witchcraft would resonate through every fibre of my being. I choose to believe that my Celtic/Teutonic bloodline is related to my attraction to the Craft, but as the boundaries between countries and cultures continue to blur as the world evolves in the digital age, it is essential for the Teen Witch to be educated in the inclusive spiritual and cultural tapestry of the modern international magickal community, and understand the importance of its diversity.

Wicca is currently the most accessible religion on the path of Witchcraft that originated from ancient Celtic culture and methods of worship. Celtic people originated in an area that is now France and southern Germany. Their culture spread extensively and included central Europe, Britain and Ireland, before they were conquered by the Romans by the first millennium BCE. Celtic culture was so sophisticated and had such a wonderful spiritual and artistic heritage that it's not surprising so many people are relating to and reviving it today. (On a lighter note, for example, the practice of 'touching wood' to ensure luck and good fortune comes from the Celtic and Druidic practice of honouring trees as sacred, magickal and the cornerstone of life.) By the way, I want to make clear that Wicca is not a genuine revival of traditional, pre-Christian Celtic religion, but simply draws some elements and a lot of inspiration from it. I also found out a long time ago that the last Witch to be burnt at the stake was Janet Horne, in 1722 in Scotland, and my adopted family tree can be traced back to Scotland. I found this to be an interesting serendipity and I once felt that this gave me the opportunity to address naysayers that I indeed have a hereditary claim to Witchcraft. But over the decades our magickal community has evolved to be less judgemental and insecure and we embrace each other without requiring a 'validation' beyond a genuine, sincere declaration of walking the path. So a hereditary bloodline is not essential to be able to claim the title and walk the path of the Witch. Let's remember that we are in a way related to every single human being on the planet, because we are all part of the same biosphere of planet Earth. So we can feel proud of, and connected to, any calling that resounds within us. 'Modern Witchcraft as it has evolved to be could be considered "a scavenger religion/spiritual path"' according to the founder of Hexfest, renowned Warlock and publisher Christian Day, reflecting on the willingness of Witches to learn from other cultures' spiritual practices. Whilst the origins of what I share in this book are rooted in northern European esoteric practice, Brujas, Black Witches and Asian Witches practise Western occultism, adding texture and contextual wisdom that expands the relevance and power of the Witch in the modern world.

Burning Times

This was a very sad time: from approximately the beginning of the 14th to the end of the 18th centuries (the 16th being the worst) the church, already well experienced in the persecution of so-called heretics, extended its hostility to those alleged to be involved in Witchcraft.

It's sometimes said that millions were tortured and killed after Witchcraft charges, but although there can be no precise numbers this figure is far too high. The most conservative historians seem willing to allow that anything from 40,000 to 60,000 women, men and children were murdered for supposedly practising Witchcraft, whilst others believe the death toll might have reached 100,000. At the height of this persecution there were hardly any village healers or midwives or independent religious leaders – all having been killed for genuine or imagined Witchcraft. The people killed consisted of anyone who threatened the powers of the church and individuals whom people of power had a grudge against. (If you want to understand how hysteria and ignorance can fuel this kind of hatred and insanity, watch the film of the Arthur Miller play *The Crucible*.) Thankfully Witchcraft is no longer an offence punishable by death in the Western world.

Gaia (pronounced 'guy-ah')

I relate very strongly to the concept of our planet as a self-regulating, living organism – Gaia or Mother Earth. Nothing is separate; each component affects and relates with each other. The waterways are Mother Earth's blood; the air, her breath; the mountains, her children; the fire, her heart. As organisms we evolved specifically from the stuff of this biosphere – so we are not separate from this earth but totally bonded with it.

Eco-conscious Teen Witch

A CHECKLIST

Make ethical and conscious choices as much as possible. Below is a mini checklist and some fun ideas to get you started.

☛ **SUPPORT LOCAL**

Skip the big supermarkets and support smaller markets and local providers.

☛ **EAT ORGANIC**

Reduce the harmful impact of GMOs and toxic chemicals; improve your personal health, physically, mentally and spiritually.

☛ **MINIMISE WASTE**

Use cloth bags; carry your own drink container; don't buy excessively packaged goods.

☛ **RECYCLE/REUSE**

Shop at op shops for great deals and cool stuff; reuse glass containers and bottles as vases and candle holders.

☛ **TRADE SKILLS, PRODUCE AND PRODUCTS**

Make soaps and trade with your Witchy friend who blends essential oils; swap a crystal with a fellow Teen Witch; trade a tarot card reading for help studying for a test.

◇◇

Witches know that their greatest responsibility is to tread as lightly as they can on this planet, to heal the damage done and prevent future damage as much as possible. Recycling, not using plastic bags and containers, composting vegetable matter and minimising your waste and being an active supporter of conservation groups are all practical ways to practise 'Gaia consciousness'.

Witches can also work magickally to honour and heal Mother Earth. The following simple ritual can be done either alone or with other Teen Witches.

Gather together in a park or on a beach. Stand, holding hands, and feel the earth beneath your feet and the sky above your heads. Breathe deeply and feel yourself centre and ground. Become very aware of where you are in the Universe, standing on the surface of a planet that floats in infinite space. Think about the myriad different life forms that share this planet with you. When you are ready, say individually (one after the other):

Gaia my Mother Earth,

(We/I) offer you (my/our) respect and love;

Thank you for your beauty and bounty;

As Witch and human with you I am one.

Now do something to honour where you are – it may be picking up all the rubbish you can see and putting it in recycling bins. It may be planting a tree. It may be just sitting, looking and pondering in wonder at how absolutely amazing the natural world is.

CHAPTER TWO

Circle Casting and the Tools of Witchcraft

One of the most daunting things for me when I started practising Witchcraft was casting Circle. There seemed to be so much to remember and I was forever getting confused about which colour candle was required in which quarter, and which guardian was which. I was worried I'd do something wrong and my Circle would not protect me from negative energies, or that I'd do something out of order and the Circle wouldn't exist at all. The information I read in various books would just blur, and my mind would switch off. Most of the time I wouldn't end up doing anything at all. What I am hoping is that this chapter will help you get your head around the basics of Circle casting so you can really get started with working magick.

If you want to try a more elaborate Circle casting, check out my book *Witch: A Magickal Journey*, or any of the plethora of other books/websites on Witchcraft.

Note: all the directions I give below are for people living in the southern hemisphere. If you read something different in another book it's likely to have been written for people living in the northern hemisphere, as directions and correspondences are based on natural phenomenon – like the way the sun appears to move across the sky or where you are on the planet in relation to the equator (the hottest/fire aspect).

There are lots of different methods and approaches to casting Circle and just about all of them will work if (a) they make sense to you, and (b) you follow the same pattern in as many of your workings as possible. There's no single correct way to cast Circle – your task is to discover the one best for you personally. The most important thing to understand and ensure is that the procedure that you choose is the one that resonates most strongly within you. You are creating a sacred space in which to work magick, and that's the most vital thing for you to remember. Understand that it's how intensely *you* feel the space to be special and sacred that will determine whether your Circle *really* exists or not.

Having said that, there's no merit in trying to invent some brand-new system for yourself. By adopting one of the standard forms, you're making it easier to share your Circles with other Witches if you choose to, as well as linking into a well-established pattern within the collective unconscious.

Your Circle is just that: a circle, with four quarter points aligned to the four cardinal directions of the compass (north, south, east and west), each one attributed to one of the four elements of traditional Western magick (fire, earth, air and water). You need to invoke the four elements into your Circle so that the magick you create in the spiritual or astral realm has a way of manifesting in the physical realm. I used to think I would never get my head around the directions, the quarters and all the correspondences but it can be done! So here it is, short and sweet.

THE FOUR ELEMENTS

There are four elements: air, earth, fire and water. Each 'lives' in a different direction.

AIR, EAST: because that's where the sun rises. It is the place of new beginnings, which is something air is good at blowing into your life. Air is represented by incense (or a feather if you can't light incense sticks/charcoal blocks at home).

EARTH, SOUTH: because it's as far away from the equator and the light and heat of the sun as you can get, and earth is about dark, contemplative energy. Earth is represented by salt, soil, sand or a crystal. (If you are in the northern hemisphere then earth is in the north.)

WATER, WEST: the sun sets in the west and it is a place of completion, where all things come to rest. Water represents all the emotions. How we feel dictates what we ultimately end up doing. Water is represented by a bowl of spring water (or tap water if that's all you have; put a pinch of salt in it to make it sacred).

FIRE, NORTH: the direction of the equator and the intense presence of the sun's fiery heat. (If you are in the northern hemisphere then fire would be in the south.) Fire is represented by a candle (or, if you can't have fire at home, something that is red or orange – you could paint a burnt stick with red paint, for example, or have a new red unlit candle).

Guardians of the Quarters: Our Magickal Friends

When we call in the guardians of the quarters we are inviting creatures that embody the qualities of these quarters to lend their energy and support to our magickal workings. You don't have to physically see these creatures or even intellectually believe in them, but one of the secrets of effective magick is to learn how to treat such beings as if they were real, living things in the Circle with you. That might sound tricky, but think back to your childhood and you'll probably discover it's a talent you had before you could spell your own name. I mean, remember those imaginary friends you had when you were really little? Whether they existed or not, they felt real to you and affected the way you saw and interacted with the world.

AIR/EAST/SYLPHS: mythological creatures of air that float and look like beautiful wispy elven characters.

EARTH/SOUTH/GNOMES: mythological creatures that live and work in the earth. We all know what gnomes look like!

WATER/WEST/UNDINES: or mermaids and mermen, mythological creatures that live in oceans, rivers and streams.

FIRE/NORTH/SALAMANDERS: a type of amphibian/lizard with vibrant orange and black markings; because of this it became mythologised as a creature of fire.

You are calling in these creatures because you are affirming the presence of the elements. There are others you can call in (some traditions use angels or power animals, for example), but we will work with these for now.

Here we go!

⊕ To Cast a Cool Circle

◇◇◇

YOU WILL NEED:

- ☞ incense or a feather
- ☞ candle (new and lit, or unlit if you can't light flame in your room)
- ☞ a bowl of salt, sand or soil, or a favourite crystal
- ☞ a bowl of spring water (or tap water if that's all you can get)
- ☞ athame or wand (or use your power finger: the index finger of you hand you write with)
- ☞ a bell or gong (not essential as you can clap your hands instead)
- ☞ a plate with some food (perhaps biscuits you have made or something yummy you have bought) and a chalice or glass of juice – or whatever you prefer
- ☞ a table or surface to place all these things on (your Witch's Altar)

DIRECTIONS

Make sure the space is as physically clean as possible: if it's your room, sweep or vacuum (yep, a good Teen Witch should be as handy with a Hoover as with a broom!).

◇◇◇

FOR SOUTHERN HEMISPHERE TEEN WITCHES	FOR NORTHERN HEMISPHERE TEEN WITCHES
NORTH – FIRE	NORTH – EARTH
SOUTH – EARTH	SOUTH – FIRE
EAST – AIR	EAST – WATER
WEST– WATER	WEST – AIR

◇◇◇

Face the eastern quarter then, using your athame, pointed index finger of your power hand, or wand, hold your arm out in front of you and turn in a sunwise (or deosil, which is anti-clockwise in the southern hemisphere and clockwise in the northern hemisphere) direction. Visualise a stream of blue or diamond-white light pouring out and forming a big circle around you as you turn.

As you do this, say:

I conjure you, my sacred Circle of power.

When you get back to the start, picture the light spreading to form a sphere (or egg-like shape) above, below and all around you. Now, still facing east, hold your incense (or feather) in your power hand and fan it as you say:

Come, guardians of air,

Bless me with your presence

And magickal assistance.

In your mind's eye take a moment to see the beautiful sylphs floating in that part of the Circle.

Now face north (if you are in the northern hemisphere face south), hold up your candle or fire representation with your power hand and say:

Come, guardians of the north/south,

Bless me with your presence

And magickal assistance.

In your mind's eye take a moment to see the salamanders writhe in, their bodies undulating like flames of fire.

Now face west, sprinkle a little water with your power hand and say:

Come, guardians of the west,

Bless me with your presence

And magickal assistance.

In your mind's eye take a moment to see the lovely mermaids/mermen floating there.

Now face south (north if you are in the northern hemisphere) and sprinkle a little salt/soil/sand with your power hand (or hold out your crystal) and say:

Come, guardians of the south/north,

Bless me with your presence

And magickal assistance.

In your mind's eye take a moment to see the gnomes, with their wise brown eyes, gather there.

Now, facing your altar (or whatever you're using as one), raise both arms in the air and say:

My Circle is empowered, bound and blessed.

Clap your hands once or strike your bell or gong and say firmly:

So mote it be.

At this point you will want to acknowledge the presence of the Lord and Lady. They are around all the time, so you're not actually inviting them in; instead you are formally connecting with their energy inside you and your Circle.

Because a spell you may be casting might call for a specific Goddess or god (or both) to be invoked a bit later, at this point you are just honouring the divinity of creation.

Now raise both arms in the air and say:

Great Lady and Lord,

Below and above,

This Circle is filled

With your divine light and love.

Now you can perform a specific ritual or cast a spell.

Note: you might be working a particular spell that doesn't specify an incense or coloured candle to use. In that case, when you are casting Circle use a stick of frankincense (or other sacred incense like sandalwood) or a feather for air. And just use a red or white candle for fire. If the spell you are casting does require a certain incense and a special candle but you need to light them separately later on and not as a part of the Circle-casting ritual, then again just use what I suggested above to cast Circle.

Raising Power

Raising power is something that is done in just about every spell-working. It is a way of creating lots of 'magickal fuel' to propel a spell on to fruition – in other words, give it a good kick start! Power raising is also used in healing rituals and any time lots of *oomph* is needed. There are many different methods, but generally you raise the power inside Circle to allow it to brew up in strength. Then, when it is peaking, you 'send' it to where it needs to go by holding your athame or wand or power finger straight up in the air and visualising the top of the Circle opening up and the power racing away to do its job. Or you might point the athame at an object you are empowering (perhaps a talisman or amulet) and focus the energy into that.

Raising power is done to empower an amulet or object or to fuel a spell that has been created within the Circle. It's like getting in a car (the shell of the spell) and then turning the ignition on to power it up before driving away. Raising power is done any time it's needed.

Ways to Raise Power

Chanting is a good one, especially when you're sharing your Circle with a few other people. A classic Wiccan Goddess chant is excellent – 'Isis, Astarte, Diana, Hecate, Demeter, Kali, Inanna' – but any relevant phrase repeated over and over can do the trick (there are some more suggestions in 'Teen Witch Tips'). This is another area where TV Witches often miss the point – it's more often than not the intention behind the words that matters, not the words themselves. Stories where magic is unwittingly released by someone muttering the words in a spell book (like in the movie *The Mummy,* for instance) exist solely in fiction. In fact, power can be raised just as effectively through wordless chant.

Another method of raising power is to run around the perimeter of the Circle as you chant, either alone or in a group. When there's more than one of you in the Circle, hold hands and chant together until you feel it peak, then you can either all raise your arms in the air and yell out 'So mote it be' to send the energy on its way or you can drop to the ground and all press your hands into the earth or floor to send the energy streaming along that way.

Another, quieter (!) way is to cup both hands together and close your eyes, focusing on all the energy building up into a supercharged energy ball in your hands. You'll feel it get hotter and hotter; when it's absolutely peaking, throw the ball into the air to race off to its destination. A group can also do this either individually or collectively – for example, you can stand in a Circle and hold your hands out to the centre and manifest the ball together. You can change it to be different colours if you like: blue for healing, pink for love, purple for power – whatever!

When you are finished the energy-raising and directing part of your ritual, eat and drink whatever goodies you brought into the Circle with you to help you ground your energy (these are called libations), saving some of both as an offering to the Goddess and god. (If you are working outside, you can crumble some food and pour drink on the ground or, if inside, give it to a pot plant or save to take outside later.) A word of warning: when I lived in a flat I used to pour my libations out the window onto the garden and one night my downstairs neighbour leant out the window at the wrong time and copped some sticky grape juice square on his head! Which was actually a kind of blessing – not that he saw it that way!

Finishing Up

Now you can close down the Circle, which means you need to acknowledge and thank the Lady, Lord and the guardians for their presence and assistance and disperse the 'energy shield' of the Circle itself.

First acknowledge the Lord and Lady:

Lady and Lord,

As above so below.

To and from you

All things flow.

Now thank the guardians of the elements.

Face east, fan your feather or incense and say:

Guardians of the air,

Hail and farewell

Until in Circle again we dwell.

See the sylphs float away.

Face north (or south if you are in

the northern hemisphere), sprinkle

some water and say:

Guardians of fire,

Hail and farewell

Until in Circle again we dwell.

See the salamanders crawl away.

Face west, sprinkle some water and say:

Guardians of water,

Hail and farewell

Until in Circle again we dwell.

See the mermaids/mermen swim away.

Face south (or north if you are in the northern hemisphere), sprinkle a little

salt/sand/soil or hold out your crystal and say:

Guardians of earth,

Hail and farewell

Until in Circle again we dwell.

And see the gnomes trundle off.

Note: you may have read in books that you need to call the guardians deosil (anti-clockwise in the southern hemisphere; clockwise in the north) and farewell them widdershins (clockwise in the southern hemisphere; anti-clockwise in the north). For this Circle casting it's fine for you to say hi and bye to them in a deosil direction.

Now hold out your athame, point your power finger or wand and turn around in a widdershins direction and imagine light streaming out and cutting through the centre of the sphere, splitting it into two halves that start to turn into mist and disperse. As you do this say:

This Circle is open but unbroken,

Carried in my heart;

Always merry meet,

Always merry part.

Strike your bell or gong or clap your hands once to signal the end of the ceremony.

The 'always merry meet, always merry part' bit makes sense if there is a group of you because you are acknowledging that it is a joyous and empowering event to gather in Circle. If you are on your own 'always merry meet, always merry part' acknowledges the joy you feel in meeting with the guardians and the formal presence of the Lady and Lord.

Summing it Up

Remember! The main aim is to ease yourself into it, gradually mastering the full process, but be aware of these basic points: you are creating a sacred space; the four elements need to be formally acknowledged and the elemental guardians called in; the divinity of creation needs to be acknowledged – that's why the Lady and Lord are honoured.

At the end you need to ground the magickal energy conjured up so you don't leave Circle feeling spaced out and uncomfortable. As well as grounding you, the food and libations (drink offered to the Lady and Lord) acknowledge your connection with the earth and your understanding of the divine nature of all creation. You are the glue that holds all this together, so be clear and confident. The passion and belief you have in what you are doing will determine how cool your Circle is!

Hold on a minute … You might say that if the above is enough to cast a Circle, why do you ever need to do anything more? Or if you've read my other books or any books on Witchcraft, you might be wondering, for example, 'What about stirring salt into the water?' or 'What about invoking and banishing pentagrams?' As I explained earlier, the Circle-casting ritual above is a special one for Teen Witches that's easy to remember and will get you started. As you get more experienced and comfortable with the ritual you will be drawn to more evocative and elaborate methods of Circle casting, which will please and empower you more and reflect your growing capacities as a Witch. An analogy would be if this were a recipe book, the Circle casting above would be something nutritious, easy-to-prepare and filling, like smashed avocado on toast. Four-course banquets will come later as you become more acquainted with your skills.

Deosil and Widdershins

◇◇

DEOSIL: southern hemisphere – anti-clockwise;
northern hemisphere – clockwise
WIDDERSHINS: southern hemisphere – clockwise;
northern hemisphere – anti-clockwise

Note: the secret to understanding the directions of deosil (with the sun) and widdershins (against the sun) is to consider if clocks were invented in the southern hemisphere the hands would move in the opposite direction that they do now . . . because they are mimicking the way the sun appears to move across the sky as it rises in the east and sets in the west. In the northern hemisphere looking 'down' to the equator it is clockwise, and in the southern hemisphere looking 'up' to the equator it is anti-clockwise . . . it's as simple as that!

Instant Circle of Pure Protection

◇◇

For when you have no props!

When you have become adept at Circle casting and you have become familiar with the feeling that a well-cast Circle provides, then you can begin casting instant Circles of pure protection at times when a formal Circle casting is not possible.

For example, when you are about to do a test at school and you want to have a calm clear space around your desk, or when you are in a group situation and there are negative people near by and you want to keep your space positive. But be aware that a real instant Circle of pure protection can only be cast when you are adept at formal Circle casting and understand the role of a sacred Circle – which is to maintain a safe, positive, sacred space within which you can work your magick and be your best magickal self.

Hold out your power finger and stretch out your arm to trace the blue/white Circle sphere in a deosil direction. As you do this say:

I conjure you, sacred Circle of power.

When you sense the glowing sphere around you, close your eyes, concentrate, raise your arms above your head and call in the elements:

Air – earth – water – fire,

All the elements manifest.

So shall this Circle now be blessed.

Now honour the Lady and Lord, and as you do this sense the Circle filling with white light:

Lady and Lord,

As above so below.

To and from you

All things flow.

Now you have created a magick Circle that, depending on how strong your powers of visualisation are and how well you understand the full Circle-casting ritual, will work just as well for simple spells and rituals.

Closing Circle is important to formally seal magickal work and also to ground and clear any excess or remaining energies. An analogy could be that it's like washing up the dishes after a meal and putting everything away ready for the next meal.

To close this Circle, all you need to do is hold out your power finger, picture blue/white light pouring out and cut through the Circle boundary as you say:

The Circle is open but unbroken.

You don't need to farewell the elemental guardians (as you didn't call them) or formally acknowledge the Lady and Lord again at this point as long as you are aware that you carry them in your heart.

Pure Power Shield

◇◇

SNAPPING IT ON – SNAPPING IT OFF

This is something you can do if you need a little protection from the outside world. Or you might want to create a mini sacred space whilst you mix up some herbs or read a book about the Craft.

Tips for Creating an Effective Instant Circle of Pure Protection

◇◇

- ☞ Really concentrate on the qualities of the elements.
- ☞ Feel air as you would feel the winds of the world rush around the planet, bringing new scents, new energies. Imagine the wind blowing your hair around. Breathe in and out deeply and be aware of its role as a major life-giving force.
- ☞ Feel earth by visualising enormous mountains and earthquakes splitting the surface to reveal layer upon layer of fertile damp soil. Sense your

connection through the soles of your feet, making your energy one with that of the earth beneath you.

☞ Feel water by visualising the oceans of the world that carry so much life and form the majority of this planet's surface. The rivers, streams, lakes and seas are the blood of our planet, so feel your own salty blood course through your veins as you meditate on this element.

☞ Feel fire by picturing the explosive sun. Concentrate on the sensation of its heat on your face and also focus on the fiery molten core of our planet and its ability to create and destroy.

☞ Hold your power hand out to your side and snap your fingers three times as you say:

Perfect power protects me,

One, two, three.

On the last snap, see in your mind's eye a cord of blue light begin to whiz around you like a super-fast skipping rope. This will deflect any negative energy until you snap it off. To do this, stretch out your power hand again, snap your fingers three times and say:

Perfect power switching off,

One, two, three, STOP!

See the blue cord disappear. I find you need to say 'stop', because as the blue light spins around you it builds up to quite a strong intensity that just snapping your fingers doesn't always manage to earth. Saying 'stop' grounds any residue of energy properly. However, if you are feeling a bit jumpy after snapping your shield on and off, just press your hands onto the earth (or floor) and visualise any excess power draining back into the ground beneath you.

Teen Witch Tools of the Trade

There are some basic tools that you will eventually want to have. However, some of you may not be allowed to own a large dagger (an athame) or light candles and incense in your room. So here is a list of things that can get you started and some important information about each.

Altar: the surface on which all your Witchy stuff lives. There are formal ways of setting up an altar, for example, certain coloured candles to be placed in certain quarters. Your altar can be a little more like a cross between an older Witch's altar and a collection of gorgeous evocative Witchy stuff. Do keep it clean and relatively uncluttered, though. You might like to have an altar cloth in a special colour like dark purple or pale blue and maybe even embroidered or painted with magickal symbols like suns, moons, stars, pentagrams or sun/star signs. My original altar cloth, over 30 years old, is now threadbare and I have my tarot cards wrapped in it. I am more organic now and do not have a cloth; I use leaves, sand and earth to denote my altar spaces, which are multiple because I am a bit of a nomad now!

By the way, it's essential to keep your altar space dedicated to your magic and keep it clear of half-finished cups of tea, school textbooks and yesterday's underwear!

Ideally your altar will be facing due south (the earth quarter; north if you are in the northern hemisphere), but if your room's not nicely centred on a north–south axis just get as close to it as you can. You will need to have the four elements represented on your altar, and if you know which way it is facing you might like to put these in the same quarters as you welcome the guardians into

Circle. So you can have a bowl of water in the west, a candle (new, red and unlit if you can't light flames in your room) in the north (south if you are in the northern hemisphere), incense (or a feather) in the east, and a bowl of salt/sand/soil or a crystal in the south (north if you are in the northern hemisphere).

If you don't know the directions, don't worry; just have these things placed somewhere on your altar, though every smart phone has a compass on it and it's also easy enough to buy a compass from a camping supply store and get things nicely aligned.

You will also want to have something that represents the Lady and Lord – maybe little statues, or pictures you've cut out from a magazine put in frames. The Lady and the Lord represent the sacredness of life, creation and sexuality, and also qualities of love, compassion and harmony between all humans beyond gender ... so put some thought into how all this can be represented on your altar.

Also on your altar you could have some flowers or a growing plant, and maybe some shells you have collected to represent the ocean. As you grow as a Teen Witch you will come across lots of special things that you might like to place on your altar, either permanently or for a little whilst. I tend to have a lot of bits and pieces on my altar (most often rocks, raw crystals, driftwood and other natural power objects that leap out at me when I am in nature) when I'm not formally using it, which I then put to one side for when I set up my altar more formally (and to make room for ingredients for spells and things) when I am performing a specific magickal ritual.

A Witch's Tools

◇◇

CRYSTALS: store-bought crystals are beautiful and evocative, and yet excessive use and consumption of them is not environmentally conscious. Consider fossicking for your own crystals or swap and trade with other Witches and take steps to limit the exploitative marketing of them, which actually limits our magickal abilities. Just be conscisous and conscientious in how you procure them and how many you have.

I usually have a couple on my altar to help intensify magickal energies or for me to hold when I'm raising power or visualising. Amethyst and selenite are my go to's. Crystals are aligned with the element of earth.

ATHAME, the Witch's dagger: traditionally a black-handled, double-bladed (but not sharp) knife used to channel and focus energy. It is symbolic of the god, being phallic in shape, as this relates to its procreative tool partner the chalice (reflecting the

Goddess and great womb of creation), and is probably the most unusual of a Witch's tools. It has a certain notoriety thanks to all those half-baked movies where Witches are shown performing human sacrifices with long, evil-looking knives. So some younger readers oughtn't get too surprised if their parents say, 'No way are you owning one of those!' Instead you can use your power finger (the index finger of the hand you write with) as a substitute or you can use a wand. An athame is never used by a real Witch to cut anything solid and it should not be waved around to show off! It is one of the most sacred and personal things a Witch can own and needs to be treated with a lot of respect. When placed on your altar, the athame is aligned with the element of air.

PENTACLE: this is a circular object that is usually made of clay or brass and has a pentagram (the sacred five-pointed star) marked on it. You can rest your athame on it, and it can also be used as a small plate to place your food on. It is aligned with the element of earth. A tip for making your own (cheap but effective) pentacle is to get a clay flowerpot base (like a flat dish), turn it upside down and draw a pentagram on it (you could paint and decorate it in earthy colours like deep orange and brown).

CHALICE: symbolic of the Goddess and basically a lovely glass or goblet used to hold your drink in. (There is another use for the chalice in older Witches' Circle casting and ritual that is mentioned in my other books, but for Teen Witches it's best as a drinking vessel.) It is aligned with the element of water and can be crystal, glass or metal – but it must only be used during magickal work.

WAND: everyone knows what a wand is! It can channel and focus energy and help conjure things into being. You can make your own: an easy one to make in Australia is to find a nice straight gum tree branch about 45 cm long and as thick as your thumb or index finger. (If you absolutely have to cut it from a tree, ask for permission first and give thanks after.) Do some research on sacred trees indigenous to where you live and let your intuition guide you to the type of branch you could procure to make your wand. Strip the leaves and twigs from it and sand it down until smooth. You can whittle both ends to a blunt point or bind

a crystal (perhaps clear quartz or amethyst) to one end with a cloth or leather cord. If you like, decorate the wand by painting meaningful symbols (perhaps some runes) on it. A wand is aligned with the element of fire.

BELL (OR GONG): you can use a bell or gong to ring in and seal the Circle or to signify the beginning or end of a ritual or ceremony. You don't need to have one – you can clap your hands instead – but I think it adds an empowering touch!

CRYSTAL SINGING BOWLS: in the years of being a Witch I have also become a devout yogini. A practice that occurs in many yoga studios now is the use of crystal bowls to create a sacred space and to commence and end yoga practice. A crystal bowl traced with the bowl striker (or your finger) will generate a soothing tone that energetically harmonises the space and everyone in it.

INCENSE: this represents the element of air and can be substituted with a feather (if you can't have a flame in your room). Different scents represent various physical and metaphysical qualities. Incense can be burnt as sticks or cones, but I prefer using charcoal discs and sprinkling powdered incense on top. You have to make sure when using the discs that they rest on sand or similar

since they get *very* hot. And make sure you put them out with some water or bury them in the sand when you're finished. *Never* leave one unattended! A good tip for getting the best, purest scent from powdered incense is to place a small piece of alfoil on top of the burning disc and place your incense on that. Not as much smoke is created, the incense burns longer and all you need to do is give it a little stir with a twig or similar occasionally to keep it cooking.

CANDLES: they are aligned with the element of fire, whether they're lit or unlit. Different colours have different magickal meanings and abilities. You will probably have at least a couple of candles on your altar – you might have little tea lights to shine some light on the proceedings (since working by everyday, household electric lights is a great way to make a Circle not so magickal!) and taller, coloured candles that are a part of specific spells or rituals. My formal altar is covered in candles. I have two: one in a sun base and one in a moon base to represent the Lord and Lady (god and 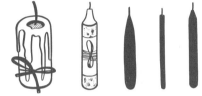 Goddess); a big fat white one that is my 'light' so I can see what I'm doing; a red one in the fire quarter to formally represent the element of fire; and then I usually have a special coloured one anointed in magickal oils that is part of a spell or ritual of gratitude I'm doing.

BOWL OF WATER: to represent the element of water, of course! The bowl can be glass, pottery or even a large sea shell with water resting in it.

CAULDRON: another notorious Witchy accessory! It's not essential and a good cauldron can be quite expensive. If you are part of a Teen Witch Coven, you might like to all pitch in and buy one together. The cauldron is very symbolic, representing the fertile womb of the Great Mother, from which all things come and to which all return. A cauldron can be used to brew magickal potions (edible and inedible!). It can also hold fire and be used to burn offerings or paper petitions.

MORTAR AND PESTLE: a handy bowl and stick to grind up incenses and powders. You can find them at any good cooking supply store. I bought mine at an Indian supermarket (where they're used to grind up all the spices used in Indian cooking).

Book of Shadows

◇◇◇

I'm sure that those of you at school or university will have more than enough books cluttering up your lives, but a Book of Shadows is really important for a Teen Witch. You are going to be learning a lot at this point in your Witchy life and you will benefit from keeping track of what you're doing. Apart from anything else, it will be fun to look back on as a wise old Witch and see how far you've come!

A Teen Witch Book of Shadows doesn't have to be a big deal (though it can be if you want!). It can even be on your computer (make sure you back it up on the cloud).

However, I think pen (or ink, crayon, coloured pencil – whatever!) and paper are ultimately more rewarding. You could have a folder with pocket inserts to slip in left-over packets of incense you used or created, or a special feather you used for a particular ritual, Polaroids you took of a gathering you had, a tape of you chanting – anything! At the very least your Book of Shadows should have notes on what you did, the results and any insights along the way.

Whilst a personal Book of Shadows is a must, some Wiccan traditions also have more formalised books of shared material, and if you are initiated into a Coven as an adult Witch you might need to copy their Book of Shadows by hand – primarily to help you learn and absorb Coven knowledge and experience.

If you are part of a Teen Witch Coven, it's a good idea for at least someone to keep a record of what you're all doing as a group. Perhaps you could take turns and have each member contribute different insights into the rituals and spells you work.

HELP! I'M A MAGICKAL MESS

I had a funny conversation with a budding Witch when she was lamenting how she had messed up a ritual. She had all her will, intention, ingredients, items and space sorted, but her magickal efforts just resulted in a magickal mess!

She had laid out a Circle of seven red tea light candles that she knocked when she moved around the Circle, spilling red wax everywhere. She left a window open and her carefully created sand sigil blew away when a gust came through the room. The worst of all was when her flowing skirt caught fire as she stood to raise energy and she hadn't noticed that it was touching a candle on the floor. Luckily she was able to put it out quickly. But her budding efforts had her wailing to me, 'I'm not magickal … I'm just a magickal mess!'

Be conscious, think ahead and mitigate liability and problems by using common sense — then you are in Circle with a powerful ritual happening, experiencing all the magick there is safely and powerfully.

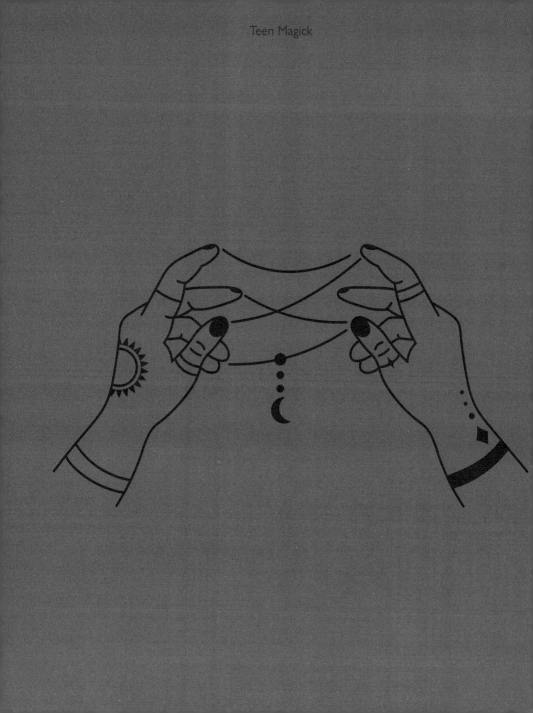

CHAPTER THREE

SLAY YOUR SPELLS

◇◇

As a young Catholic I used to make the sign of the cross before entering church or after communion, and now as a Witch I make the sign of the pentagram as a quick mini-ritual of self-blessing and protection. I find this helps me focus and strengthen my Witchy powers. First touch your third eye, then your right nipple, left shoulder, right shoulder, left nipple and then third eye again to trace out the sacred five-pointed star.

EMPOWER YOUR INGREDIENTS

◇◇

Before you start any spell or ritual it's good to cleanse and empower what you're working with. After casting Circle, hold your hands over your altar and the ingredients (the herbs or objects) you are using. Take a moment to close your eyes and inhale deeply. Feel the palms of your hands tingle and grow hot as you focus your energy there.

When you are ready, in your mind's eye see pure white light streaming from your hands and into the objects as you say:

I cleanse these objects of negativity
With light that's pure and positive.
I empower these objects to work my will
For the good of all and with harm to nil.

WHEN SPELL-CASTING ...

Believe that your magick will work, and fuel it with your passion and intent. Try not to cast spells when you're feeling really sad or angry, unless you feel very confident about being able to channel these emotions as fuel for your workings.

If you're feeling scattered or vague, wait until you feel clearer. You could try a candle meditation to clear your head.

Memorise the incantations: it might be a hassle, but trust me – it's worth it. When you know the words and you're not looking at a book, you can really focus on the energies you are conjuring.

Part of my television work involved me memorising long spiels to say to camera. I used to look at the paragraphs in front of me and think, 'Oh my Goddess, how am I going to remember all this?' But gradually, after repeating line by line, it would sink in. Then I got really good at it (memorising is an art you can learn) and now I can memorise long passages with no trouble. And usually it's stuff I'm not that personally attached to! When I'm memorising things that I'm absolutely passionate about, like incantations and invocations, learning things by heart is a pleasure!

Be resourceful: you may not have the right coloured candle, or it may be the waning moon and the spell says to do it on a waxing moon. Do the spell anyway. Here are a few suggestions:

- ☞ A white candle can replace any other candle except black.
- ☞ You can substitute herbs by understanding what they are used for and finding ones with similar qualities. If I don't have an unusual herb, I find lavender is easily obtainable and a good substitute for just about everything. It has great transformative and nurturing qualities, and can effectively charge up just about any spell.

Research: when you need to invoke a Goddess or god for a spell, make sure you know what you are welcoming. Do some research, so that you know exactly where they're coming from and what their primary energies are. Don't just call in a name; call in a presence.

⊕ Spell-sealing Charm

◇◇◇

Unless there is a specific suggestion for a spell ending, it's a good idea to seal it off with this:

This I ask for the good of all
So that harm may come to none.
So mote it be.
My will be done.

Magickal Meditations

A lot of the symbolism in spell-working and ritual needs to be charged up by the powers of your mind's eye and your emotions. There are simple things you can do to improve your powers of visualisation and your psychic abilities.

To improve my overall powers of visualisation, I like colouring in landscapes – I let my eyes relax and I start to change the colour of leaves on a tree from green to pink. I see the colour change as if the tip of the leaf has been dipped into a pool of pink water and is absorbing it like a sponge. You'll be amazed at how quickly you can master this. Of course, in the physical world the leaves aren't turning pink, but in the inner reality I have created they are.

There is another fun visualisation practice that I call 'rubbing it out'. If I am waiting for an Uber or whatever I will focus on a distant building (city skylines are good) and start 'rubbing it out' as if I have a giant eraser. I will do this until I can visualise the skyline minus the building I have rubbed out. (If you find that the buildings are actually getting demolished in real life whilst you're doing this, you're obviously too good – stop it immediately!)

Another good discipline to develop psychic powers is the candle meditation. Light a candle in a dark room and gaze at the flame. When you are ready, try to make it flicker to the left and right at your will. See if you can make the flame grow long and short at your will. Keep playing with the flame until you have mastered its movements. Now, you might think this sounds impossible – but try it out, I dare you! It's likely you'll be amazed at the results!

THE MAGICK OF LIFE

People can get hung up on the Hollywood hocus pocus results of spell-casting. They expect results like the ones the girls from *Charmed* get. But real magick is far more profound than this: if life were like *Sabrina* or *Charmed* everyone would take it for granted and we would become bored, demanding and out of sync with the tidal ebbs and flows of life.

When we understand and contemplate the interconnectedness of all things, then we see that the 'special effects' witchcraft of movies and TV is not as exciting and moving as real, natural magick. However, anything's possible. Don't forget that only 80 years ago if someone had said there would be a small box sitting in the corner of your living room in which people could talk and move around in different environments, they would have thought you were insane. Of course, we now know that box as a television – and it's not a box, it's a flat screen!

Even science (especially the field of quantum physics) is now explaining what Witches have known instinctively all along what we imagine can and will happen: we can affect reality by the strength and passion of our minds (not just by snapping our fingers!). And when we become adept at harnessing and focusing the elemental powers as well and start making magick, anything is possible!

◇◇◇

CHAPTER FOUR

A Witch's Sacred Days

◇◇◇

Sabbats are the eight seasonal festivals celebrated by Witches (think Christmas and Easter but a lot more often!) that correspond with both traditional agricultural events (like the sowing and harvesting of crops and seasonal changes) and astronomical events (the solstices and equinoxes). We celebrate the sabbats as a way of keeping ourselves attuned to the cycles of life as they come and go outside us and within us.

The four major (agriculturally based) sabbats are Samhain, Imbolc, Beltane and Lammas, and the four minor (astronomically based) sabbats are Yule, Ostara, Litha and Mabon.

The Wheel of the Year is the name of this cycle of festivals and the Wheel of the Year myth is the story that enhances our understanding of and insight into these sacred times. Here I would like to offer some simple, enjoyable and empowering ways that Teen Witches can honour and celebrate these sacred times and the turning of the Wheel of the Year in a unique and easy way. The suggestions below can be incorporated into a party-like gathering, a small meeting of one or two people or as a solo experience.

Whilst Teen Witches can celebrate the eight sabbats, many of you will most likely still be expected to (and want to!) celebrate the Christmas and Easter holidays. This is fine; just be aware of the ancient origins of these celebrations and the underlying fact that they are about love and sharing good times together.

SAMHAIN

1 May (southern hemisphere) | 31 October (northern hemisphere)

Samhain is a time to remember our ancestors. Get together with your Witchy friends and each bring a photo of a loved one (or loved ones) who has passed on and share your favourite memories of them. Dress in black and burn patchouli and myrrh incense to honour their spirits. The northern hemisphere correspondence of this festival has been commercialised as Halloween and is marketed as a time to go trick or treating and scaring each other. However, as long as you remain aware that it is also a special time to respect the dead, you can have a bit of fun with Halloween props like jack o' lanterns and pointy hats and broomsticks! Even the most serious Witches' festivals like this one honour the role death plays in life in a light, joyous aspect.

YULE

◇◇

20–23 June (southern hemisphere) | 20–23 December (northern hemisphere) (depending on the actual day of the solstice)

I suggest that everyone bathe in chamomile (pour a cup of the tea into the bath) before dressing in reds and purples.

Gather together for a bonfire or a fire in an open fireplace at someone's home. Tonight you will be celebrating the longest night of the year, and at sunrise it is the beginning of the ascent of the sun. From now on the days will be longer and get warmer as the journey towards spring has begun.

Get the fire going and place a Yule log in the centre. Traditionally the Yule log is oak, but I have used gum tree wood and decorated it with gold and red ribbons. As it burns, I sprinkle myrrh and frankincense resin on it.

You can also throw on handfuls of gum leaves (or any oily leaf that makes a thick smoke) and make wishes as the smoke swirls towards the newborn sun, which will catch it and infuse it with its growing life force.

Have a big feast of your favourite winter foods, like soups and casseroles and puddings, and drink warm, honey-spiced grape juice. If you are allowed to sit up all night to welcome the sun in, do so! As it rises, everyone can light a red candle from the sparks of the Yule log in honour of the new sun/son. Everyone can also take home some of the charred Yule log in a little green bag tied with gold ribbon. Put this under your bed to ensure a safe and happy home.

IMBOLC

◇◇◇

1 August (southern hemisphere) | 2 February (northern hemisphere)

New beginnings and new inspirations are to be experienced during Imbolc. Do a big clean out of your room and get rid of anything you don't need any more. Have a gathering where everyone writes a list of things they want to achieve by the next sabbat (Ostara is seven weeks away) and then turn it into a poem. All wear white and bring a white candle and flower to the gathering.

Stand in a circle and read out your favourite poems (or ones you have written yourself) and then together ask the Goddess to bless your goals. Raise energy by holding hands and chanting Goddess names: 'Isis, Astarte, Diana, Hecate, Demeter, Kali, Inanna.' When the power peaks, throw your hands in the air and shout: 'May all our dreams come true!' Have a feast featuring pasta with pesto (basil, one of the main ingredients, is a sacred herb at this time). Wrap your poem around a bay leaf and keep it on your altar or in your Book of Shadows. Now is also a good time to buy a new pentagram necklace (if you wear one).

OSTARA

◇◇◇

20-23 September (southern hemisphere) | 20-23 March (northern hemisphere) (depending on the actual day of the equinox)

Ostara is the Witches' Easter – it's a time to celebrate that spring is here and the land is alive and regenerating. Get dressed up in gorgeous colourful clothing, put flowers in your hair, get everyone together and go for a picnic.

For southern-hemisphere Witches, those chocolate Easter eggs that you saved from the commercial Easter earlier in the year can be eaten now. (That's if you managed to save them, which is one of the ultimate tests of a Teen Witch's self-discipline – lol!) You can also decorate real eggs, painting them with symbols meaningful to you, and place them on your altar.

BELTANE

31 October (southern hemisphere) | 1 May (northern hemisphere)

Beltane is the fertility festival, a time to honour creation itself. Choose a beautiful natural setting and make a big circle of ivy or other leafy green vine to sit in. Feast on lots of fresh fruits like strawberries and apples – luscious, succulent things. Talk openly about your feelings and affection for the important people in your life. Share a loving cup (all take a sip from one cup) and pass a kiss around from one to the other as an open expression of unconditional love. Each person should bring a passage to read from a book or a poem that inspires their passion and reverence for life to share with everyone else.

LITHA

20-23 December (southern hemisphere) | 20-23 June (northern hemisphere) (depending on the actual solstice)

Litha is the longest day of the year and the time the sun is at its peak. From now on, the days will gradually grow shorter and the descent towards winter has begun (even though, as climate change occurs, Australia and other parts of the southern hemisphere are hitting their hottest weather). It is traditional at this time to throw lavender on a fire to ensure safety for the coming year – but it's likely there will be a fire ban! Instead, burn lavender incense and scatter rose petals around your feasting table.

Have a dinner early in the warm evening and enjoy the balmy weather. As this is the commercial Christmas time in the southern hemisphere, you could bond with that energy and exchange gifts of opulence like richly scented incense and candles, lucky coins and amulets. (Whilst some southern-hemisphere Witches save the present-giving business for our own Yule festival, a lot of us like any excuse to share gifts with those we love and are more than happy to do so at Litha as well as Yule.)

LAMMAS

2 February (southern hemisphere) | 1 August (northern hemisphere)

Lammas is a time to honour the harvest, not only of the land but of the rewards reaped for our hard work in all areas of our lives. Gather together and bake bread with sunflower seeds, being aware of how the combining of skills can create new opportunities. As you are feasting on the freshly baked bread, make sure to offer some to the Goddess and god. Together, trade stories of your successes and share insights you have achieved over the last year so that you can learn from and inspire each other.

MABON

◇◇

20-23 March (southern hemisphere) | 20-23 September (northern hemisphere) (depending on the actual date of the equinox)

Mabon is the final harvest of crops before winter, and is a wonderful time to look back over the past year and at what you have achieved. Write down what you feel most proud of and throw the paper into a fire with a handful of sage or eucalyptus leaves as an offering to the Goddess and god, asking them to bless and acknowledge your efforts.

For Moon Children...

◇◇

THE ESBAT

Another important time for Witches to gather together is every full moon, a potent time for magick of all sorts and a very appropriate time to honour the Goddess at her most visible. The occasion is also often celebrated by a beautiful traditional ritual called 'drawing down the moon', where the Priestess of a Coven will draw down the lunar essence to empower and bless the Coven.

I am spontaneous when honouring and celebrating the full moon, but I always do something. Maybe I will go outside and gaze at her full face as she rises over the horizon and do some deep meditative breathing and witchy prayers of gratitude or chant Goddess names. At other times I may do a full-blown ritual involving casting Circle and reciting the 'Charge of the Star Goddess', a beautiful reworking by Starhawk, of Doreen Valiente's original charge, to draw down the energy.

Charge of the Star Goddess

STARHAWK – THE SPIRAL DANCE:
A REBIRTH OF THE ANCIENT RELIGION OF THE GODDESS

Hear the words of the Star Goddess, the dust of whose feet are the hosts of heaven, whose body encircles the Universe …

I who am the beauty of the green earth,

The white Moon among the Stars,

And the Mystery of the Waters, I call upon your soul to arise and

come unto Me.

For I am the Soul of Nature, which gives life to the Universe.

From Me all things proceed,

And unto Me they must return.

Let My worship be in the heart that rejoices,

For behold – all acts of love and

pleasure are My rituals.

Let there be beauty and strength,

Power and compassion,

Honour and humility,

Mirth and reverence within you.

And you who seek to know Me,

Know that your seeking and yearning will avail you not,

Unless you know the Mystery:

For if that which you seek you find not within yourself,

You will never find it without.
For behold, I have been with you from the beginning,
And I am that which is attained at the end of desire.

Whilst writing this book I experienced an extraordinary full lunar eclipse. I was staying in a beautiful mountain country house with gorgeous landscaped gardens and natural bush settings, and on the night of the eclipse it was extremely cold with not a cloud in the sky.

With two friends I watched the moon rise blindingly white from a clearing in the bush. Gradually, the shadow of the earth softened the moon's glow until it took on a rosy hue. We stood spellbound as the moon became a soft pink pearl floating in the sky. At this point I cast Circle around the fire we had lit and I said the 'Charge of the Star Goddess' in honour of this special night, and then we each threw handfuls of lavender into the fire and made wishes. As the smoke swirled into the sky in offering to the Goddess, we knew our wishes would come true.

It was a truly magickal night and we stayed out for hours until the fire had burnt down and the moon had returned to a beaming white orb.

It is appropriate for Teen Witches to create their own meaningful ritual for the full moon, leaving formal drawing down the moon rituals until you are a little further down the path of your Craft. Rituals that you create yourself, with full awareness of the process involved, will be more magickal and honour the Goddess more than something complicated you get out of a book and perhaps don't fully understand. So light candles, sing songs, make wishes and give thanks for all the good things in life, knowing that the Goddess is smiling down upon you.

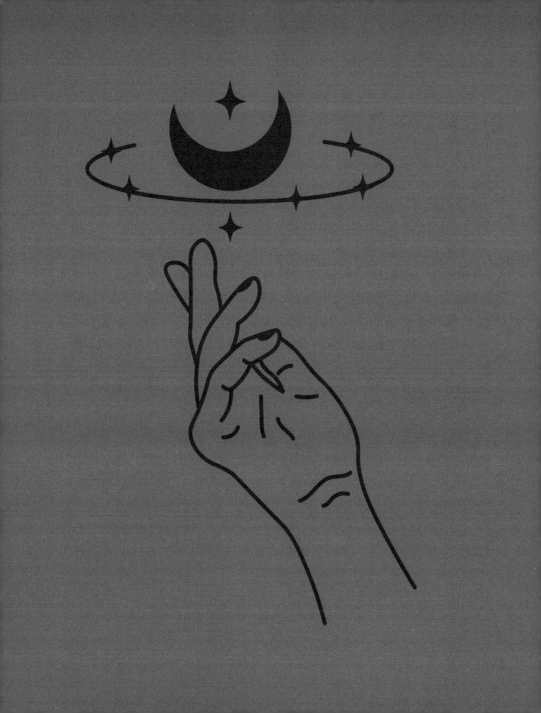

CHAPTER FIVE

It's Only Natural

When I was writing the original conception of this book I was blessed to stay at a grand country home in Mount Macedon, Victoria. Mount Macedon is right next to Hanging Rock, the beautiful and eerie place that is the setting for the story of the disappearance of four schoolgirls in 1900, immortalised by Joan Lindsay in her novel *Picnic at Hanging Rock*.

It is a magickal area, incredibly lush and fertile even in the winter months. Since Witchcraft is a nature-worshipping religion, I couldn't imagine a better place to write a book for budding Teen Witches. Each day I would take long walks, all rugged up in the cold air, and just allow the awesome natural beauty around me to seep into my consciousness and make me feel at one with myself and the world.

Alone I would stop and listen to the silence. Of course, it was never completely silent – I could hear the rustle of grass and bushes, the sweet calls of birds, the hushed roar of the wind as it whisked across the tops of the huge gum trees. My work back then was often very demanding and saw me in hectic urban environments and crowded smoky nightclubs and venues, which could stress me out and leave me feeling really depleted. So being away from cars, radios, people's voices, machines and clutter was enormously healing and put me in touch more than ever with the ultimate meaning of being a Witch. I sometimes wandered off the dirt road into the bush. I would just keep going, clambering over mossy rocks and fallen logs and gurgling waterways that had formed after the heavy rain the night before. Thick piles of composting, russet red leaves would squish under foot as I made my way deeper into the magickal weave of giant, glowing green ferns and tangled twigs and branches of shrubs and bushes. I sipped rainwater that had pooled on big flat leaves and stopped when I sensed it was right to – just to breathe and listen. Once I was sure I could hear the groaning of a giant red-barked gum as its twisted trunk eased its way up out of the ground through the canopy until its leaves nestled high in the grey mist above. I meditated on that spiralling trunk, seeing in it all of life and nature – a DNA coil, the cone of a sea shell, incense smoke released with flame, the swirl of light I see in a cone of power raised in Circle.

I went for a walk one morning after a long night of writing. My eyes were tired and I had switched on my computer, but something just made me get up and leave its blank, blue screen and walk outside. I descended the long driveway looking up at the towering gums, feeling the cold air on my cheeks and the lightest mist of rain on my face. As I took a few more slow steps, my gaze travelled across to the mesh of dripping green leaves of a giant fern, my feet crunching on the gravel. Then I felt the impulse to look up again. Perched in the high fork of a gum tree sat a koala looking at me sleepily. The branches she was nestled in held her like a cradle, rocked by the wind. We watched each other for a whilst, with her occasionally looking away to observe the oncoming misty clouds that floated across the top of the mountain. Every now and again a stronger blast of wind would come: 'Hang on!' I laughed, as I watched her sway wildly back and forth. As she craned her neck I could see a fluffy, white fur collar under her chin that contrasted with her short, sleek, grey body fur. Eventually she stretched, turned around and started to make her way further up the slim trunk, her big black claws gripping effortlessly. Perched higher, she lazily reached out to grab some gum leaves to munch on. It was the first time I had seen a wild koala and I was overwhelmed standing there, a lone human sharing this beautiful animal's space.

Back then and even more so now in our hyper-connected world, it never ceases to amaze me how it is so easy to get caught up in the extreme stress and stimulation of living in an urban environment, so much so that we lose the innate sense of peace that we all have a right to feel. Across all my years as an urban Witch, no matter how spiritually diligent I was, I still got caught up in pushing myself to do more and more, trying to get to a point where I felt satisfied with my efforts. The pressure of my people-pleasing city life cut me off from a rewarding sense of self and I got tricked into thinking that by 'doing' I would reach that point of fulfilment. However, the answer doesn't lie in 'doing' but in 'being' — just stopping and being in the moment. Then everything is enough. I eventually moved to a remote tropical island in the

Caribbean seven years ago and rebirthed my life as a commercial pilot flying passengers and humanitarian aid. This experience helped me get connected in the moment, and peaceful.

So, if you are ever feeling really cut off from enjoying life and nothing you do seems enough, take yourself off into the country, or a lush park or open beach, and let your mind wander. Breathe deeply. Connect with your natural self – this is one of the best Witchy disciplines I can suggest.

There are many spells you can cast and rituals you can perform that work with natural energy and objects; you're only limited by your imagination. Often, the more remote and untouched your environment is, the more natural magick there is to tap into. Remember: you don't have to cast Circle for these but can if you like, although you are already in a naturally sacred space, perfect for these spells and rituals.

River Blessing

Follow a flowing stream or river, observing its methods and sharing its space. When I do this, I reflect on the beauty of the moving water and imagine what it would feel like to *be* water – spilling over rocks, swirling in pools and rushing through channels. I focus on feeling my blood moving through my veins and connect with how, in a small way, my body reflects the great waterways of the planet.

To honour and to receive a blessing of the stream or river, it is appropriate to perform the pentagram salute.

THE PENTAGRAM SALUTE: dip your index finger in the cascading water and trace from third eye (the space between your eyebrows) to right nipple to left shoulder across to right shoulder to left nipple and back to third eye.

Tree Thoughts

Let yourself be drawn to a tree. You might be attracted to a lush and beautiful young jacaranda tree or you might be drawn to the old, gnarled, textured branches of a gum … maybe you are at the base of a giant ancient sequoia redwood. Kneel at your chosen tree's base and offer your respect. Meditate on the absolute magnificence of trees and become aware of their essential and amazing presence on this planet. Acknowledge that they are so taken for granted. When you are ready, leave something of yourself as an offering (like a lock of your hair or a kiss bestowed on the tree's trunk, or trace your initials in the dirt at its base) and join a conservation group if you are not already a part of one.

Bird Call Divination

Ask a question and wait to hear a bird call: one means no, two means yes, three means ask again and silence means the outcome is unclear or that it is better for you not to be certain at this point. A whole cacophony of birdsong means everything you desire will come to you!

Flower Divination

This works very well with roses, but any flower bud can be used. Gently tie a small white ribbon around the stem of one bud and a small blue one around another. Then make yourself known to the plant by saying:

I respectfully ask, oh flower divine,

To reveal the answer to this question of mine.

Pour an offering of spring water on its roots and ask your question. If the white ribbon blooms first, the answer is yes; if the blue blooms first, the answer is no.

It's worth noting you need to ask really straightforward questions where a yes/no answer will suffice. You need to do this spell using only one species of plant as some bloom faster than others, but rather than tying ribbons you could choose two plants of the same species but with different flowers in different colours. Decide which colour will be 'yes' and which 'no'.

Earth Divination

Go somewhere where there is lots of cracked dried earth. I like doing this at the beach on a very hot day where the top layer of sand has become baked and has separated into a latticework of patterns. Using a stick, trace a metre-diameter circle in a deosil (sunwise/anti-clockwise in the south, clockwise in the north) direction and as you do chant:

Circle of earth revealing

Scenes of my future being.

Now sit and gaze at the patterns formed by the cracked sand (or earth). Ask a question and allow your eyes to go out of focus and your subconscious to open up. You will be amazed at what is revealed. You might see pictures form in the sand or words might just float into your head. When you are finished, open the circle by tracing back over it in a widdershins/clockwise direction in the south and deosil/anti-clockwise in the north.

River Spell

◇◇◇

This is for when you've been having a hard time and you want to move on.

Go to a flowing river at sunrise. Hold a stick in your hand and focus all the thoughts of things you want to let go of into the stick. When you are ready, cast it into the river and watch it float away as you say:

As the river flows, I let go.

Yesterday, its story told; I go forth wise and bold.

Another day starts to unfold.

Turn around and walk away without looking back.

Stone Spell

◇◇◇

Stones are wonderful for absorbing problems that need to be dealt with. This is a banishing ritual that works wonders.

Choose a soft stone that you can mark with another, harder stone. Focus on what you want to get rid of – it might be a bad habit like biting your nails, overeating, irrational fear of something or even a person who is giving you grief and you want them to stop bugging you. As you do this, dig a hole in the earth at least 20 cm deep.

When you have a very clear image of what you want to get rid of, carve either the name of the thing or a symbol that represents it (for example, you might draw fear as a big 'X'; just make sure your symbol is meaningful to you and that you allow your intuition to choose it). When you have done this, hold the stone in both hands and say:

Begone, begone, begone from me,
I cast away and bury deep
That which no longer works for me.
With harm to none so mote it be.

Drop the stone into the hole and cover it up. Walk away without looking back. You can also do this at the ocean's edge or, better yet, standing on a cliff over the ocean and throwing the stone into the water. You can cast this spell as often as necessary, but depending on your power of visualisation and focus you might need to repeat it a few times.

To maximise effectiveness, try to perform this spell during the waning moon and for even more empowerment on a Saturday ruled by Saturn, the planet of binding and banishing.

Chanting

I often chant when I am alone in nature, and I recommend it to you! During magickal work chanting can raise power (see 'Raising Power' page 50), but chanting can also calm the mind and connect you with a peaceful sense of the Divine. I love either the classic Wiccan Goddess chant: 'Isis, Astarte, Diana, Hecate, Demeter, Kali, Inanna', or a Sanskrit chant my yoga teacher gave me – the ancient Gayatri mantra.

Gayatri Mantra

<><><><><><><><><><><><><><><><><><><><><><><><><><><><><><><><><><>

Om bhur bhuvaḥ svaḥ tat savitur vareñyam bhargo
devasya dhīmahi dhiyo yonaḥ prachodayāt

Translated: we meditate on that most adored supreme presence, the creator/ess, whose effulgence (divine light) illumines all realms (physical, mental and spiritual). May this divine light illumine our intellect. Word meanings: *om*: the primeval sound; *bhur*: the physical body/physical realm; *bhuvaḥ*: the life force/the mental realm; *svaḥ*: the soul/spiritual realm; *tat*: that (god); *savitur*: the sun, creator (source of all life); *vareñyam*: adore; *bhargo*: effulgence (divine light); *devasya*: supreme Lord; *dhīmahi*: meditate; *dhiyo*: the intellect; *yo*: may this light; *nah*: our; *prachodayāt*: illumine/inspire.

When I chant to honour nature, I focus on how the sounds emanating from my natural instrument, my voice, blend and weave with nature's instruments around me: leaves rustling together, branches rubbing and creaking in the wind, water cascading over stones or falling as droplets into a pond. Birds and animals vocalise along with me too — all sounds seem to speak to me, centre me and share their wisdom.

An important practice of Australian spirituality is 'singing to the land'. Aboriginal and Torres Strait Islander peoples honour and reinforce their ties to the land by doing this. Those of us who are from other heritages and are not initiated into ancient Aboriginal traditions and songs can honour

our unique and divine land spirit by offering our own songs and hearts.

Fire Meditation

There's nothing quite like sitting outside at night and staring into the dancing flames and glowing, shimmering coals of an open fire. Fire like this encourages contemplation and insight. I like to do smoke divination by throwing gum leaves on the fire and looking for pictures and images in the heavy swirling smoke. An effective magick ritual is to write your wishes and hopes on little pieces of coloured paper (check out the colour correspondences in 'Slay your Spells') and throw them into the fire so that its energy will help make them come true. Remember, though – always check fire regulations first and whether there is a ban in place.

Faeries and Nature Spirits

According to one theory, the original faeries were the pre-Celtic Pagan peoples of the British Isles, France and Germany. Evidence of this can be seen in both custom and language – for example, one of the races living in Britain before the Celts was the Picts, which is almost certainly the source of the word 'pixie'. The skeletal remains of members of these races show that they tended to be smaller and more lithe in build than subsequent arrivals to these regions, hence the notion of faeries as being the little people. They lived in harmony with the natural cycles of the land and, when driven into hiding by later contenders for the land, they gradually became mythologised as mysterious inhabitants of the wild country possessed of supernatural powers gained through their adherence to the oldest religion.

The Irish still believe the faerie folk or 'Sidhe' live in the hills of Ireland in burial grounds and graves and emerge at certain times of the year (during festivals like Samhain). For the majority of people now, however, faeries are popularised as gorgeous little winged creatures that bestow blessings and good fortune, and a complicated and elaborate mythological world full of different types of faerie folk has evolved.

Whatever their origins, faeries are also often considered to be spirits of nature, which is how I related to them as a child – subtle beings living not only close to the land, but inside it. When I was younger I used to make homes for faeries in the bush. I would fashion stones, twigs, moss and flower petals into little abodes at the base of a shrub or under the big, flat, exposed root of a tree. Whilst writing this book I would often sit next to a small waterfall, and as I became mesmerised by the silky, dancing water I could swear I saw sparkling little creatures hopping from rock to rock, splashing through the thin sheets of water.

The way to see faeries is to open your heart to the possibility that they exist and fuel that with wonder and love. Better yet, create your own garden and invite them to share it with you. If you can, have a small part of your yard all to yourself (or if you live in a flat, planter boxes and pots of your own). Make sure your garden is fertilised organically – which means no artificial chemicals or pesticides!

Talk to your plants and let them know you love them.

Grow and nurture lots of coloured flowers and scented herbs – faeries love these! Breathing in the scent of flowers and herbs is also healing for the human soul; my favourites are gardenias, camellias, roses, jasmine, lilies, lavender, rosemary and basil. Stud the soil around your plants with crystals and shells and tie coloured ribbons on stems and branches to attract faeries. With a silver pen you can write wishes and goals on the ribbons and ask the faeries to help make them come true.

CHAPTER SIX

Magickal Social Media

The biggest change in the 16 years since I originally wrote this book is the advent of social media. It's incredible to think (considering how completely enmeshed in our lives Facebook, Instagram, Snapchat and Pinterest are) that it didn't exist that long ago but it has impacted our lives forever and changed the way humans interact in, not even, the blink of an eye.

It's important that as a modern Teen Witch you understand how social media works and not let it manipulate you. It must be a positive presence in your life, not an energetic drain that exploits or smothers your individuality.

During the writing of this rebooted book I was at a private family Christmas party in Los Angeles and I witnessed a 'famous' girl who has 6.5 million followers on Instagram and her brother who has 250,000 followers behaving the same as girls and guys with a few hundred followers. They spent a lot of the evening taking carefully constructed selfies, tweaking them with effects and then uploading them and laughing about how many likes they instantly got and then looking at other people's feeds and commenting on those. They are incredibly attractive human beings in a culturally accepted aesthetic way, and yet they would retake photos over and over again to get themselves looking their 'best'. I noticed this with interest and thought how another friend's 16-year-old daughter with her 700 followers does exactly the same thing – there is exactly the same amount of personal fear in not being accepted enough, satisfaction when you are and elation when there's more than you expect. The whole phenomenon is not geared towards unconditional personal acceptance and celebration; it's geared towards other people's approval in a fickle and 'unreal' environment.

At the same party I listened to an impassioned conversation between two teen girls about how they were planning plastic surgery to adjust the tilt of their noses so they would look 'better' in selfies. Rather than rolling your eyes and thinking how idiotic it is – it's worth having compassion, not judgement; see it for what it is – observe but don't get involved. But it's disturbing.

No teen is immune to the pressure of social media – and it's extremely addictive. But you can make social media a powerful part of your personal magickal practice; however, it is bucking the superficial trend and forgoes having over a million followers by posting provocative selfies and perpetuating that the greatest value an individual can have is how they look, not who they are.

It does connect you with other magickal people – it can empower and build your personal practice and be a tool for mystical learning. If you consciously share Magick in your posts and make each one not about 'you', per se, but as a tool of service and sharing positive energy, knowledge and your lessons learned … as new to being on the path as you are, then the Magick can become cyclical and empowering for all who interact with the post.

Tips for Making Magickal Social Media Posts

Create a sacred space before you post. Light a candle, burn some incense and only post from in front of your altar during ritual. This will slow the obsessive-compulsive desire to post things that have had less thought and expansive magick channelled into them.

Make a rule that you won't post multiple selfies, that you will only post images created with context. Before you post anything run these questions by yourself:

Does it need to be said?

Does it need to be said right now?

Does it need to be said by me?

Is it of service?

Is it celebrating my magickal existence?

Align your posts with the phases of the moon and magickal qualities and planetary influences of the day (see Chapter 16 Magickal Meanings) and consciously imbue them with magick. Don't just post pics of your crystals because they look pretty and cool.

Add some words on the magickal meaning and significance of what you are sharing.

Rather than posting with the aim of how many likes you will get, think about the quality of comments that will be shared underneath those likes based on the depth of sincerity that your post contains. Think how it can be aspirational, inspirational, motivating to others, how it can inspire stimulating, uplifting conversation, shared love and high vibes.

Magickal Social Media Checklist

◇◇

SET YOUR INTENTIONS

Before making any changes to your social media habits, take some time to think about *why* you use Facebook, Instagram, Twitter or whichever social media platform you are most passionate about. For example, I want to:

- ☞ stay connected with far-away friends and family, both genetic and magickal
- ☞ share positive energy
- ☞ learn about spells and magickal knowledge from people I might not meet offline

Once you have clear guidance:

- ☞ set boundaries
- ☞ firmly commit to this concept – if someone, or something in my feed is bothering me, draining my energy and not related to one or all of my three goals, I hide, mute or un-follow that person or account
- ☞ let go of the negative

Once you've identified the reasons you use social media, it's time to clean up your feed. To do this effectively you'll need to cultivate an awareness of your reactions.

Just like in meditation when you observe your breathing as a way to understand your existence and state of being, spend some time observing your reactions to your social media feed. If that school mate's gossipy rants make you crazy, let that person go. If a family member posts nothing but political rants, give yourself permission to hide, un-follow or un-friend that person – family or not.

Feel free to delete posts from your own feed that you may have published in the past that are not harmoniously aligned with your new magickal social media goals.

If there are comments on your well-meaning feeds that are negative, feel free to delete the comments without giving it a second thought.

◇◇

One of my earlier websites from the 90s had a message board on it (the original version of social media!). This meant that people could pick a topic and then leave messages on the board that everyone could see. People wrote so much awful shit about me! Seriously. It was vicious and cruel. And guess what I did? I left it up! Like I owed something to these awful people. (They are called 'trolls' now.) One day after spending hours trying to be answerable to every horrible criticism and mean bitchy comment directed at me, I realised something pretty extraordinary: I could just delete the whole message board. That meant letting go of some of the lovely things people had offered on it, but the negativity had infected the entire space like a virus.

So I just got rid of it all.

DELETE

Are you sure?

DELETE

It felt amazing, and it was one of the most magickal things I've done in my life. It showed the profound effects on many levels, of taking positive action in the face of overwhelming negativity.

After deleting this message board I did something that I have continued to do when dealing with negativity occasionally popping up on feeds I see. I intentionally replace the space with something positive. It might mean stepping away from your computer or putting down your smart device and stepping outside to allow the sun on your face so that the shadows fall behind you, and saying a prayer of healing:

Universe, I give thanks for the freedom I can exercise in allowing only positivity into my space. I pray for the healing and peace of mind of those stuck in the negative rat race.

Practise Random Acts of Online Kindness

Just like internet trolls might randomly place negativity in feeds, do the opposite: plant random comments and posts of gratitude, celebration of the good things in life and positivity.

And the incredible thing is the high level of judgemental negativity from my own witchy community directed at me in general pretty much vanished at the same time I deleted that message board. I had radically shifted my boundaries and parameters and chose to see and allow only the good in people to congregate around me. This prepped me very well for the day that social media took over as a personal promotion vehicle and I was able to keep my side of the internet highway clean (cheesy way to put it, but true.)

Cleaning up your social media circle becomes more difficult with people who are meaningful to you or important in your life but who have a social media presence you find upsetting or irritating. If there's someone in your feed you can't jettison, you'll have to work on managing your reaction to this person.

First, think about why this person is upsetting to you. Are they succeeding in an area where you're struggling? If that's the case, take time to recognise your own strengths. Be compassionate to yourself and honour their success – see that they are a mirror helping you know yourself.

Then, think about what small, concrete steps you could take toward reaching the goal that person you may be jealous of has achieved. Put your energy toward achieving that goal instead of worrying about what that person is sharing on social media.

CONNECT WITH THE WORLD IRL

With so much of our lives shared online it's easy to forget there is a big 'IRL' (in real life) world out there that unfolds in real time. Take the time to put down the smartphone or make plans with friends to do something magickal together. Don't let the connection you feel through social media take the place of frequent and regular in-person interactions.

When you talk with your friend over dinner you learn about everything your friend has left out of the social media feed, and in turn you can share the things that are too personal for you to reveal online. The person whose life looks shiny and perfect on Instagram may be struggling with some of the same issues as you, but you'll never know if you don't reach out. Watching that girl I mentioned earlier, who is one of the most famous on Instagram (and whose best friend IS the most famous at the time of writing, with 156 million followers), exhibiting all the very same insecurities, paranoias and extreme approval needs that I saw a young girl in the suburbs of Sydney, was eye-opening. Usually nothing is what it appears on social media. All that being said, I will be accountable and say for the most part I do make my social media posts tangibly reflect my lessons and joys … because I've positioned myself as an inspirational, aspirational person. I'm grateful for the opportunity to have this meaning and usefulness in people's lives. That is the main reason along with staying in touch with far-off friends and family and my magickal community :)

Positively Manage Social Media Time

Even a well-edited social media feed can be a waste of time and an unnecessary distraction. If you find yourself getting sucked into Facebook and Instagram when you should be studying or paying attention to those around you, try to positively manage your time on social media. Consider, like I mentioned earlier, only posting in a sacred space and maybe only at a certain time of the day, like sunrise. Limit what you do online at night before sleep.

Consider charging your phone outside of your bedroom at night. That way you resist the urge to check it if you wake up. It's better for your brainwaves and sleep not to have it switched on next to you.

In answer to the impact of invasive feeds and the spreading thin of our focus caused by social media there are now apps you can install on your laptop and across all devices that block, limit and give you options to set time boundaries for social media and certain websites and help you positively channel your focus and intentions. At the time of writing the Freedom app was increasing in popularity as being a well-designed positive assist for setting personal online boundaries.

Stop Stalking and Engage in Posts: Don't just Lurk

Even if you don't clean up your friend list or set limits on your social media time, an easy way to make social media a positive force in your life is to engage instead of lurk. International research has shown that teens who comment and connect with friends are happier on social media than those who scroll without commenting – passively observing, or 'lurking', and not having a sense of conscious mindful involvement starts to deteriorate our personalities.

Of course, not all commenting is created equal. Arguing with people or getting into fights with strangers is not a good way to engage. Stay positive and supportive, and don't make a comment online you wouldn't say to that person's face.

If you're in a Facebook group get involved. Share your own struggles and successes and support the ups and downs of others. Real communities can be formed online but, just like in real life, being part of a community is a two-way street. During my time in flight school I joined an online female pilot's closed group. It was hugely helpful in me meeting my aviation goals as I could share anything on that group – especially my gender-driven frustrations with my male co-workers in the unfortunately still often sexist environment of aviation. After I achieved my commercial ratings I was then able to share my lessons and tips for success with other pilots. Not only that, I was able to have a good laugh too. Laughter heals so many wounds. It's very healthy to not take life and yourself so seriously sometimes.

⊕ Stop Stalking Spell

xxxxxxxxxxxxxxxxxxxxxxxxxxxxxxxxxxxxxxxxxxxxxxxxxxxxxxxxxx

This is a spell for when, despite your best efforts, you are addicted to online stalking someone's social media — a boy you like, a girl who dumped you … whatever, whoever, sometimes a spell can help you heal and move on.

YOU WILL NEED:

- ☞ a single screenshot of the feed you are addicted to printed out on a piece of paper
- ☞ a black candle (white for purity and release if you can't get black for binding)
- ☞ a sharp feather quill or pointed stick
- ☞ a space outside to bury in dirt

DIRECTIONS

Do this spell immediately when you need to.

Note: you really have to want to be free of your stalking tendencies. Magick works with the intent with which you fuel it.

Carve the person's online name into the candle with the quill/stick.

Light the candle and drip wax onto the paper as you say:

I bind myself from stalking thee. I release my attachment willingly. I make space for healing within. I am free — my life can again begin.

Repeat this charm as many times as you feel appropriate as you drip wax until the paper image is completely obscured.

Whilst the wax is still damp, roll the paper into a tube and breathe through it three times, saying between each breath:

I release thee.

Finally, bury the paper at least 30 centimetres in the ground. Cover thoroughly with dirt. Stamp on the surface three times and walk away without looking back.

STOP BEFORE YOU CYBER STALK

One of the most damaging aspects of social media is its coercion into spying on people who we decide make us feel less than, not enough, or angry. Especially in the case of young love – you feel compelled to spy on someone's social media feed to try to glean information about their likes and dislikes, who they are into right now or were last year and how you may be able to manipulate that to your advantage – whatever you decide is advantageous in your current injured moment. Generally nothing good comes of this, but it's still so hard not to do once you unleash the beast. It can make people crazy as they get sucked into the spiralling black hole of insecurity and paranoia. So, here is a checklist that my closest girlfriend created for herself when she could see that her cyber fears of the life her boyfriend had before her had her looking at his old girlfriends online. She knew it was totally unhealthy so she created this list, which I think is really powerful and she kindly allowed me to feature it here:

- ☞ Why are you doing this?
- ☞ Is it in your highest good?
- ☞ What could you do instead?
- ☞ Is this person really a threat?
- ☞ Can anything positive come out of it?
- ☞ Know your worth.

CHAPTER SEVEN

Parents: Can't Live With Them, Can't Live Without Them!

I had a very tumultuous time growing up with my parents. And when I hit my teens all hell broke loose! I am the oldest child, so as I was finding my feet as a human being my parents were finding their feet as parents.

Unsurprisingly, we all made lots of mistakes! From when I was as young as 12 there were many times when all I wanted to do was run away – and I would. I would pinch some biscuits from the pantry, get a bottle of cordial and my toothbrush and set off. I don't think I was seriously intending to run away; more just searching for some attention and trying to get my parents to understand how desperately unhappy I was. I would start walking through the bush but never go much further than a few kilometres before I would turn around and go home and sneak the stuff back into the pantry, leaving my parents none the

109

wiser. I really felt I didn't want to be there, but I couldn't really leave. I guess being adopted didn't help. It's very easy to feel alienated from your parents as a teen, and add to this all the adoption issues and it's extra trouble. I remember when I was 14 or so being at one of the big family Christmas gatherings where everyone would get together to celebrate the season of peace and goodwill by spending most of the day gossiping about each other. One of my relatives came up to me and said, 'Your mother will never love you as much as I love my children, because you're not really hers. You're not really anyone's, are you?'

This was not very helpful and nurturing for a neurotic 14-year-old!

It often seemed that I had nothing in common with Mum and Dad. We argued over *everything*. To make matters worse, my parents held on to the attitude they experienced themselves as kids of 'spare the rod and spoil the child', i.e. lots of punishment. The rift between us grew larger and larger and one of the strongest memories of my teens (and why I decided to move out at 15) is of crying myself to sleep every night. I know my parents were doing the best they knew how and that their own upbringing dictated how they raised me. I was very opinionated and headstrong, but even then I could sometimes be a bit too easily led and tended to fall in with the wrong groups at school. I'm the first to admit that I must have been a handful for my parents.

Funnily enough, one of the things that started me searching for alternatives, which ultimately led to the path of Witchcraft, was rebelling against my parents by not eating what they did! Mum used to put salt on everything, so I started to refuse to use salt. Mum and Dad ate meat, so I decided to become a vegetarian. This was very hard because Mum would insist that I ate like the rest of the family, but if I managed not to eat everything on my plate I felt I had succeeded in defying them. Out of this I started to become aware of vegetarianism and healthy eating which, although now is common, encouraged and commercialised, back then was something people dismissed as silly and to be mocked at.

☾ To Eat or Not to Eat... ☾

Teen Witches strive to tread as lightly on the earth as possible and honour their sacred ties to this magnificent natural world. To many, veganism and vegetarianism make the most conscious sense, limiting and even completely erasing our use of animals in the food and produce supply of our lives.

Our bodies are our temples – the most sacred structure we can ever hope to own and inhabit – and it's been well documented that eating meat, especially when it is procured in a mass-market exploitative way and not harvested humanely and peacefully, can be flooded with hormones that can lead to toxic physical and mental conditions in humans.

If a Teen Witch chooses to eat meat or fish and poultry – especially if they live in a region where that food is culturally insisted upon or the only food available – then ensuring it is organically and humanely sourced and saying a prayer of gratitude before consuming are positive and appropriate ways to honour the animal's sacrifice:

I gratefully thank thee, [animal], for your nourishment and life force that will now express itself through me, and I promise to live a good and useful life in honour of your sacrifice.

As I have mentioned, I only started practising Witchcraft in my late teens, so what would I have done differently if I had been a Teen Witch from an earlier age?

For a start I would have been a lot more forgiving and tolerant of my parents.

I would have realised that the harsh injustices they seemed to be heaping on me were a reflection of their own childhoods and they were trying to protect me from harm and misfortune. I would have been more appreciative of how hard Dad worked to keep three kids clothed, fed, healthy, educated and with a roof over our heads. I would have been more connected with my mother's challenge of raising three kids of different ages, all having different mothering needs.

The wonderful thing about the Craft is that it heightens your sense of personal power whatever age you begin practising it. When you're a teenager you can sometimes feel extremely disempowered by your home life and take every opportunity to rebel just to give you a sense of your own power. But as a Teen Witch the important thing to focus on is realising all the power you will ever need is inside you and then it doesn't become an issue to prove it to yourself and others. For example, a real martial arts expert feels no need to pick fights for fun, so a talented Teen Witch doesn't need to create all the battlefields other kids require as a testing ground.

◇◇

Personal Self-worth Strengthens With Every Circle, Spell and Ritual You Do

◇◇

Some of my friends at school had great relationships with their parents – they experienced a positive, supportive home environment – and whilst having a few of the usual family disagreements it was all ultimately constructive and healthy learning experiences for everyone... and then some thought their relationship with their parents was great, but it wasn't for a different reason.

One girl was allowed to do pretty much whatever she liked. She only had her mum (her dad had left them when she was very young) and she was an only child. Looking back now I think her mum let her do anything because she felt guilty that there wasn't a father around. This had good and bad effects.

She could go out as late as she liked, she could have boyfriends and friends over, she could say what she liked, swear/cuss, and when she was 14 she was even allowed to smoke. Basically her mother didn't say 'boo' to her and the girl thought it was great. However, in the end, she didn't do well at school – not because she couldn't, but because she never studied or did her homework since her mother never forced the issue with her. She could also get her mum to write her sick notes for days off school and spent her free time at the local shopping centre, where she took up stealing cosmetics – and eventually got busted for it. By the age of 15 she was pregnant to one of the boys her mother used to let her hang out and drink alcohol in the loungeroom with.

This is an extreme but unfortunately increasingly common case. My dad wasn't a great explainer and both my parents were really tough on me, but I got to see that there were reasons for some of the restrictions they enforced. They did instill in me basic values of discipline and hard work and the story of the girl at school highlights what can happen when you don't have those boundaries. Not that I'm pretending to have been a model child, of course! As it was, my parents often thought my behaviour was terrible, but if they'd known what I really got up to sometimes they would've locked me in my bedroom and never let me out! The logic behind some of their strictness rubbed off on me, and just before I would go too far I would stop myself.

My friends and I were all jealous of our friend's 'dream life' but ultimately her lifestyle did her no good at all.

An important part of being a Teen Witch is understanding that the Craft is a discipline, and you're not going to get anywhere in magick without a lot in the way of self-control. Probably only one or two of my friends had a family life that was really happy, where parents and children all got along and there was lots of love to share around. Unfortunately it's almost mandatory that a lot of the time teens and parents do not mix. It's part of life's journey, and the challenges of your teens can teach you to be strong and know yourself. I like who I am now and I am that person because of everything I've been through, and that includes the way I was brought up.

A challenging home life means that you have something to learn. Often the most special people have had the hardest lessons, and you can use a difficult home life and the ups and downs of getting along with your parents as fuel to become a better person and a more powerful Teen Witch. I wasn't a Teen Witch, so I didn't make my home environment work for me. I was expelled from my school at 14 and put into a special school for gifted but troubled children at 15, which I left before I finished Year 10 because I got a job as model/receptionist for a clothing company. Mum and Dad didn't try to stop me – in fact, I think they were relieved to see me go! Things were really horrible at home and it was starting to badly affect my younger brother and sister. We had reached a dead end.

Looking back I know that if I'd been practising Witchcraft I would have had a better appreciation of myself and have been less inclined to prove myself by rebelling and doing risky things that, although at the time seemed thrilling and fun, were ultimately destructive.

Teen Witches know that, no matter what their parents say, no matter what the toughies at school say, they are special, sacred and an essential part of the Universe.

Through their rituals and spells they can always be in touch with their inner magick, and no one can take this away from them.

Of course, this sense of personal power can also be used to create positive changes, rather than simply making the hard times less uncomfortable. There are spells and rituals you can do to bring more harmony into your relationship with your parents, and spells and rituals you can do to make you a better person, more loving and appreciative of your parents and more at ease in your own skin.

When you have this understanding, home problems don't tend to bother you as much. If your parents do or say something that you think is unfair, you're more able to let it go rather than taking it on board and feeling that you have to defend yourself. You may even end up agreeing with them and realising that they are right! And, funnily enough, the more this happens the less your parents will give you grief and you may actually start to get along.

There will always be problems, of course – they're a fact of life no matter how old you are – but challenges and obstacles are there to make our lives ultimately richer and more rewarding.

HONOURING YOUR ELDERS: A SACRED ACT

Traditional societies and cultures place great emphasis on honouring grandparents and elders and the essential role they play in the support and structure of family and community. In the modern Western world, elderly grandparents are often sent to a nursing home when they become too difficult to care for, and then it is sometimes seen as a chore to visit them. It's a very sad and upside-down way to address the sacredness of all life. At the time of working on this book there was a situation where the world shut down because of a virus that is of greatest risk to the elderly. It was a sharp wake-up call to the importance of honouring elders and upholding their comfort and needs as a sacred duty when living as a conscious magickal human.

Maiden/mother/crone and youth/warrior/sage are equally divine and empowered stages of human life experience reflecting the journeys we all take as Witches. Teen Witches see it as a sacred duty to respect and treasure elders and seek out opportunities to do so.

When I was at high school I had a chance to volunteer my afternoons at a nursing home for the elderly as part of my elective subjects. At the time I didn't realise how significant this was as a magickal, life-affirming practice. Witches are healers and strive to serve the community. I learned a lot in my time there.

◇◇

Before we get on to spells to help a difficult home life, I want to remind you that attempting to change your parents' opinions or behaviour through spells is an extremely bad idea and they will certainly either fail to work or backfire horribly. Remember one of the Witches' Laws is: 'Do what you will, but do not interfere with another's free will.' Trying to manipulate anyone is disrespectful no matter how good you think your intentions are. As far as your parents go, using spells to try to force them to change makes the chances of you ever having a good relationship with them extremely remote. Manipulative magick is self-destructive at the best of times but becomes more so when directed at those we're closest to.

The spells I offer here are completely non-manipulative and work toward change in yourself and increasing your sense of balance in the world.

⊕ THE FORGIVE AND FORGET SPELL

This is a spell for when you are really not getting along with your parents and no one can open their mouths without saying something nasty. You are totally hurt and over it, and they are fed up with you. Remember that in a situation like this neither you nor your parents are empowered; it's likely you are all just playing out a game of pre-programmed reactions. The person who really has their personal power together is the one who stops behaving like a terminator and turns back into a human being. This spell is a way for you to do this.

However, it's a fairly demanding three-part spell that will require a strong commitment of time and focus – but it works! It's also carried out over three phases of the moon: the waning moon, the waxing moon and the full moon.

As you progress through the spell you will notice things starting to improve, but the maximum positive impact will be felt around the full moon and onwards.

φ PART ONE

Best time: a waning moon.

YOU WILL NEED:

- 1 black candle
- 1 black piece of paper
- 1 black pen
- 1 bulb of garlic

- 1 cooking knife to slice garlic
- 1 block of ice
- 1 sharp feather quill or pointed stick
- 1 stick of patchouli incense, or a charcoal disc and leaves of patchouli crushed to a powder

DIRECTIONS

Cast Circle, using the full ritual or snapping in an instant Circle (snap your fingers three times by your side and visualise a skipping rope of protective blue light around you). Light the incense and gaze at the spiralling smoke, calming your mind. Sit and meditate on the problems you are experiencing with your parents. Go over individual arguments in your mind and dwell on hurtful things that were said. When you are ready, carve your first name and your parents' first names into the black candle with your quill/stick, then lick your thumb and trace it over the names to seal them. Now light the candle, take a deep breath and intone:

Flame of night
Burning bright,
Illuminate within me
A spark of light.
Power of fire,
Lift me higher,
Purge from me
My darkest hour.

Now pick up the black pen, and on the black paper write out all the sadness and anger inside you. It may come as sentences, it may come as words, it may come as pictures.

Write on both sides of the paper and, if necessary, write on top of other writing. When the paper is coated with your feelings, pick up the bulb of garlic and slice the top off it with your cooking knife.

Hold the garlic in the hand that you write with and trace a big 'X' on both sides of the paper from the top to the bottom. As you do this say:

I release pain and woe,

From within me sadness flows.

I am ready to forgive and forget,

New ways of being come for the best.

Now light the patchouli incense and into your Circle invoke the ancient Greek Goddess and patroness of Witches, Hecate, by saying:

Hecate, Goddess of old,

May you bless me with your presence threefold.

Feel the powerful and magickally transformative energy of Hecate manifest herself in your Circle. When you feel her presence, wrap the paper around the block of ice and say:

Hecate, in your dark night,

Freeze these words so that I might

Be free to think well and good,

New ways of being are understood.

Now say your spell-sealing charm:

This I ask for the good of all

So that harm may come to none,

So mote it be,

My will be done.

Now thank and farewell Hecate, close your Circle and bury the paper and the garlic under a tree, thanking it for its help in sealing your spell.

φ PART TWO

Best time: a waxing moon.

YOU WILL NEED:

- 1 light blue candle
- 1 blue ribbon
- 1 stick of lavender incense (or burn lavender on a charcoal disc)
- a picture of you and your parents together
- half a cup of crushed almonds (or, if you have a nut allergy, half a cup of sea salt)
- a sharp feather quill or pointed stick

DIRECTIONS

Cast Circle, either in the full ritual or the instant, and light the incense as a part of this. Carve your first name and your parents' first names into the candle with your quill/stick, and again seal them by licking your thumb and tracing over the names.

Light the candle and sprinkle the crushed almonds around it in a circle. As you do this invoke the Goddess of the waxing moon, Artemis.

Artemis, bless me with your presence

As you float in starry heavens.

May our love grow strong and good

As you grow waxing to full.

Feel the silvery maiden, Artemis, and her blossoming, loving energy fill your Circle. Hold the photo in your hands, picturing your parents and yourself laughing together and enjoying wonderful happy times. When this is clear and strong in your mind, wrap the blue ribbon around the photo three times and tie five knots as you say the following:

By one, my will is done.

By two, it will come true.

By three, so mote it be.

By four, for the good of all.

By five, so shall love thrive.

Thank Artemis for her blessing and close the Circle. Keep the photo and the candle in your bedroom and, every night leading up to the full moon, light it for a whilst and hold the photo in both your hands as you gaze into the candle, picturing you and your parents getting along happily, having great conversations and sharing lots of love.

φ PART THREE

Best time: a full moon.

YOU WILL NEED:

- ☛ 1 white or silver candle
- ☛ 1 stick of jasmine incense
- ☛ 1 white flower, perhaps a gardenia or a rose
- ☛ 1 silver ribbon
- ☛ 1 piece of rose quartz crystal
- ☛ 1 white velvet cloth bag or white cardboard box
- ☛ a picture of you and your parents together

- sea salt
- a sharp feather quill or pointed stick

DIRECTIONS

Cast Circle, either in the full ritual or the instant and lighting the incense as a part of this. Again, carve your first name and your parents' first names into the candle and seal them by licking your thumb and tracing over the names.

Light the candle and sprinkle the sea salt in a circle around it.

Hold the flower and the crystal in your hands and invoke the Goddess of the full moon, Selene:

Queen of the sky, Great Mother, Selene,

I ask you to bless my parents and me

That we may live in harmony

Growing together happily.

As you feel Selene's wise and intensely loving presence fill your Circle, place the flower, crystal and photo with the blue ribbon in the bag or box. Wrap the silver ribbon around it and tie seven knots as you say:

One is love.

Two is truth.

Three is sacred.

Four is balance.

Five is power.

Six is passion.

Seven is strength.

Now you have a magickal amulet that will continue your spell-working so that your relationship with your parents gets better and better. It will also work to help you move through and learn from the challenges that will naturally present themselves, rather than getting caught up in destructive and unproductive patterns.

To finish the forgive and forget spell, hold your amulet and say your spell-sealing charm:

This I ask for the good of all

So that harm may come to none.

So mote it be,

My will be done.

Thank Selene and close your Circle. Keep your amulet either on your altar or somewhere safe. You can charge it up whenever you need to by lighting the silver candle and again asking for Selene's blessing as you did above.

Sorting Out Your Siblings

When your sisters and/or brothers are sending you around the bend, you can use the spells suggested here to harmonise your relationship with them too. Just substitute their name/s and instead of saying 'parents' say 'siblings' or 'sister/brother'.

The Spreading Love Ritual

This is one of the simplest things you can do. It may sound obvious, but the more love you give out the more you will receive back. So do something unexpected and nice for your parents. Don't wait for their birthdays or Christmas celebrations – buy or make them a present. Give them a card in which you've written a poem about how much you appreciate them and all they've given you. Surprise them by cleaning the whole house when they are out one day. Just remember, the more spreading love rituals you do the more love will come to you.

⊕ The Quick and Easy Perfect Parents Spell

Best time: any time!

This spell will help you shift your perception of your parents and allow you to experience them in a more positive and harmonious way. By changing ourselves we can change the world around us.

The blessings of the elements will also protect you from negativity.

YOU WILL NEED:

- ☞ 1 white candle (for spirit and the element of fire)
- ☞ 1 stick of strawberry incense or any floral/fruity scent that lifts your heart (for fun and the element of air)
- ☞ a bowl of salt (for purity and the element of earth)
- ☞ a bowl of spring water or tap water with a pinch of salt (for emotions and the element of water)

DIRECTIONS

Snap in an instant Circle and light the candle and incense.

Look at all your goodies and let the heady scent of strawberry fill your heart with joy. Now say firmly:

I respect and love my parents;

They respect and love me;

We can live and learn joyfully.

Hold the candle and say:

Fire, speed my wish to me.

Hold the incense and say:

Air, bring me new energy.

Hold the salt and say:

Earth, make me strong.

Hold the water and say:

Water, fill me with love.

Snap closed the Circle – the spell is done!

Powerful Affirmations

This affirmation is great for when you are in the middle of an argument with your parents and you want it to stop. To do this, you have to stop fuelling the argument. Say inside your head (and heart):

I let go of anger, I let go of sadness. Life is sacred. I can stop this madness.

Except for a few extreme cases, most parents do deserve their children's respect. The job of a parent is surely the most difficult and underrated on the planet. It's important that as a Teen Witch you respect your elders as well-intentioned human beings regardless of whether you agree with everything they say and every choice they make. The bottom line is most of the time they are doing the best they can at a very demanding job. As you get older you'll discover this – especially if you become a parent yourself.

An excellent affirmation for appreciating and getting along with your parents is very simple. Say:

Goddess, help me to understand, love and respect my parents.

She will.

CHAPTER EIGHT

◇◇

School Crafting!

◇◇

Of all the requests for spells and rituals I get from Teen Witches via my social media, it's always school and love that come across as the most pressing issues. And why not, since you spend most of your teenage life in school and intimate relationships with significant others is an exciting new world to awaken to? In this chapter I have put together lots of spells that hopefully will provide you with the tools you need to get the most out of these important years.

Note: don't forget to check out the magickal properties of the herbs, crystals, colours and so on that you are using in the 'Magickal Meanings' chapter.

⊕ Boring Class Spell

Here is a spell to cast to help you stay focused in the class that causes you to fall asleep – whether it's the subject or the teacher, the boredom is killing you!

Best time: when you need it!

YOU WILL NEED:

- ☛ a yellow candle
- ☛ a teaspoon of celery seed
- ☛ lemon essential oil
- ☛ a yellow piece of paper
- ☛ lemon juice
- ☛ a feather to use as a writing quill
- ☛ a sealable envelope or small bag

DIRECTIONS

At home, light the yellow candle. By this light dip your feather quill into the lemon juice, writing the following on the piece of paper (you don't need to see the words – just trace their intent onto the paper – but keep dipping the quill into the juice to harness the clarifying energy of the lemon):

I [name] do declare

The powers of mind

Are strong and clear;

Fascinating is my course

I enjoy with magick force.

Now fold the paper over until it is a small triangle and drip three drops of the lemon oil on it. Place this and the celery seeds into the envelope or bag and seal. Hold the charm between both hands and gaze at the candle flame as you repeat the incantation three more times.

Take the charm with you to class and, when you feel you are drifting off, shake the charm so that the seeds rattle and say the invocation to restate the spell. You will immediately feel clearer and more able to enjoy the class.

Keep charging up this spell by rattling the seeds as often as necessary.

⊕ Horrible Teacher Spell

◇◇

Teachers are only human and capable of making mistakes, but when I was at school I used to put them on a pedestal and was either worshipping them, terrified of them or hating them. Teaching is one of the most demanding and yet undervalued jobs in Western society (along with motherhood), so it's important that you respect your teachers and acknowledge they are most likely doing the best they can in an often difficult and frustrating system.

Some are brilliant and inspiring, but for those who are just plain awful be tolerant. If you find yourself lumbered with a teacher who seems to enjoy torturing students, here's a spell to help sort them out. Note, though, that this isn't a curse or anything nasty!

Best time: it can give extra impact to do this spell on a Saturday (ruled by Saturn) during the waning moon (for banishing negative energies), but any time is appropriate.

YOU WILL NEED:

- a black candle
- a white candle
- 4 senna pods (or ½ teaspoon of the powder)
- some soil scooped from the imprint of the teacher's footprint (you may have to be ingenious to get this; make sure they don't see you do it!)
- a small pot of heart's ease (a type of violet; pansy or a small flowering rose can also work)
- a sharp feather quill or pointed stick
- a piece of black paper
- a black pen
- a small jug of spring water

DIRECTIONS

Carve your teacher's name with the quill on the black candle, and then on the piece of paper write down with the black pen all the horrible things they do and say, covering both sides of the paper if necessary. Now stand the black candle on the paper, light it and say:

On this paper, dark and forlorn,

The written words are hurting.

I bind these so they have no form,

Now letters with no meaning.

Fold the paper over once and drip a drop of wax on it, then fold it again, dripping one drop of wax each time until the paper is folded into a small square.

Now burn the paper in the flame of the black candle, being careful to keep the ashes.

Carve the teacher's name into the white candle and light it. Focus on the healing and renewing energies of the pure white candle and its fire.

When you are ready, mix the ash from the paper in with the soil from your teacher's footprint and sprinkle in a deosil direction (anti-clockwise in the southern hemisphere; clockwise in the north) around the pot plant. Then press the four senna pods into the base of the pot plant (or sprinkle the powder around the base).

Now slowly pour the water over the soil as you say:

Nourishing the energies of love and compassion,

So grows this plant with healthy abandon.

Blessed and honoured is this new situation,

Free from the past, new patterns created.

Now say the spell sealing charm:

This I ask for the good of all

So that harm may come to none,

So mote it be,

My will be done.

Keep looking after the little plant and watch your relationship with your teacher improve!

Note: this spell can be adapted to include other people with whom you have a poor relationship. You are not seeking to change their behaviour beyond their free will; you are just banishing sadness and hurt and encouraging new, more loving and compassionate energies to blossom.

⊕ Leave My Things Alone Spell

〈〉

I remember the first time something was stolen from me at school – I was devastated! My parents had just taken us on a holiday to Tasmania. I was 12 and I had a fantastic time, the highlight being our visit to an enormous lavender farm. (I must have been Witchy even before I was consciously aware of it – I was fascinated by the herb and its uses. Maybe that's why it's one of my faves to this day!)

In addition to dried lavender, lavender oil and lavender jam, I also brought home a strange souvenir. It was a dried apple fashioned into the head of a little old wise woman wearing a white cap, white kitchen apron and chequered skirt. She was carrying a little straw broom and was very Witchy! I kept her in my desk at school and every chance I got I would open the desk and look at her. I felt I had a special friend hiding away in there (especially as I didn't have any friends outside my desk). I usually remembered to put her away in my locker if one of my classes wasn't in my home room, but one day I didn't. When I returned she was gone. I remember being really shocked that someone would take something that wasn't theirs. This may sound naïve, but at the time it really freaked me out and I took quite a whilst to get over it!

So here is a little ritual that you can do to help protect your belongings from interference by another. Of course, you have to take appropriate action on the physical plane – don't be careless or leave things lying around that you don't want others to fiddle with – but this ritual will help assure your belongings' safety.

DIRECTIONS

With your power finger or your athame, trace a pentagram surrounded by a circle over the object or area you want protected.

In your mind's eye see the pentagram form as electric blue light. Now all you need to do is empower the protective shield by directing the palm of your power hand towards the object. Feel the palm of your hand heat up as you channel your energy and desire into the pentagram shield, which you should see glow and pulse in your mind's eye.

The object is now protected. You can create this shield over just about anything, not just objects but also doorways, to discourage unwanted people entering or even whole buildings. When I was writing this book in a very beautiful but remote country house, on the nights I was alone I would trace a giant blue circled pentagram over the roof of the house with my mind's eye to protect me as I slept.

Note: don't physically touch the object. I know some Witches who trace pentagrams into the dusty bonnets of their cars to protect them, but it's really better to do it in your mind's eye even if it's just to avoid arousing the interest of anyone who doesn't understand the sacred meaning of the five-pointed star. Unfortunately the symbol was for a long time debased as a satanic and negative symbol (though this has  changed a lot since originally writing this book) and you don't want any hassles – you want your stuff left alone!

⊕ Quick Help for Studying and Exams

YOU WILL NEED:

- a piece of citrine quartz
- a piece of clear quartz
- rosemary oil
- an oil burner

DIRECTIONS

Before you study for an exam, burn five drops of rosemary oil in water on the oil burner. Hold the citrine in your right hand and the clear quartz in your left, inhale the scent of rosemary and say:

My mind is clear, my knowledge good.

Success is mine, be as it should.

Start studying. Before your exam, place a drop of rosemary oil on your temples and place the crystals in your pocket whilst you do your exam.

⊕ A Spell to Help Deal With School Bullies

I was bullied at school. I don't know why – I tried to fit in – but whether it was older girls pushing me down the stairs or my so-called friends one day just deciding to ignore me for a week, there was always something wrong. The following spell will give you strength to deal with those peers who make your life a misery. You'll be able to cope with their poor behaviour and eventually they will give up and leave you alone ... or at least stop playing dumb mind games on you.

YOU WILL NEED:

- a handful of borage blossoms or leaves or any dried small flower and its leaves that you are drawn to
- dragon's blood powder: this is the powdered resin of a tree easily obtained online
- sandalwood powder: also available online if not in your local witchy store
- a piece of tiger's eye (which is a crystal)
- a yellow silk pouch
- a red candle
- bloodprint ink (see page 31); you can also use a small lock of hair

DIRECTIONS

To a handful of blossoms or leaves, add a teaspoon of dragon's blood powder and a teaspoon of sandalwood powder. Grind these together using your mortar and pestle and add the piece of tiger's eye.

Dip your power index finger (the hand you write with) in the bloodprint ink and stamp on some paper. Wipe your finger with a cloth. If you are performing this spell for someone else, take their stamp. If preferred, you can use a lock of hair instead.

Place all this in the yellow silk pouch and light the red candle. Holding the pouch in both hands, call on the Judeo-Christian angel Archangel Michael, who is a fierce protector of the innocent; his sword can cut through the physic cords of negative energy that bullies use to bind themselves to their victims. Say:

Archangel Michael, avail me of your mighty sword

Cut away my oppressors. Free me to be whole.

Carry the pouch at all times to ward off problems, and recharge its powers by lighting the red candle and calling on the archangel.

⊕ The Freeze-off Spell

This spell is one of my favourites. It will help to freeze the actions of people picking on you or giving you grief. Write on a piece of black paper the name or names of the people who you want to stop tormenting you (or write on white paper with a black pen) and put it in an ice cube tray with a clove of garlic with an 'X' carved into it. Pour water over it and freeze. The creeps will leave you alone.

⊕ The 'I'm Not Nervous' Amulet

Whether it's the school play, the night before exams or having to make important decisions about your future, keeping this amulet with you can enhance your personal vibrations and align you with fortuitous energies.

Best time: Sunday, to infuse with positive solar energy.

YOU WILL NEED:

- ☞ a purple velvet or silk pouch or bag about the size of your palm
- ☞ 1 teaspoon of powdered sandalwood
- ☞ piece of white agate crystal or clear quartz
- ☞ 6 pinches of St John's Wort herb or lavender
- ☞ 1 gold candle
- ☞ your favourite perfume or essential oil blend (one that makes you feel fabulous and focused when you wear it)

Note: the scent needs to be sprayed, so if it's an oil blend maybe consider putting a few drops of the oil with a teaspoon of isopropyl alcohol in a spray bottle.

DIRECTIONS

Lay the first four things out, light the gold candle and spray three squirts of perfume over the flame (be careful as the alcohol in the perfume will flare up) as you say:

I infuse these objects with my will,

Pure power is mine to have my fill.

Confidence and bravery come to be

When this amulet is with me.

Now put all the objects into the amulet bag and spray with a squirt of perfume or oil blend. Hold the amulet pouch in both hands, gaze into the flame and concentrate on being able to remember your lines, study for your test or make your decisions easily and effortlessly. Say the charm one more time and snuff the candle; the spell is done. You can recharge the amulet any time by holding it and repeating the charm.

How to Snuff a Candle Flame

◇◇◇

In the interests of not being a magickal mess, here are my best tips for snuffing candle flames safely and with the least mess.

Best choice: buy a proper candle snuffer; they are easily available online.

Next best choice: lick your thumb and index finger generously and quickly and confidently pinch the wick. Have a cloth or tissue nearby to wipe the residue off your fingers.

If the candle you are using is in glass and has a lid or similar, just put the lid on it to starve the oxygen from the flame and it will gently extinguish.

⊕ The 'I Am Losing the Plot' Spell

◇◇◇

Sometimes the pressure of exams or homework can just do your head in and you start losing the plot. The following spell is one of healing and re-empowerment and will help you get back on track and coping again.

YOU WILL NEED:

- ☞ a silver candle
- ☞ a blue candle
- ☞ 3 drops of cinnamon oil for those identifying as boys or neroli/orange blossom for those identifying as girls; you can substitute any earthy woody oil for boys and floral/fruity for girls, but these are the best aligned for this spell
- ☞ 6 drops of rose geranium (calming, healing and loving); lavender will also substitute here very well
- ☞ a sharp feather quill or pointed stick

138

DIRECTIONS

With the quill/stick, carve your name into both candles. Using your finger, anoint over the carving with the blended oils. Light both candles. As they burn imagine streams of silver and blue light swirling together around and above the candle flames. Picture yourself feeling calm and well, and at peace with your place in the world. Then call on the Witches' Goddess:

Lady of light, I now call forth

For I need your strength and form,

Light my steps, clear my head,

So I tread the path for which I'm meant.

Keep focusing on the swirling blue light and then see in your mind's eye an image of yourself with that light swirling around you, healing and strengthening. When you are ready, snuff the candles and repeat this spell at least once a day until the situation improves.

⊕ You're On a Witch Hunt

Here's a spell to deal with schoolmates, teachers or anyone who is ridiculing you or hassling you for being a Witch.

Of course you can always do the freeze-off spell to get them to leave you alone, but this one can work more specifically not only to stop them bothering you but also to help heal them from their prejudice and lack of compassion.

Best time: a Friday (ruled by Venus, planet of unconditional love) during the waxing moon.

YOU WILL NEED:

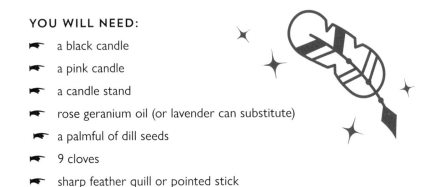

- 🐾 a black candle
- 🐾 a pink candle
- 🐾 a candle stand
- 🐾 rose geranium oil (or lavender can substitute)
- 🐾 a palmful of dill seeds
- 🐾 9 cloves
- 🐾 sharp feather quill or pointed stick

DIRECTIONS

Cast Circle. Carve the names of the person/people whom you want to accept your choices without judgement into the black candle with the quill. If there are too many or you don't know their names, carve a line for each one. Lick your thumb and trace over the carvings with your spit to bind your energy to theirs for a short time.

Place the candle in a stand and, around it, place the cloves in an even circle. Light the candle and hold your hands over the warmth of its flame, channelling your energy into the candle (be careful when you do this; once when I did it the candle flame leapt up really high and strong and burnt my palm!).

As you project your energy, slowly say this incantation:

I reverse all that is adverse,

Bound to me, no longer cursed;

Ill feelings gone, the tide is turned,

I am free, no longer spurned.

Now with your left hand (or the hand you don't write with) gather the cloves up in a widdershins direction (clockwise or against the sun in the southern hemisphere; anti-clockwise in the north) to release your binding to these people. Put the candle and the cloves to one side to be buried later.

Now anoint the pink candle with a few drops of rose geranium oil, rubbing in well. Sprinkle the dill seeds around the base in a deosil direction (sunwise, anti-clockwise in the south; clockwise in the north). Light the candle and sit and meditate for a moment on the qualities of compassion and love. Think about how really powerful people don't hold grudges or resent others for their lack of knowledge or lack of understanding, and instead seek to heal unpleasant and unbalanced situations with love.

When you are ready, use your quill or stick to carefully mark an 'X' on the heart area of the candle (about three-quarters of the way up) as you say:

Here I declare

Love to feel

Love to share.

Do the same at the 'throat area' (a bit higher up) and say:

Here I declare words are kind, words are fair.

Finally, carefully mark an 'X' at the third eye area (higher up again) and say:

Here I declare thoughts that care.

Now hold your hands over the flame and project your energy as you say:

Let no person, thing or time

Undo the charm I set to rhyme.

Then, for extra impact, you could add the spell-sealing charm:

This I ask for the good of all,

So that harm may come to none.

So mote it be,
My will be done.

Now, if you like, you can leave the candle burning or snuff the flame and keep the candle and dill seeds wrapped in white cloth and hidden in a drawer somewhere for at least another three full moons to keep the spell charged.

After closing Circle, bury the black candle and cloves in some dirt. After three full moons you can bury the pink candle and dill seeds. If the problem persists do the spell in full again.

⊕ Pencil Shavings Spell

This one is really easy; you can even do it in class! It's great for releasing blocked energy, dispersing unpleasant situations or keeping heated situations under control.

YOU WILL NEED:

- a piece of white paper
- 1 lead pencil
- 1 sharpener

DIRECTIONS

On the paper, write down the problem with the pencil, for example: 'The student behind me keeps bugging me to tell her the answers to the test.' Next, take the sharpener and sharpen the pencil three full turns, letting the shavings fall on the paper, then fold the paper and repeat the process. By now the student should have stopped doing it. If there is tension between you and another classmate or your teacher, you could write: 'Energy is blocked, the situation stopped.' Keep writing, sharpening and folding to keep the situation from blowing up further. Throw the paper and shavings in the bin when you're done (or in the incinerator if you don't want people to read what you've written!).

⊕ ERASER SPELL

◇◇

This is another easy one to do in class. It's great if you're having trouble learning something.

YOU WILL NEED:

- ☞ 1 lead pencil or pen
- ☞ a piece of white paper
- ☞ 1 eraser or white-out liquid

DIRECTIONS

Write the problem on the paper, for example: 'I cannot understand this maths equation.' Look at what you've written and be aware of the emotions inside you as you contemplate your problem. You may become aware that you have always been told by your father, 'You'll never succeed at anything because you never stick at anything long enough.' (That's what I was always told!) Or you may become aware of a deep feeling of pressure because you are so scared of getting something wrong that you'd rather not attempt it in the first place. Try to isolate the real problem: it's probably not the difficulty of the maths equation or how smart you are; it's more likely your feelings about your capabilities.

When you are confident you have isolated the emotion or thought, channel it into your hand, pick up the eraser or white-out liquid and rub out that emotion by erasing your written sentence. When it is gone, know that you have removed the problem and get on with solving that equation!

⊕ Another Study Spell

This is another good one to help with studying as it helps create a conducive environment for absorbing knowledge.

This spell involves making Merlyn's powder of knowledge.

YOU WILL NEED:
- 1 purple candle
- frankincense or lavender incense
- Merlyn's powder of knowledge:
    - 3 teaspoons powdered nutmeg
    - 2 teaspoons crushed patchouli leaves (if you can't get these double up on the lavender)
    - 1 teaspoon black pepper
    - 1 teaspoon crushed lavender
    - 2 teaspoons cornflour
    - some filings from your nails (use a nail file and capture them on paper; if you bite your fingernails use your toenails and do the self-love spell on page 171 later so that you stop eating yourself up!)

DIRECTIONS

Mix the ingredients for the powder of knowledge either with your fingers in a glass or china bowl or in a mortar and pestle (this is best).

Cast Circle, lighting the purple candle and incense as part of your Circle casting. Call on the magickal master of learning, knowledge and wisdom, Merlyn:

I invoke thee, Merlyn,

Master of learning;

Avail me of your ability

To know and learn easily.

Merlyn's presence will feel solid and comforting, but also tingly and intellectually stimulating. Merlyn makes learning fun and exciting no matter what the subject! Feel imbued with his power: everything is magickal and possible and you will become aware that all the knowledge you absorb will be put to profound and good use.

Now that you are charged up, pick up the knowledge powder and hold it towards the candle flame, saying:

I charge this powder with learning powers

As Merlyn decrees my knowledge flowers.

Focus on the powder, absorbing Merlyn's essence; the ingredients will be receptive to this energy and absorb it well.

When you are ready say 'It is done' and close Circle in the usual way, thanking Merlyn for his assistance.

You can use the powder by sprinkling a little around where you are studying, whether it's on the floor or around your books or computer. If you are worried about making a mess, sprinkle some around the base of the purple candle and have that burning as you study. Or have a small bowl with some of the powder in it. You could place a citrine or clear quartz in your study area and sprinkle a little around that. You can also put some of the powder into a little cloth bag (purple is a good colour) and carry it with you; if you do this, pop a piece of the quartz in with it.

For an extra hit of knowledge power, throw some of the powder onto a lit charcoal disc as incense.

⊕ Colour Spell

This is another really simple one!

Check the colour correspondences in 'Magickal Meanings' for colours that correspond to your goals and needs. For example, you would like more pocket money so you can afford to buy a new outfit to look great, so choose green for money, yellow for intellect (to help you make the best choice) and pink for self-love.

On white paper, draw a pentagram with each colour over the top of each other, focusing on your desire. Kiss the magick sigil (a sigil is a sign or symbol with magickal power) three times and fold the paper into a small square. Every day for seven days open the paper, stare at the sigil – focusing intently on your wish – before kissing it three times and folding it up again. Do this morning and night and within the week your wish will start to manifest.

⊕ Quick Calming Spell Amulet

This one's great for when you're feeling nervous: before an exam, before an interview with an employer (if you are getting a part-time job outside of school or have left school and are starting work), or even to have in your pocket before getting off the school bus because the boy or girl you like is there.

YOU WILL NEED:

- ☞ a piece of amethyst crystal
- ☞ a handful of chamomile
- ☞ a teaspoon of sandalwood powder
- ☞ a blue mojo bag

DIRECTIONS

Mix the chamomile and sandalwood together with your power hand as you say this incantation:

> Powers of sacred herb and sacred wood,
>
> Calm my nerves so all is good;
>
> Restore a sense of peace to me,
>
> So I conquer fear and am at peace.

Place the mixture in the bag together with the amethyst crystal. The amethyst will amplify the soothing and restorative energies of the herb and wood so that your energies align with their peaceful presence, your mind will be clear and you will be capable of your duties. Keep the bag in your pocket and give it a squish with your hand when you need to churn up its powers.

Another good tip for keeping your cool is to wear a sandalwood bead necklace or bracelet (try Indian import stores and new-age stores). Sandalwood also helps making learning easy so wearing it at school is a good move.

Also, upon awakening on a potentially stressful day, place slices of cucumber on your eyelids for five minutes and in your mind's eye picture a vast calm ocean. This will soothe you and take any puffiness from a restless sleep away from your eyes. Cucumber can open up the powers of the subconscious and help you be more in touch with the big picture of your life.

⊕ Sleep Tonic

Speaking of restless sleep, here's an excellent sleep tonic that will knock you out and give you a peaceful night's rest the night before that exam, sporting carnival or big date. Drink one hour before bed.

YOU WILL NEED:
- half a handful of hops (lavender can substitute)
- a small handful of clover (pick it fresh from a garden or park; use common sense and choose an area that is unlikely to have dog pee)
- 1/4 teaspoon of tarragon
- three pieces of lettuce, chopped

DIRECTIONS
Steep the ingredients in a saucepan of almost boiling water for five minutes, then strain and drink – and go straight to bed!

The other option is to buy a sleep blend herbal tea. In the years since this book was first written herbal remedies have become common and can be found in supermarkets and easily purchased online. Any blend that has ingredients like hops, valerian or chamomile will be excellent. It's the conscious act of making the tea and quietly drinking it that imbues the ritual with magickal intent as well as the gentle medicinal properties of the herbs in the tea.

If you have been having nightmares because you are stressed out over school, or anything really, place a piece of amethyst crystal under your pillow for good dreams and a restful sleep.

⊕ Square-peg-in-a-round-hole Spell

Peer pressure is the worst, except for perhaps having no pressure because no one acknowledges you exist! I copped both extremes at school. One of my main memories of school is of finally having a group to hang out with but always being on the edge of the pack. Walking down the hill from the bus stop to school I was always on the perimeter of our group, leaning in, straining to hear what the coolest girls were saying and trying to laugh and bitch at the appropriate times. The following spell puts you in touch with your inner power. At this point it's worth mentioning that all the things that are valued as cool at school are the least important attributes when you leave. So if you don't fit in, take it as a sign that you are capable of doing something really spectacular when you leave. Get everything you need out of school selfishly; don't let others distract you from your personal goals and power.

And remember: when people are jerks to you it's because they are actually insecure, fearful and over-compensating with bullying and bitchy behaviour, so have compassion for them. The meaner they are the more compassion you can use to put out their negativity. This compassion doesn't have to be verbally delivered to them or even made directly known to them. It's one of the first and most powerful magickal lessons a Teen Witch can learn – that the world answers according to the questions you ask of it. If you exercise inner compassion you stop feeding the negative things around you … and like magic they fade away and you will find that paths around you to happier experiences and times will be shown to you.

Best time: Sunday as the moon waxes (this time is important as you need to make the most of the prevailing solar and lunar energies).

YOU WILL NEED:

- 1 green candle
- 1 pink candle
- 1 small magnet
- 1 tablespoon sunflower oil
- 3 drops rosemary oil
- 2 drops lemon oil
- 1/2 teaspoon dragon's blood powder
- nag champa incense (as mentioned earlier in this book, you can get it from just about every health food and new age/Witchy supply store; it's a wonderfully inspiring blend from India)
- 1 hair from your head

DIRECTIONS

Burn the incense as you mix the oils together and stir through the dragon's blood powder. Place in a small bottle and pop the magnet in.

Anoint the green and pink candles and light. Now anoint yourself: a dab on your third eye (between your eyebrows), over your heart and over your solar plexus (just below the rib cage) and get ready for maximum empowerment!

Inhale slowly and connect with your deep sense of self, the one that goes beyond other people's opinions of you or even your immediate opinions of yourself. Deep inside there is a place Witches call the 'green': it's the fertile and eternally renewing essence of your personal power. Sometimes its presence may only be perceived as the tiniest of sparks; at other times it may be an enormous, lush, glowing sphere. When you are connected hold your hands towards the candles and let the fuel of their sacred fire be drawn inside you to the green, stoking it up so that your whole being feels strong, passionate and unique (it's your personal power). When you are ready pick up the oil, holding it towards the candle flame and intone:

Sacred oil of dragon fire,
Potion of power heed my desire;
By day and night fuel my might
Growing stronger – ever bright.

Feel the bottle of oil grow hot in your hands as energy pours into it. Place your hair in the bottle, binding your physical and spiritual essence to its contents.

When you are ready, snuff the candles and keep the bottle safe – somewhere private; no one must use this oil except you. Every morning dab a little on the soles of your feet so that you always take empowered steps. This oil is not only for empowerment but also attraction, and you will find as you use it that people will genuinely start to seek out your company because they will sense your new strength and be drawn to it in a positive way.

⊕ Leaving School Spell

Okay, you've decided to leave school. Whether you're about to enter college or university, start a job or go backpacking around Europe so that you can have a break, this spell seals the high school experience, helping you to consolidate your time there, release it and move on to the rest of your life. It's good to do this spell the morning after your final school day.

Best time: just before dawn.

YOU WILL NEED:

- ☞ a handful of dried rue (lavender can substitute)
- ☞ a handful of dried sage
- ☞ small branches of willow (fallen from the tree and dried) for a small fire, or use eucalyptus wood and be very mindful of fire safety
- ☞ 1 teaspoon sandalwood powder
- ☞ 1 dark blue candle
- ☞ 1 pale blue candle
- ☞ paper

DIRECTIONS

Mix the sage, rue and sandalwood together in a bowl.

Make a small (safe!) fire with the willow and paper and set the blue candles up on either side. Light the fire and wait for the sun to rise. As the sun rises, throw one half of the herb mix into the fire as you say:

Sacred herbs and fire light,

Rising sun new and bright.

Bless my efforts of the past,

Launch me on my future path.

Sit quietly and meditate on your time at school – don't judge anything as good or bad – just let memories flow through your mind like water. When you are ready, throw the second half of the herb mix into the fire and say the incantation again. This time, meditate on your plans for the future. Again, don't judge; just let your ideas flow throw your mind.

When the fire has burnt down, collect some of the ash and place it in a container. You can use this ash for future spells requiring extra strength or transformative powers as it has absorbed your presence and the essence of your efforts from your school years. Just add a pinch to any incense blend or herb mixture.

Snuff the blue candles and get on with the rest of your life!

What Do I Do With All My Used Candles?

◇◇◇

When doing spells, being safety conscious and not leaving candles burning unattended and also working with the parameters suggested in the individual spells (like snuffing flames for magickal effect or burying them to sell a spell), you may find you have a surplus of slightly used candles.

It's totally okay to repurpose used spell candles for new spells. If you have carved your initials or anointed candles with oil you can hold the candle gently across a flame and slightly melt and soften the wax with the previous spell marks. Using waxed paper (away from the flame), gently rub the softened wax to smooth out the surface and erase and make the candle 'new'. The other option is just to use your previous spell candles for lighting and ambience when doing any ritual work. Modern Teen Witches are conscious of avoiding excessive waste and consumerism, so be inventive and positive in how you repurpose your magickal cabinet!

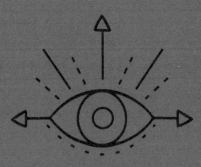

<><><><><><><><><><><><><><><><><><><><><><><><><><><><><><><><><><>

DOING WHAT YOU WILL

<><><><><><><><><><><><><><><><><><><><><><><><><><><><><><><><><><><>

Unfortunately, some Teen Witches have to keep their spiritual path a secret because their parents, friends or teachers don't understand or tolerate their interests. For this reason, I've written a special chapter for those who are on the path but have to put up with people trying to push them off!

You may have tried to help those people understand that you do not do evil things, that you do not worship Satan – all the worst misconceptions about the Craft – but they will not listen. If you do need to express your Witchcraft secretly, it's not about being sneaky and lying – both of which will inhibit your personal magickal development – it's about being resourceful and inventive so that you don't have to abandon your Craft until a time when you are able to express yourself freely.

In this book I've addressed ways of exploring the Craft if your parents, teachers and/or friends are not very accepting or approving of your interests. As a young person it's a brave and wise thing to make a choice to willingly explore a spiritual path, especially Witchcraft … because it's one of the very best!

Whether it's the best for you or not (only you can decide that), one thing is certain: the Craft is one of the most widely misunderstood of all the Western world's religions.

So here, in a nutshell, are a few tips on 'doing what you will'.

First and foremost: how do you tell your parents and friends that you are a Witch? Well, before rushing into this, ask yourself whether it's really necessary to do it at all. I didn't let anyone know about my growing interest in the Craft for quite a few years; I just read about it, explored it and tried things out in private until I felt confident in coming out of the broom closet (That phrase, by the way, makes a strong statement about this whole issue: being drawn to the Craft can raise exactly the same sort of issues as being gay can. Whilst more and more people in our society are cool about both subjects, coming out as a Witch or gay can still be

difficult depending on how your family and friends feel about the subject. Also, different people will feel differently about just how 'out' they want to be, and it's completely right for them to make up their own minds. I refer to my dear Witch friend Michael Herkes, aka the Glam Witch, who says: 'Being gay isn't a choice, and one could argue that the call to being a Witch is not a choice either.' However, if you do want to tell your parents, or if your mum found some Witchy things in your room and asked you 'What the hell is all this?', what can you say?

Reassure them that, despite what they may have heard, Witchcraft (or in particular Wicca) has nothing to do with satanism or hurting people, animals or yourself. Let them know that as a Teen Witch you find nature sacred, you acknowledge not only a god but also a Goddess and you do rituals to honour these. You also cast spells to help and heal and to get the most out of your life. You could also tell your parents that there are three laws that, as a Witch, you must abide by:

1. Do what you want to do as long as you don't hurt anyone.

2. Do what you want to do as long as you don't interfere with another's free will.

3. That which you send out returns upon you, threefold – minimum!

When or if you talk to your parents about Witchcraft it's important that you emphasise you're interested in magick because you love being alive, and that you want to make the most out of your life and be the very best you can be, which is what Witchcraft is all about.

If they won't listen or don't understand or are worried or ridiculing you, stop referring to your Craft as Witchcraft and call it Wicca (the recognised religion of Witchcraft) instead (even if you are a spiritual Witch not practising the religion); you may find that not saying such a provocative word will provide breathing space whilst they get used to the idea.

Remember, the way to address fear and ignorance is with love and knowledge. No one is perfect, adults included, and sometimes things that are different freak people out and they react by judging and rejecting those things. Just be patient and remember as a Teen Witch you don't have to prove anything to anyone: the path you follow is the one you forge yourself.

THE CLAYTONS ALTAR

◇◇◇

Back in the 1980s there was a non-alcoholic drink called Claytons. It was a sugary cordial that was packaged to look like whiskey and it was promoted for adults as the 'drink you have when you're not having a drink'. The drink is now forgotten but the word 'Claytons' has stayed in urban vernacular as describing something that looks like one thing but is actually another. So you can have an altar without having an altar ... the Claytons Altar.

Your parents may forbid you to have an altar in your room, or they might even destroy one you have set up. This can be very distressing – I remember my father breaking my vinyl records when I accidentally played one too loud because I didn't realise he was in the house. No questions were asked; he just came in, tore the record off the stereo and broke it and the few others I was allowed to own. That really upset me, and I can't even begin to think how I would have felt if I'd had an altar in my room and he'd smashed that.

You can have a Teen Witch's altar in your room that doesn't attract attention and doesn't look obviously Witchy. You only need to have the elements represented and something for the Lady and Lord. For example, you could have a feather for air, a crystal or stone for earth, an unlit candle for fire and a vase with water for water and fresh flowers for the Lady and leafy branches for the

Lord (of the forests).

Or you could have a photo altar, setting up photos in frames or even sticking them on the wall. Water could be a picture of the ocean, a volcano or sun can be fire, the sky and clouds for air and a mountain for earth. And a photo of a special woman and man for the Lady and Lord (I have some beautiful esoteric cards featuring amazing-looking men and women to reinforce the presence of the Lady and Lord at my altar).

What about toys? Even stuffed ones! A bird for air, a snake for earth, a bee or cat for fire (the golden colour of honey represents the sun and the Egyptian sun Goddess, Bast, is often represented as a cat) and a fish for water.

When you understand what the symbolism and roles of the traditional altar pieces are, then you are only limited by your imagination as to how you make your own Claytons altar meaningful and potent.

Part of being a Teen Witch is being just that: a teen. So don't feel you have to do things exactly like adult Witches.

Whilst you are living with your parents or guardians, you have to respect the fact that you live under their roof and it is appropriate and honourable for you to respect their rules and expectations. You just need to be resourceful and use your intuition to get around certain obstacles (like them not respecting your interests).

I'm Burning Up

As I have said before, candles and incense may pose a threat to your parents because they don't want the house burnt down: fair enough. When I was living at home I was forbidden to burn incense because my dad thought the sweet-smelling smoke was drugs! No matter how much I tried to tell him incense wasn't intoxicating, he wouldn't listen.

Teen Witches can use candles of every colour without lighting them. Until you are allowed to burn them, visualise them burning instead by being aware of the qualities of heat and the powerful moving and shaking energy that a flame conjures.

You can power-up unlit candles by using a pin to carve your name (or the intent of a spell) and then rubbing a few drops of appropriate essential oil (the one suggested in the spell or ritual, or if none is suggested use lavender) over the carving as you visualise the element of fire.

You can also use a feather instead of incense to represent the element of air. Perhaps even place a few drops of essential oil (relevant to your spell or ritual) on a feather and wave that through the air to enjoy the scent and invoke the mood and energies you normally would by lighting incense.

Put That Knife Down!

An athame looks pretty formidable and pretty lethal to those who don't understand what it's for. It's never used for cutting anything solid. It is used for directing and focusing energy and for cutting portals in the etheric and astral planes; for example, in adept Witches' Circle-casting rituals, the invoking and banishing pentagrams for each quarter are created when calling on the guardians of the elements).

Instead of an athame, you can use your power finger (the index finger of your right hand or, if you prefer, your left if this is the hand you write with). Or you can use your wand or even a feather. I don't often use my athame and use my power finger instead, especially when I'm travelling a lot and carrying a big knife is just not feasible.

The Invisible Book of Shadows

A lot of Teen Witches have told me that their parents, on finding their Book of Shadows, promptly burnt it. Maybe you could leave it in your locker at school or keep it on a computer drive (though as I say in the section on Book of Shadows on page 66, handwritten and embellished hard copy is often more satisfying). Do a leave me alone charm to help keep it undisturbed. A Book of Shadows is an important part of a Teen Witch's knowledge and experience, documenting as it does this fertile time of your Witchy development – so don't leave it lying around. If you have to hide it, make sure it's in a good spot. (How about inside the trunk of a hollow tree? Wrapped in something waterproof and mouse-proof, of course.)

For the Book Witch

Reading is always a big part of Witchy research and you might want to consider using libraries for your Witchy research rather than filling your shelves with books your folks might take exception to. Or maybe do most of your research using the Internet – although it is possible that your folks may keep an eye on what sites you've been to, material you've saved and so on, so don't assume your computer is private space unless you know way more about computers than your parents!

Can I Please Have Some Privacy?

◇◇

Circles outdoors in a safe place are often even better than Circles in your room, especially if you're worried you'll be disturbed at home. However, I must stress that the place needs to be very safe: certainly not in the middle of nowhere, unless you are with a group of older people who can handle any situation. Even protection spells are not entirely infallible, so always be spiritually safe and tell someone you trust where you are going.

And Finally...

◇◇

You don't need to go around advertising that you are a Witch and making a big visible statement about it all the time. Being a Witch is not about rebelling against your parents, or about what you wear, or bragging or having power over other people. It is about tapping into the power inside you; it's about being the best you can be; it's about love and getting what you want out of life. So be proud of your choices and don't take any criticism personally. Don't feel you have to be on a crusade all the time to make people understand you; just be true to yourself and your goals and use your Witchcraft to help you achieve them.

Teen Witch in Love

From when I was 13, I was obsessed with boys, and often to my detriment. I went from being an A-grade student to a D-grade student in a term – seriously! I guess it was normal enough, but I lost all sense of myself and thought that the best I could be was based on whether some boy liked me. The girls in the group I hung out with were a bit older than me and were sort of tough and, to me, seemed to have their act together a lot more than I did. Their boyfriends were older and cooler, but I got stuck with guys who were just as nervous as me. My friends set me up with this guy who, when I sat down next to him at the bus stop, jumped three inches off the seat! We didn't last very long!

The next guy I went out with, Sam, was a bit more confident, but one day two of my girlfriends and I jigged school to go and see the movie *Saturday Night Fever,* which had just come out (I'm showing my age here!). My two friends sat behind Sam and me with their boyfriends. It was so humiliating: the whole way through the movie they kept issuing instructions like, 'Okay, Sam, put your arm around Fiona', 'Give him a cuddle, Fiona. C'mon are you chicken?' By the end I was leaning so far out into the aisle that Sam's arm was nearly popping out of its socket as he attempted to keep it around me. When we were outside I tried to be cool and said, 'Good movie, huh?' but Sam just walked away. The next day at school one of my girlfriends came up to me and said, 'Sam says to say, "You're dropped".'

For weeks after this I was increasingly pressured by the girls in my group since I was the only one who hadn't been kissed and they were starting to call me frigid! There was another boy, George, who had been acting keen for a whilst. He wasn't too bad – he had the bluest eyes I'd ever seen. But on my 14th birthday my day of reckoning had come; there was no escaping it. The girls had set it up that I would meet George by the side of the sewing cottage at my girls-only school and there the deed would be done. I was standing there feeling so nervous that I was about to throw up (which probably wouldn't have made the whole thing any less romantic, now I think of it), and then George sauntered along. He looked cockier than he probably felt. My group was standing a short distance away eyeing us both off. George and I exchanged a few words: 'Hot, isn't it?' 'Yeah.' Then, all off a sudden, my vision was blocked by his blurred face and – whack! – it landed on me. What 'it' was isn't easily described. It definitely didn't seem to have a lot in common with any screen kisses I'd seen at the movies. Perhaps I could best describe it as a 'slobbering chin chew'. He'd missed nearly all of both lips, which was quite an achievement at such close range, but he managed to catch a bit of the bottom one. On the good side, most of his tongue didn't get anywhere near the inside of my mouth. On the not-so-good side, it spent most of the interaction slobbering all over my chin. I couldn't move or breathe, and then finally, after what seemed an eternity, it was over. 'See ya this arvo at the bus stop,' George said. And then he was gone. Yep, he was every bit as romantic with words as he was with his kisses. I slowly lifted my hand to my chin and wiped his spit away as the girls ran over. 'Why didn't ya put ya arms 'round him?' they asked. I tried to tell them that he'd grabbed me so fast they'd stayed pinned against my chest, where I'd had them crossed before the alleged magic moment, but I found I didn't really want to talk about it. I just felt sad that something I'd hoped would be so special turned out to be so disappointing. As kisses went it had been about as magickal as being hit in the face with an over-ripe mango!

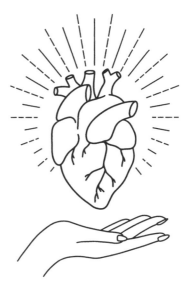

Since I wouldn't wish that sort of fiasco on anyone, and since some of you might have that first-kiss experience in front of you, the following is a spell to help you prepare for that big event in your life. Whether you are nervous and want to wait, or eager and want to hurry up, this spell can work for you. It is primarily a confidence spell, but it's also a time spell that will act to help you through the experience and also ensure that it comes along at the right time: when you are ready.

⊕ First-Kiss Bliss Spell

◇◇

Best day: Friday, ruled by Venus, the planet of love.

Best time: just before dawn (the shift from night to day is a good time for magick).

Moon phase: best during a waxing moon, but full is also good.

YOU WILL NEED:

- ☞ 1 large pink candle
- ☞ 1 handful each of lavender and dried rose petals
- ☞ a teaspoon honey
- ☞ peppermint (if you want to hurry the kiss along) or rosemary (if you want to let it take its time)
- ☞ a wind-up clock set to the current time
- ☞ a small bowl of olive oil in which a rose quartz crystal has sat overnight
- ☞ a red ribbon

DIRECTIONS

Assemble everything outside where the sun's first rays can fall on you. If you can't do this, stand near a window where you can see the first light awaken the day.

Cast Circle, preferably with the full ritual, but if you feel sufficiently practised blast a Circle of pure protection: visualise a sphere of white light around you keeping negativity out and positive power in.

Place the candle in the centre of Circle, and dip your power finger (the index finger of whatever hand you write with) into the oil and touch your forehead, lips and heart as you say:

My thoughts are clear, my heart is true, my intent is good and pure.

With your power hand (the one you write with), sprinkle the mixture of lavender and rose petals around the pink candle deosil or sunwise direction (anticlockwise in the southern hemisphere; clockwise in the northern hemisphere). The sun should be starting to lighten the horizon now and, as it does, light the candle and say:

As the sun rises to warm my face,

In perfect time and perfect grace,

So shall my first kiss take its place.

Repeat this until you feel the warmth of the sun settle upon you. Now, pick up the clock and if you want your kiss to happen soon, wind the clock hands forward three full revolutions as you say:

Through time and space speed to me

My perfect kiss easily.

Now bind the peppermint to the clock with the red ribbon.

If you want to take your time, wind the clock hands backwards three full revolutions as you say:

I take my time for peace of mind

When I am ready, the kiss is mine.

Bind the rosemary to the clock with the red ribbon. Now place the teaspoon of honey in your mouth. Savour its sweetness and say:

Honey pure, honey sweet,

The perfect kiss is mine to keep.

The main part of the spell is done but there is a final affirmation – the love spell sealing charm – that requires the most focus. Stand with your arms outstretched to the sun and say:

I am perfect and whole,

Blessed and essential,

Unlimited is my potential.

My life is unfolding as it must

For the good of all is this magick cast.

Then say:

In return for my perfect kiss, I kiss the sun three times twixt.

Spin deosil/sunwise three times and blow a kiss to the sun. Snuff the candle and place it in a box with the clock, the lavender and rose petals. You can cast this spell again to speed things up or slow things down on the following two Fridays. By then you will have either done it or the pressure to do it will be off!

I Think I'm in Love

You are in love with the gorgeous quiet boy or girl at the back of the classroom, but they don't seem to know you are alive. You've tried everything, from passing the word around that you like them, to smiling invitingly at them, to catching the wrong bus home – the one, coincidentally enough, they happen to take. But whatever brilliant strategy you come up with, still they will not respond. It's got to the point now where they are all you think about and you can't concentrate on your schoolwork. Seeing them in class is all you look forward to and you are convinced you're in love with them. But you are a Teen Witch and have the power, with the right spell, to make them fall in love with you – right? WRONG!

Love spells will always backfire or just plain fizzle when you break the second of the Witches' Laws: 'Do what you want but don't interfere with another's free will.' Your spell might do an effective job of tying the object of your affection to you, only for you to find out that the person's not at all who you thought they were: boring, selfish or an out-and-out weirdo and not in a cool way! But you've woven your spell so well you can't get rid of them.

Before you do any kind of 'come to me' love spell, you should consider doing a self-love spell first to make sure that your personal energies are aligned and you are very clear about why you want a partner and what qualities you seek. It's natural for you to experiment in love but you will go through some pretty intense learning curves as far as human interaction goes. All the same, try not to let these changes in your life treat you any harder than they need to. There's so much pressure now on teenagers to grow up quickly, and spend their money on looking good (well, magazines' and Instagram followers' ideas of what looks good), and just about every music video is overloaded with fierce sexy images. This can all be great fun and cool entertainment, but the underlying effect can pressure you to keep up and compete with each other to have the most fierce clothes, friends, boyfriends, girlfriends … whatever.

Teen Witches are different from regular teenagers in that they can be aware of all this pressure and decide how much they want to take on and how much they want to stand apart from it. If there's one thing a Witch needs to be able to withstand, it's peer-group pressure and the temptation to conform to other people's idea of what their lives should be like. The misinformed sometimes refer to the Craft as a cult, but the reality is that a 'conformist' Witch is an absolute contradiction in terms. Our independence is one of the main sources of our power.

Finding that independence isn't the easiest thing in the world, of course. When I look back at the diaries I kept in my teens, every second paragraph was about some guy and how hard it was to keep him happy, first, and then keep myself happy, second. Every other paragraph was about how fat and ugly I felt. Let me encourage you to enjoy your solo time instead of dedicating your every waking moment to seeking the approval of others. Spend your energies on being the best version of you that you can be – perfecting your Witchcraft and doing cool spells and rituals that help and heal the planet, your family, school, your friends and yourself. You will attract people in your life who will teach you the lessons you need to learn.

I have to admit that this is all your classic case of 'do what I say, not as I did'. Unfortunately, absolutely every relationship I had, from my first kiss at 14 to all the boyfriends I had through my 20s were pretty much disasters, but this was because I didn't value and respect myself. After a short time of bliss my relationships would descend into destructive, often violent (mentally and emotionally) affairs. A pattern had been set in my early teens: I did not consider myself worthy of love and I attracted people into my life who continued to fit into this vision of life I had for myself. If I had been a Teen Witch then I would have addressed those deep underlying feelings of self-hatred and sadness straight up, and not had to have so many hard lessons to realise I am fine as I am and do deserve love. Now that I've got over those self-destructive thinking patterns, I know I'd rather be single than have a bad boyfriend. In other words, I've learnt to enjoy and value my own company and that of my friends instead of feeling compelled to sort out someone else's problems and blaming myself when things go wrong. That being said, it takes two to have an argument and sometimes our perceived adversaries can be our greatest teachers.

The following spell to help you appreciate your own worth is awesome and will leave you feeling amazing if you are uncentred, lonely or just a bit lost in the world. It will reinstate a strong sense of self and what your needs are, and when you are in that 'together' state you can make an enlightened decision as to whether you want to bring a partner into your life or wait for the Universe to get around to it in its own perfect time.

So here's the ...

⊕ Awesome Self-love Spell

Do you know the chorus of the old song 'Scarborough Fair': 'Are you going to Scarborough Fair? Parsley, sage, rosemary and thyme.' The herbs in the song are for love and healing and this spell uses all four.

Best day: any (but Friday is good: ruled by Venus, the planet of love).

Best time: when you need it.

Moon phase: any, but preferably waxing or full.

YOU WILL NEED:

- a picture of yourself aged between one and five, another aged between five and 10, another aged between 10 and now and a very recent picture
- a small bunch of parsley
- a small bunch of sage
- a small bunch of rosemary

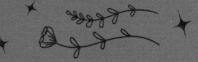

- a small bunch of thyme
- a lock of your hair
- a silver ribbon if you're a girl or a gold ribbon if you're a boy
- a silver candle if you're a girl or a gold candle if you're a boy
- a sharp feather quill or pointed stick
- an apple cut across to expose the pentacle arrangement of the seeds
- cinnamon
- some beautiful instrumental music

DIRECTIONS

Start the music softly and cast Circle. When you have done this, lay out the four photographs with a different herb lying across each. Carve your full name and your magickal name (if you have one) in your silver or gold candle with the quill, lick your thumb and trace it over your name to seal it, then light the wick.

Invoke the Goddess of love, Aphrodite, and ask for her blessing:

Goddess of love, Aphrodite,

Bless me with your glorious presence;

Fuel my self-appreciation.

Fill my soul with sweet elation;

May the waters of your heavenly home

Cleanse my soul and make me whole.

Sense Aphrodite manifesting in your Circle as a swirling pink sea of light; in your mind's eye you may see her float in on her shell. Know that she is here to magnify your finest qualities and bring out the very best in you.

Now pick up the apple (which is sacred to Aphrodite) and sprinkle some cinnamon on it (for purification and strength). Slowly eat the apple and be aware that you are taking in Aphrodite's power. When you are finished, save five seeds and put them aside.

Now pick up the bunches of herbs and, placing the lock of your hair in the centre, wind the ribbon around the stem five times and tie a big bow as you say:

I weave the strands of my life together,

With these sacred herbs I bless my endeavours.

I am good, I am whole, I am proud to be me.

I share this love with the world gratefully.

Inhale deeply the pungent scent of your herb charm as you look at the photos of your progression in life as a growing, evolving human being. Feel a deep, unconditional sense of appreciation for yourself and where you've come from and where you're going. If you feel your mind wandering and settling on unpleasant memories, focus on Aphrodite's perfect pink presence inside you and around you in your Circle, breathing in her pink light, feeling it enter your lungs, warm and loving.

Now say the love spell sealing charm:

I am perfect and whole,

Blessed and essential,

Unlimited is my potential.

My life is unfolding as it must,

For the good of all is this magick cast.

When you are ready, thank the Goddess Aphrodite for her assistance and close Circle. Take the five apple seeds outside and plant them as an offering to the eternally renewing forces of life and hang your bunch of herbs in your window or somewhere they can dry and be kept for as long as you like, or until you do the spell again.

Okay, you've done the awesome self-love spell and you still want that guy or girl. There's no way around it, so here's …

⊕ The 'I Have to Have You' Spell

As I mentioned above, it's not a good idea to try to attract a particular individual in case your glowing judgement of them isn't all that accurate. After all, you're obviously not that close to them or you wouldn't be needing this spell. Instead what you need to do is look at what attracts you to them and define all those alluring qualities that you perceive them to have (be aware you're often looking at them through rose-coloured glasses).

As a teen I used to get crushes on famous people — and funnily enough, because of my work, I've met quite a few of them and they've turned out to be a long way from the perfect creatures I thought they were. In fact, a couple of them have been horrible! It's disappointing when you find out that the person who wrote and performed your ultra-favourite song is a loser, but that's life sometimes in the world of music! Having said that, some I've met are nicer than I ever imagined them to be. People are people with good and bad points, no matter whether they're a number one rock star or the gardener.

Anyway, this spell works to draw to you your perfect partner.

Best day: Friday, ruled by Venus, the planet of love.

Best time: the early evening.

Moon phase: it would be perfect when the new crescent moon makes her first appearance of the month in the sky, but any time during the waxing crescent and before full is good.

YOU WILL NEED:

- ☞ a strawberry herbal tea bag
- ☞ a pink candle
- ☞ pink, rose or mixed flower-scented bath salts, or maybe a bath bomb (Lush make an excellent one for this spell in the shape of a heart with nine rose buds embedded in it)
- ☞ rose potpourri
- ☞ a pink cord 33 cm/one foot long (you could buy silky, present-wrapping cord)
- ☞ 1/4 cup olive oil that a rose has floated in overnight
- ☞ a piece of paper and a pink texta (sharpie)
- ☞ a white cup filled with nearly boiled water

DIRECTIONS

As a part of the ritual, before casting Circle light the pink candle and take a bath using the bath salts as you drink the cup of strawberry tea from the white cup. As you soak, meditate on the qualities of your ideal partner. If a particular person enters your mind, think about what you like about them then let their image float away. When you feel focused and ready, get out of the bath and carry your candle to where you're doing your ritual (try not to let the flame blow out if it's lit). Then cast Circle and invoke Aphrodite:

Aphrodite, bring me perfect love

For the good of all, with harm to none.

On your piece of paper write down all the things you want in your dream partner – not just personality qualities; you can even specify hair colour or eye colour (just don't think of a specific person!). When you are ready, put the paper down and sprinkle a little of the potpourri on it as you say:

Flower of love,

Bless my request,

Manifest the person

That will suit me best.

Do this two more times so you have recited the charm three times in total. Now, fold the paper around the potpourri to contain it inside.

Next, pick up the cord and tie five knots, spacing them evenly. As you tie them you must focus clearly on your desired person coming to you.

Tie the first knot at the right end of the cord and say:

By one, this spell's begun.

Trace a pentagram with a little of the rose-infused olive oil on the knot. Then tie the next:

By two, it shall come true.

Trace another pentagram on this knot, then tie the next:

By three, so mote it be.

Trace another pentagram and tie another knot:

By four, for the good of all.

Trace another pentagram and tie another knot:

By five, love comes alive.

Trace a pentagram on the final knot.

You have now created a magickal cord that is charged with your spell.

Thank the Goddess Aphrodite and close the Circle. Take the cord and put it somewhere safe with your folded piece of paper (maybe you could place both in a clean, white, cotton pillowcase and put them away in a drawer). When your new love arrives on the scene, you need to release the magick of the cord and burn it. Place the cord on the ground and trace a pentagram in the air over each knot (without touching it) as you say each time, 'This magick is released, the spell has done its work.' When you've done all five, burn the cord. You can burn the paper charm with the cord. I think it's important to release the magick of this spell once it has worked because you want to allow the other person's input and energy to take your relationship further and in new directions that perhaps you hadn't thought of. If you have really fixed ideas about how you think a relationship should be, you won't grow as a person. As much as I've had some hard, sad times I have benefited from my difficult relationships. As the negative patterns of the past gradually shifted, and whatever their good and bad points might have been, all my partners showed me things about myself that ultimately led to me becoming a better and happier person.

Note: you can adapt the above spell to bring a best friend, or just more friends, into your life. As you do the spell think about what you would like in a friend, what things you would like to do together and fun times you would like to share. When you invoke the Goddess Aphrodite ask her to bring you perfect friendship.

⊕ Make Your Own Enchanted Love Bath Salts

YOU WILL NEED:

- ☞ 1 cup sea salt
- ☞ 1 cup Epsom salts (from the chemist/drugstore)
- ☞ 1/4 cup dried rose petals
- ☞ 1/4 cup coconut or almond oil
- ☞ 11 drops lavender oil

DIRECTIONS

Blend all of the ingredients in a glass container, cover with a lid and store in a dark cool place.

Don't have a bath? Make a foot bath and soak your feet so that the steps you take are blessed with love.

⊕ Unconditional Love Spell

This is a spell to do for anyone just because you love them. They could be your best friend, your sister or brother, your teacher or your girlfriend or boyfriend. This spell works to send them lots of positive energy and it also lets the Universe know how special this person is and so attracts good fortune to them.

Best time: any time!

YOU WILL NEED:

- ☞ a light blue candle
- ☞ lavender oil
- ☞ a sugar cube
- ☞ a really beautiful flower in a vase
- ☞ a sharp feather quill or pointed stick

DIRECTIONS

Cast Circle and trace the name of your loved one into the candle with the quill, lick your thumb and trace over the name. Light the candle and place just one drop of oil on the sugar cube as you say:

For love and friendship, pure and sweet.

Now pop it in the vase with the flower. Hold the vase and gaze at the flower as you say:

Universe, I ask [their name] be blessed;
She/he fills my life with happiness.
Return to them three times three
The pleasure they have given me.

Now close Circle and give the flower to your special person. If it's impossible to give it to them, keep it in the vase and think of them every time you look at it.

⊕ Rose Potpourri: Make Your Own!

⟨⟨⟨⟨⟨⟨⟨⟨⟨⟨⟨⟨⟨⟨⟨⟨⟨⟨⟨⟨⟨⟨⟨⟨⟨⟨⟨⟨⟨⟨⟨⟨⟨⟨⟨⟨⟨⟨⟩

Pluck the petals from about five lovely, big, scented red roses and spread them over waxed paper in a dry, warm place.

When they are completely dry, sprinkle them with two tablespoons of orris root (order online or find at a good health food grocery) and, with your hands, mix it all up together in a glass bowl. As you do this, visualise pink light streaming from your hands into the bowl as you take a deep breath in and on every exhale say the word 'love'.

Finally, a few drops of rose oil – or ylang ylang, tuberose or any other luscious heady floral scent that you intuitively feel drawn to – mixed in will enhance the scent and seal in strong love attracting power.

What is Orris Root Powder?

⟨⟨⟨⟨⟨⟨⟨⟨⟨⟨⟨⟨⟨⟨⟨⟨⟨⟨⟨⟨⟨⟨⟨⟨⟨⟨⟨⟨⟨⟨⟨⟨⟨⟨⟨⟨⟨⟨⟩

Traditional potpourri is made by adding essential oils to dried flowers and herbs and sealing them in a jar together for a few weeks to let the fragrance develop. Unfortunately, most essential oils are volatile, which means they are likely to evaporate over the space of a few hours or days, leaving the potpourri with no fragrance. A fixative is any material that prevents this rapid evaporation; it absorbs the oil and keeps it in the potpourri. Orris root powder, which is the powdered dried root of the iris lily and smells like violets, is one material that does this, but there are many others. Suitable fixative may be particular tree resins, flowers, roots, leaves or seeds as well as less volatile essential oils. Here are some you could try:

- 🐾 gum benzoin, myrrh and frankincense

180

- cinnamon powder and sticks
- cloves and nutmeg
- cumin, coriander and angelica seeds
- vanilla pods
- oakmoss
- chamomile flowers
- geranium roots
- leaves of lemon verbena
- oils of sandalwood, cedarwood, patchouli and ylang ylang

⊕ SIMPLE SPELL TO ENJOY SINGLE LIFE

Sometimes you can feel really left out when all your friends have boyfriends or girlfriends and you don't. In addition to the awesome self-love spell, here's an easy one to help you feel happy and empowered.

Best time: whenever you need it.

YOU WILL NEED:
- a white feather
- a clear quartz crystal
- a white candle
- a glass of spring water
- a piece of white paper
- a silver pen
- a white velvet or other cloth drawstring pouch

DIRECTIONS

For this spell you're going to make an amulet. This can be done in a fully cast Circle or, if you prefer, visualise a pure power shield (a sphere of white light around you keeping positive power in your space and negative energy out). Either way, make sure you empower your objects (see 'Slay your Spells'). Light the candle, hold the crystal and say:

My mind is clear for my intent.

Drop the crystal in the water, take a sip and say:

My life is mine, my goals are met.

Now, on the paper and with the silver pen draw a pentagram with a circle around it touching the five points and around that write your full name. Take the feather and trace over the pentagram three times with it as you say:

Feather of air and star of earth,

Empower me as fire burns; I am free, my will flows deep;

No need to be in another's keep.

Snuff the candle, put the feather and the crystal in the pouch with the paper (you can fold it up) and pour the water onto a plant. Snap off the power shield.

Keep your amulet with you so that you can hold it and repeat the charm whenever you're feeling lonely or left out.

CHAPTER ELEVEN

◇◇◇

Let's Talk About Teen Witch Sex

◇◇◇

In the 16 years since the first version of this book was released the world has become radically 'PC' (politically correct), which has led to an almost hypocritical and convoluted 'correct practice' of language that doesn't deeply address underlying fears, ignorance and prejudice. As a result, there appears a surface change in cultural consciousness whilst the real problems fester unaddressed.

So before continuing, here's the score: I haven't written this chapter to tell you how to run your sexual lives, when to begin them or what other choices you ought to be making on the subject. What I'd like you to think about is the fact that your body and your sexuality are your own and it's not up to anybody –

your friends, family and definitely not an author you've probably never met – to tell you what you should be doing.

That doesn't mean you should disregard all advice automatically, a practice as robotic and self-negating as doing everything you're told without question. If you're still pretty young, it's a safe bet that your parents will have some pretty heavy-duty opinions on your sexual behaviour. Because a lot of parents are uncomfortable discussing the topic with their kids they often express these opinions as completely black and white, 'thou shalts' and 'thou shalt nots' that tend to disregard your own feelings. The challenge for you in that situation is to keep in mind that however their opinions might be expressed, you can be pretty sure they're motivated by concerns for your health, safety and happiness. Perhaps they're trying to protect you from making some of the bad choices they made at your age. A lot of teens end up making precisely those same mistakes (or much worse ones) by automatically rebelling against ultimatums from their parents. So, before you make any decision on your own sexual life, be very clear that you're not falling into that trap.

The same thing applies when your friends try to make your choices for you by telling you you're being a wimp or a loser for behaving in a certain way around sexual issues. Every time you make a decision on this subject, be 100 per cent clear who's making that decision: is it you, or someone you're giving your power of choice to?

But I do have a few strong recommendations about your sexual life. The main one is simply to educate yourself on the subject as much as you possibly can. This book is not a sex-education manual, but there is a lot of other really helpful information out there so make it your business to soak it up.

For Witches, sexuality is always held to be a powerful and sacred thing. But just because you might be a Teen Witch doesn't mean you're safe from the dangers out there in the sexual world. Find out all you can about safe sex, contraception and, just as importantly, how to treat your future (or maybe even present) lovers with respect, kindness and understanding and how to ensure you're treated the same way. I suppose the first thing to realise is that it's illegal to have sex until you are 16 years old, so you should bear this in mind whenever you are making decisions about your sexual activity.

All of the above applies to all teens, of course, but here are a few tips for those who also have the advantage of being able to whip up a little magick! The following are some spells to deal with some of the really big events that will confront you as you awaken sexually.

BODY AWARENESS

I spent so much time torturing myself about my appearance when I was a teen. I had no bosoms and my lips were apparently too big (my nickname at school was 'Fish Lips'). When I left school and started work as a model/receptionist for a clothing company, all of a sudden I was too fat. And when I started having sex, I was even more hyper-critical of myself. I used to turn around and look at my bum in the mirror and hate it. There is so much pressure on young girls, and increasing pressure on young boys, to conform to particular body types — the kinds of bodies that only a tiny fraction of the human race have naturally, and only a slightly larger fraction of the human race can achieve with masses of ridiculously hard work. At a time of supposed enlightenment and liberation, never has there been so much insidious advertising and so many disempowering messages in the shows we watch on television and the feeds we follow on social media, about what our bodies should be like.

Teen Witches need to have a good hard think about how much they want to absorb from the world around them about how they should look. For a start, the three girls from the original *Charmed* are portrayed as powerful Witches but they are all skinny as rakes (Prue especially) with big bosoms, dressed in designer clothing and looking as fresh as daisies whether they're waking up, going to a nightclub or zapping a demon. Buffy and Willow barely ooze a drop of sweat when vanquishing vampires; Sandra Bullock and Nicole Kidman didn't have an ounce of excess fat between them in *Practical Magic* and more recently Sabrina, in *Chilling Adventures of Sabrina*, is as cute and perfect as they come whether she is a freshman at high school or the queen of hell. And there are older Witches in classic movies like *The Witches of Eastwick* portrayed by the likes of Susan Sarandon, Michelle Pfeiffer and Cher – all very beautiful, in a standard, exceptional movie-star way. And more lately glamorous Sarah Paulson and Jessica Lange cementing powerful awe-inspiring Witches as iconic physical perfection in *American Horror Story*.

As a Witch, you need to be able to value your physical self whatever shape, age or state of health it might be in.

Whilst not every Witch needs to work skyclad (naked) in shared Circles if she or he chooses not to, every Witch should be able to stand skyclad in front of a full-length mirror and respect and love what's reflected back. If that reflection causes embarrassment, anger or even disgust, your magick will always be diminished. All spells and rituals require the Witch to say, either actually or metaphorically, at some point: 'As I will so mote it be.' If there's some part of that 'I', that sense of yourself, that you can't respect, there's no way your powers can be firing on all cylinders.

Besides which, if you allow the media's idea of the right shape or features for a human being to poison your respect for your own body, you're falling for one of the oldest con tricks on the planet: if you give in to feeling like an underachiever, you'll keep spending money to catch up or to compensate (and this is exactly what the media, or advertisers, want!). Once again, it's your choice whether you want to believe this or not.

Working on stage and in the public eye for so long myself, I guess I could be accused of being part of the same conspiracy, but let me assure you that just about every photo you've seen of me over all the years has been airbrushed to the max (it's all makeup and lighting, darling!).

The most lasting and extraordinary beauty in these artificial, commercial times is that which comes from within – that inner light and sense of pride, compassion and celebration an individual has within themselves. Our bodies are the lampshade, our spirit is the light that shines.

Are You a 20-watt Bulb or a 100-watt Bulb?

◇◇

It's now becoming more fashionable to have booty curves and natural breasts. The plus-size model phenomenon is very positive because it celebrates girls who don't conform to the stick-figure type. And yet extremes on both ends of the scale are not ideal – the best expression of health, vitality and magickal beauty lies somewhere in the middle. And it doesn't escape me that my giant fish lips for which I was mercilessly teased are now coveted. What does it all mean? Well, what does it mean to you? If you can step outside the trends and truly connect with what you feel passionately inspired by as you forge your visual stamp on the world at this coveted commercial age (aka 'youth'), then you can see the trends for what they are and decide to be the light that others follow. Establish your creative parameters on how you embody and celebrate your physical form. I don't gauge my attractiveness on physical looks any more; I gauge it on how healthy, motivated, supple, efficient, energised and peaceful I feel everything else falls into place.

Here are some spells to celebrate and empower yourself with.

⊕ Bright Water

YOU WILL NEED:

- ☛ 1 cup orange blossom flowers (if you can't get these, peel the skin of two oranges and cut into small pieces)
- ☛ 1 cup spring water
- ☛ 3 drops of frankincense oil (this is expensive, so if you can't afford it buy pure frankincense incense sticks and stir the mixture with three of these)
- ☛ 3 pinches of dragon's blood powder (you can buy this at a witchy supply store or online, but if you can't get it in your mortar and pestle crush a teaspoon of rock salt together with a pinch of cinnamon and a pinch of nutmeg)
- ☛ a clear quartz crystal
- ☛ orange non-staining food dye

DIRECTIONS

Soak the flowers or peel in the spring water overnight in a glass. Strain the liquid in the morning and add the oil (or stir for five minutes with the incense sticks), then sprinkle in the dragon's blood powder. Drop the crystal in and add three drops of the dye. Hold the glass in both hands and say:

Crystal of light,
Charge this water
With moonlight and wisdom,
Sunshine and laughter.

⊕ Sacred-self Bath Salts

YOU WILL NEED:

- ☛ 3/4 cup semi-ground rock salt
- ☛ 1/4 cup Epsom salts (from the chemist)
- ☛ purple food dye (from the supermarket)
- ☛ 5 drops essential oil of rose geranium (smells divine and can be burnt in an oil burner to help continue the spell working)
- ☛ verbena (also called vervain; a herb you can buy at the health food store)
- ☛ chamomile (also at your health food store)

DIRECTIONS

Grind the two herbs in your mortar and pestle until they are mostly powdery. As you grind say this chant:

Herbs of power, herbs of worth,

Assist me in my magick work.

Mix the rock and Epsom salts together and drop in a few drops of the food dye. Give it a good shake as the salt absorbs the colour. Mix through the herbs, and drop in the oil and mix it through. (A good trick is to put it all in a waxed paper bag and shake it around.)

⊕ The 100-watt Light-bulb Spell

Best time: a waxing to full moon.

Best day: Thursday, ruled by Jupiter and good for confidence.

YOU WILL NEED:

- 📖 a cup of bright water
- 📖 a full-length mirror
- 📖 a torch
- 📖 four white candles
- 📖 to be skyclad for this spell!

DIRECTIONS

Cast Circle and then set up the four white candles to form a circle in front of your mirror. Turn the lights off and light the candles. Sprinkle the bright water around you deosil (sunwise, or anti-clockwise in the southern hemisphere; clockwise in the northern hemisphere).

Dip your power finger (or your athame) in the bright water and trace a pentagram on your third eye, over your heart and over your solar plexus (between your belly button and the bottom of your ribcage).

Shine the torch on your third eye as you look at yourself in the mirror and say:

[Your name], you are bright to see;

In your light no shadows be;

The fire of the sun,

The glow of the moon,

The sparkle of stars,

Flow from you.

Now shine the torch over your heart (not the reflection) and repeat the incantation, then over your solar plexus and repeat the incantation.

When you have done this, look in the mirror and use the torch to trace a large pentagram of light in front of you fast so that the light of the torch blurs and seems to draw solid lines. Raise power in whatever way you like; a good method is to hold your hands over your heart and chant your own name over and over, and feel your body heat light up as all the inner beauty you have gets revved up and charges to the surface. When you feel the power peaking, throw your hands into the air and say:

I am divine, shining light;

I am Goddess/god

Pure and bright.

From stop to go, I switch on my inner[or 'fierce'] glow.

Stand with your arms in the air, exulting in your glowing self. When you are ready, close Circle. Every morning, after washing, dip your finger in the bright water and trace a pentagram over your heart to help your inner beauty/attractiveness glow all day.

Your Body is Sacred

<><><><><><><><><><><><><><><><><><><><><><><><><><><><><><><><>

I mentioned the disaster of my first kiss in the chapter Teen Witch in Love. Well, things didn't get dramatically better after that complete dud of a first experience. I was petrified the first time I had sex and for at least the next year after. Apart from not knowing some of the elementary physical tips for young lovers, my real problem was that I had no concept of my self-worth and the sacredness of my body. I was just trying to fit in and do what I thought a girlfriend was supposed to do.

Teen Witches think long and hard about their first sexual experience.

I would have been in touch with the sacredness of my body and approached the whole experience of my first time completely differently in retrospect.

Here is the body sacred spell, which you can do to strengthen your sense of self so that you will make the right choice for your first time. It can also help you if you've already had a disappointing first experience and want to make sure the next time is way, way better.

⊕ BODY SACRED SPELL

◇◇

Best day: Friday (Venus again!).

Best time: in the evening before going to bed.

YOU WILL NEED:

- 🖝 sacred-self bath salts (see page 190)
- 🖝 a purple candle
- 🖝 purple paper (if you can't find purple paper use a coloured pencil and decorate a white piece of paper with swirls and spirals of purple)
- 🖝 a gold pen
- 🖝 a sharp pin
- 🖝 rose geranium or neroli oil for girls and cinnamon or pine for boys, or any oil that you feel intuitively aligned with

DIRECTIONS

Run a bath and cast Circle in the bathroom. Trace a pentagram, your sun/star sign symbol and your name and age on the candle with the pin.

Lick your thumb and seal the carving with your spit, then dip your finger in a little rose geranium oil and trace over the pentagram with it.

Pour the sacred-self bath salts in the water and stir deosil (anti-clockwise in the southern hemisphere; clockwise in the north) in a big circle seven times with your power hand as you say:

Mystic be the number seven

I call upon the powers of heaven

To bless and manifest my goal:

Perfect harmony body and soul;

As is my will so it will be,

For the good of all but most for me.

Get in the bath and soak; feel the water caress every pore of your body and know that you are utterly unique and deserve only the very best in what you choose to experience.

Meditate on this, and when you are ready get out of the bath, write on the purple paper with the gold pen your name and underneath it the pentagram, and then the following:

I am [name],

Child of the divine, I am special and proud,

Good and blessed

My first time [or next time if you've already done it and you want to improve on the next experience] shall be truth and bliss

A sacred rite that deeply is

Love to receive and love to give.

Close Circle, and for the next six nights before going to sleep burn the candle and read your declaration. Keep both the candle and paper wrapped in white cloth when you're not working the spell.

This spell can be redone regularly, but it is good to perform it when you think you've met someone you really like and with whom you might be considering taking the plunge.

Oops ... I Did It Again!

◇◇

Recently a young male friend of mine asked if he could discuss with me a 'problem' he was having. He was 17 and dating a 16-year-old girl who he really liked but he was having so much trouble with sex.

He could not have sex for more than a few seconds before he came, and got really embarrassed. She would feel disappointed and embarrassed too. They would try, but the same thing would happen again. I told him his 'problem' of premature ejaculation was totally natural and most teenage guys experience it. It has to do with nerves and the pressure to perform. Girls, of course, suffer from the same pressures but for them the reaction is the reverse and they often don't reach orgasm at all. I encouraged him to stop having sex with her for a whilst and to focus on building up other areas of their relationship — like doing fun things together, having lots of yummy cuddles and kisses and talking about their hopes and dreams. I also suggested a spell for him to try. A few weeks later he called me and said the problem was solved! When the pressure to perform was off and he could relax, he felt more comfortable and the spell worked to align the energies of his head and heart so that he could feel integrated and in touch with his body.

⊕ The 'It's All Good' Spell

Best day/time: Sunday at sunrise.

YOU WILL NEED:

- ☛ a gold candle
- ☛ charcoal disc (most health food stores sell them, as well as Witchy supply stores and online; see the Teen Witch Tips chapter for how to light them)
- ☛ frankincense resin (available from Witchy supply stores and online)
- ☛ a plate filled with a 20 cm circle of sand a couple of centimetres deep
- ☛ bell, gong or crystal singing bowl

DIRECTIONS

As the sun rises, cast Circle and light the gold candle. Light the charcoal disc and drop a pinch of frankincense on it.

With your athame or power finger, trace your name in the sand and then a circle three times in a deosil/sunwise direction around it. As you do this chant:

In light of the mighty sun,

I align myself to the powers above;

My potential is great, my intentions are good;

All shall be as it should.

Sprinkle a few more grains of frankincense on the disc and say:

As is my will, so mote it be,

The spell is cast — one, two, three.

Clap your hands or strike your bell or gong as you count 'one, two, three'.

Sit for a whilst, enjoying the sunrise and sprinkling grains of frankincense on the disc as an offering to the sun. When you are ready close Circle and don't worry – it's all good!

ORGASMS

◇◇◇

I got into heaps of trouble when I was busted masturbating in my bedroom when I was nine. It was fire cracker night (when they were still legal in Australia) and I was bored waiting for my family to leave to attend a big bonfire and party in my suburb. I had been masturbating for a whilst by that time in my life, and I always was very careful to be extremely discreet because I was told that playing with yourself was really bad.

However, on this night Mum walked in on me and, after looking at me in horror, sent Dad in to tell me off. He very helpfully told me that it was a sin and dirty and said, 'It's bad to do it.' I remember saying innocently, 'But it feels so nice', which in retrospect probably wasn't very tactful in the circumstances – but I was nine and genuinely confused. All I knew was that I had discovered a wonderful thing that I could do all by myself and which made me feel like I had magick inside me. Which is precisely what it was.

Sex and sexuality and the pleasure associated with them are the most natural things for humans and absolutely essential parts of our lives – in fact, it is the only reason we are alive. If sexual pleasure wasn't so blissful the human race would have died out long ago! In other words, humans have a wonderful ability to feel intense physical joy and for many people orgasm is about as close to spiritual ecstasy as they'll reach in their lives. It isn't just a pleasure like eating when you're hungry or resting when you're tired. It's a fire that makes you feel at one with the forces of all life and creativity.

When I orgasm, as a Witch I feel all the joy that churns at the very centre of the Universe. I feel utterly divine and blessed and transcendent (which is why I sometimes use orgasm as a solo power-raising method in ritual).

This couldn't be further from what I was taught as a young Catholic shrouded in fear – that sex and orgasm should be suppressed and considered dirty.

All acts of love and pleasure are sacred to the Goddess.

A Teen Witch understands these words from our charge of the Goddess and the deeply sacred and divine nature of their bodies, and knows they have nothing to feel ashamed or even confused about. They are beautiful, handsome, unconditionally perfect and loved by the Goddess and god as an expression of the brilliant and powerful force of life. Orgasm is a sacred gift, as well as being one of the coolest and most fun things to do – it's free and easily available! (Having said that, if you have trouble orgasming then don't stress; take your time, keep practising and it will work itself out.)

The only other thing I'd like to add on the subject of masturbation is that every time you do it you're tapping into a great source of magickal energy that you might as well use some of the time instead of just frittering it away, however pleasantly.

A sacred orgasm ritual is very simple. Just do it! Don't be in too much of a rush (that sets a bad precedent for later life, especially for guys!).

Don't let anyone make you feel guilty or worried about doing it. And dedicate each beautiful feeling you have to someone or something special in the Universe. Oh, and a final tip: do a private space spell so you don't get interrupted by people barging into your room without knocking!

The Rainbow Witch

◇◇

At its core, Witchcraft embraces the magnificent diversity of humanity in all its colours, shapes, sizes and preferences. We encourage evolution and change, and one of the most dynamic modern aspects of the Craft is its challenging of patriarchal gender roles.

Witchcraft is a religion that honours the life force as sacred and is primarily matriarchal, though many Witches are tending more and more to a Taoist-like balance of female and male energy that is not gender specific in how it manifests in humans. The Goddess is still often given extra emphasis, but that's largely to help correct the imbalance of the masculine over the feminine that many of our cultures have. However, as the gap between men and women's power in society becomes narrower, the need to exult the Goddess above the god becomes less necessary.

Witches also do not see the emotional and physical union of heterosexual couples as superior to that of lesbian and gay couples. Love and pleasure are sacred to Witches, and all Witches are free to explore these in whatever way they choose. Reproduction of the species is not the only expression of love or pleasure, nor the only form of fertility. We acknowledge that absolute masculinity and femininity exist only in the abstract. In practice, each of us has male and female elements to our personality and energy.

Not surprisingly, the LGBTQIA community took the rainbow as the symbol of the richness of variety in our species. In many ways, especially in the past, Witches and gay people have a lot in common. Throughout history, both groups have often been treated as outcasts and minorities to be hunted down and persecuted. In these modern times, Witches and gay people have been increasingly encouraged to come out of their individual closets (for a Witch the broom closet, of course!), and though there is still prejudice directed at us there is considerably more freedom for us to express ourselves.

In fact, prior to the dominance of the Western patriarchal religious mindset, there was a rich history of the profound role homosexuality played in the spiritual evolution of humanity. It is only since the Christian era that the idea of a woman or effeminate man as a spiritual leader has been denigrated.

In ancient temples and primitive cultures the gay, effeminate man and virgin Priestess (virgin meaning complete unto herself) were all seen to have great psychic and magickal abilities. Also, if you do a bit of research you'll find many of the Goddesses and Gods of old had lesbian and gay encounters. Hermes, the Greek god of magick, medicine, intelligence and communication, was portrayed as androgynous and bisexual. And going further back in time to one of the greatest ancient Syrian Gods, Baal was often portrayed as being one with his female counterpart, Astarte, and invoked as 'Baal – whether god or Goddess'.

The infamous isle of Lesbos was colonised by Amazons in the sixth century BCE. The women of this island were revered as poets, musicians, artists, lovers and Priestesses in service of the great Greek Goddesses Artemis and Aphrodite. Even though during the early Christian era most traces of this colony were destroyed, today some Wiccan Covens exist as female only – the roles within the Coven being based on the perceived structure and function of these ancient temples.

Some traditions in the Craft teach that energy polarity is like a battery, and to raise power during magickal ritual it is essential to have the opposites of male and female acting together. But these energies are given gender-specific definitions based on the archetypal behaviour and roles of women and men in our society, not on some profound universal truth of what it is to be male and female. We all have the Goddess and god within us. A perfect example of this is raising power as a solitary Witch: when firing up alone you are expounding on the totality of your personal being, celebrating the fact that all things exist within as well as without.

In Witchcraft, gay, lesbian, bisexual, transgendered, queer, intersex and asexual humans can find a sense of spiritual peace and integration.

There are inspiring role models, Gods and Goddesses to relate to and a tolerant and compassionate magickal community to be a part of. Everyone can turn the Wheel of the Year, dance the spiral dance of the cosmos and take their rightful place as divine children of the Universe.

Yin and Yang

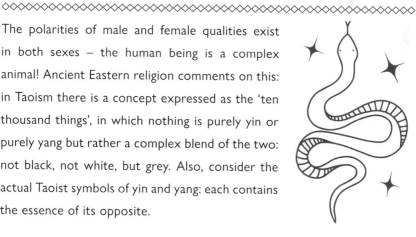

The polarities of male and female qualities exist in both sexes — the human being is a complex animal! Ancient Eastern religion comments on this: in Taoism there is a concept expressed as the 'ten thousand things', in which nothing is purely yin or purely yang but rather a complex blend of the two: not black, not white, but grey. Also, consider the actual Taoist symbols of yin and yang: each contains the essence of its opposite.

CHAPTER TWELVE

◇◇

OUT OF IT

◇◇

Drugs: well, what can I say besides suggesting: 'Don't do it.' In my book *Witch: A Personal Journey*, the chapter 'Flying High' talks about why drugs and magick don't sustainably mix for older Witches and that goes for Teen Witches too. I'm not saying this to be straight or to sound like a mum or dad. I'm saying this because I know – I've been there and done it … and drinking and drugging didn't help my Witchcraft, only diluted and reduced it's focus and power.

As an adult I had my time over-indulging in the legal drug alcohol, and it became a very dark force in my life. But before it killed me (or I killed myself with it more accurately) I got sober in a program and at the time of writing this I have been sober from all substances for seven years. It's truly magick.

Witchcraft is demanding and challenging and often when you get it happening in a big way the rush is better than any artificial high you could experience on drugs.

With Witchcraft there's no come-down, no health problems and it's relatively free. It won't make you do things you regret either.

Alcohol is something most Teens at one time or another will experiment with and even abuse. Alcohol, cigarettes and e-cigarettes cause more grief, illness and death than just about anything else, and yet are legal and promoted to the max! Giant corporations and a corrupt system benefit from you hurting yourself and spending all your money. It's kind of disgusting – consider being sober to give the system the middle finger if nothing else!

Many eco-conscious Teen Witches choose not to drink alcohol, smoke cigarettes, nor vape. For cigarettes, the first most obvious reason is that they pollute the environment; the second is that they kill you and the people around you; and the third is that if you buy them you are supporting huge multinational corporations who are responsible for massive amounts of ecological damage.

Same goes for vaping. It totally disrespects the temple that is your body and is totally bad for the environment. 'What?' you say. 'There's no carcinogenic smoke ...' No there isn't, but the plastic non-biodegradable vape sticks will be around polluting long after you are dead. Plus it is another huge multinational business feeding giant corporations and a few elite patriarchal pockets.

And alcohol is another heavily marketed and exploited substance that contributes to so much sadness and destruction in people's lives, thus eroding our planet's health. I remember the first time I got drunk. I was 14 and there was a school dance and, surprise, surprise, I was actually allowed to go! My group of friends decided to meet at the basketball court first to get smashed before we went in. I sculled half a goonie bag (the silver foil bag inside a wine cask) of very cheap Moselle. I didn't really want to do it but everyone else was having some and I always overdid things in an attempt to impress people so that hopefully they'd like me.

We started walking down to the school hall and all of a sudden I felt like I was floating. I started giggling uncontrollably. Now, you may be thinking, 'Cool, that sounds like fun', but half an hour later the scene was anything but. I ended up in the lap of an older boy, pashing (kissing!) him in front of everyone. Then I got busted by the headmistress, Sister Cecelia, and she called my parents. I had to sit outside to wait for them to pick me up early, and when they arrived I threw up in the gutter. It was not cool; not only was I grounded for months, I was branded a slut at school.

Teen Sex in 2020

Recent surveys indicate that 30 per cent of teens say their parents have never spoken to them about sex. Recent data also indicates that 40 per cent of high school students have had sex and 10 per cent of these have had sex with four or more people. Thirty-eight per cent of teens have sex without using protection. The numbers back when I was a teen were not this high. Social media, online dating and hooking up with apps have made sex a commodity to be used and exchanged, rather than meaningful relationships and fierce awareness of personal health and boundaries being forged at a pivotal age. (You could say that meaningful relationships are important at any age, but especially when you are forming your mature views and opinions about the world.) 'Quality over quantity' is a value-based concept lost in translation when posting a selfie posed in front of the mirror with your butt framed provocatively gets you 3K likes and ultimately has you valuing yourself more for vague clicks and sexual overtures than anything that celebrates the totality of who you really are – and all you are capable of being. It's natural and healthy and essential to be curious about sex. As a Teen Witch you emphasise personal boundaries and the sacredness of sex and as such don't feel in a hurry to go all the way. It's healthy to explore your evolving sexuality and the transcendental sensual states of being with private sacred masturbation and self-care, but you don't have to be in a hurry to share and especially give away this magick to others.

I was actually quite shy, especially when it came to this kind of stuff, so I was devastated. I couldn't believe I'd done something so stupid and so embarrassing.

In fact, I barely remembered doing it at all.

If I had been a Teen Witch at that age I would have had a lot more respect for myself and my body. I wouldn't have felt the need to show off and try to impress my friends. What's more, I would have had a great night. (My friends who stayed on said the night was unreal.)

But unfortunately my stupidity didn't end there. Six months later it was suggested it would be best for me to leave my school because I got caught taking pills. One of my friends had a dad who was a musician who toured on the road with his band a lot. He had pills called Avils, for car sickness. I took a handful of them and was found wandering around the schoolyard in a daze when I was supposed to be in my science class.

Again, I did it to impress a tough gang of girls who I hoped would stop picking on me. But, no, they just thought I was an idiot and I got expelled. This totally sucked – my already precarious relationship with my parents was trashed and they were utterly heartbroken. My sister and brother were really embarrassed to be related to me and my teen hell just descended into even deeper depths of despair.

So many of the dumb things I did were because of peer pressure and just me needing to feel like I was someone special who belonged somewhere. If I'd been practising the Craft back then, I would have known I was both these things already and would never have made my life so difficult for myself.

There is an enormous amount of pressure on teens to be cool and fit in, and sometimes it might feel easier to just say, 'Okay, I will.' But you will most likely be fitting into a scene that's not going to do you any favours and certainly not give you a leg-up into awesomeness – you will just be wasting your time when you could be doing something ultimately far more rewarding. Basically, if you think that e-cigarettes make you cooler, visit a lung cancer ward. If you feel drinking alcohol will improve your life, ask a family who's lost a loved one in a drink-driving accident. If you believe illegal drugs will make you happier, talk to someone who's wasted years of their life trying to get straight again, or anyone who's done time in prison on a drugs charge. Well, call me prejudiced again but I've got a theory that teenagers who are drawn to the Craft are probably more together than most and don't need to do any of those things – certainly not to excess and to the point where they are screwing up their own lives.

⊕ Just Say Nope Spell

Best time: either a Saturday during the waning moon or when you need it.

YOU WILL NEED:

- ☞ a black candle
- ☞ a lemon
- ☞ a sharp feathered quill or pointed stick
- ☞ hot black tea
- ☞ an ice cube
- ☞ a black cloth

DIRECTIONS

Cast Circle either with the full ritual or an instant Circle of pure protection. Light the black candle and, using the quill, carve the name of the problem (for example, drugs, or a particular person who is trying to make you take drugs) into the side of the lemon. Then, using all your powers of visualisation, imagine the problem. When you have a clear image in your mind, take a sip of the tea and blow five hot breaths over the lemon as you say forcefully:

[Problem], I sour your power over me.

You now have no hold on me;

I am free, my resolve is great.

I have the power to decide my fate.

Now snuff the candle. Open the Circle and take the candle, lemon (wrapped in black cloth as you transport it) and the ice (you could use a thermos to keep it frozen if you have to travel a distance). Go to where the problem occurs: at your school, at the bus stop, in the person's street. Unwrap the lemon and bury it as close as you can to the problem place.

Stand the black candle on the earth and light it, saying the incantation again. When you have done this, put the ice in your mouth and then blow five cold breaths on the earth over which the lemon lies, with the final breath blowing out the candle. As the lemon decomposes into the earth, so will your problem recede.

⊕ Naturally High Spell

This is a spell you can do before you go out so that you are feeling naturally buzzed!

YOU WILL NEED:

- ylang ylang essential oil (a beautiful euphoric oil from topical flowers – clary sage is also good – or if you have a favourite blend that when you take a deep breath of it you feel uplifted use it)
- an orange candle
- a yellow candle
- a feather
- a chalice (beautiful glass or goblet)
- berry juice (either strawberry, blackberry or cranberry or a mixture)
- honey
- a silver spoon

DIRECTIONS

Cast Circle, either with the full or instant ritual.

Light the candles and take a few deep breaths as you gaze at the flames to calm and centre yourself. Now stir half a teaspoon of honey into the berry juice in the chalice with the silver spoon deosil (sunwise or anti-clockwise in the southern hemisphere; clockwise in the north). As you stir, repeat faster and

faster the following incantation until you feel the powers in the cup peaking:

Love, joy, power grows,

This magick brew does bestow.

(Watch out: it's a bit of a tongue twister!)

Now drink the juice until it is finished. Feel its magickal charge send a buzz through your body. Next, place three drops of ylang ylang on the feather and, fanning it in front of your face, deeply inhale its divine scent.

Then, holding the feather out in front of you, trace a large Witches' pentagram in the air and step through it; then turn around, trace another and step through it; and then once again, turn around and do the same.

Holding the feather above your head, say:

Three times blessed am I,

Powerful and naturally high.

You can say 'super-naturally high' if you like!

My charm is great,

My intent is good,

This time is mine, be as it should.

Touch the feather to your third eye (between the eyebrows), throat and heart. Close Circle and, if you like, wear some of the ylang ylang oil as perfume – it's great for girls and guys. Be careful, however, if you have sensitive skin: mix a few drops in a teaspoon of almond, olive or jojoba oil and wear it diluted.

Twinkle, Twinkle, Little Star

Back in 2004 I put a request up on my then website for contributions from Teen Witches, which is how I met Jessica. She sent me an amazing email about her internet Teen Witch meeting place called NightStar Teen Pagan Network.

All these years later Jessica has obviously grown up; I tried to find her with some internet sleuthing but didn't have any luck. Jessica, if you are reading this reboot please send me a message; I would love to reconnect with you!

I think what is really amazing about what she shared with me back then is that it still resonates now. The basics are all similar and can be used as a current and vital template for establishing online Teen Witch communities, so I have kept this interview to inspire you.

As I connect with people around the world on social media, and from my own internet sleuthing, I can see there are many online groups and online shops that offer special events like Teen Witch Sunday: every third Sunday of the month this adult 18+ store makes available readings and workshops for Teen Witches aged from 13 to 18 accompanied by an adult. At the time of writing the world lockdown means that everything is now online and virtual, but when the physical world opens up again there will be physical in-store teen gatherings like Teen Witch Sunday so do your research and find out where there is an opportunity near you! And if there isn't one, ask your local Witchy supply store to host one.

In the meantime you can type #teenwitch #babywitch and so on on Instagram and Pinterest to get ideas and connect online, but meeting in person and/or being in a tangible learning group that encourages ongoing deeper-quality interaction and learning, over brief surface scratching aesthetically pleasing photos, is a great balance for all the immediate gratification stuff.

Enjoy this interview!

I wanted to meet Jessica in person straight away after she responded to my request and organised to have a coffee together. Little did I know the trouble she went to for what was to be a clandestine meeting, with her jumping every time her cell phone rang. Jessica is one of many Teen Witches whose family unfortunately doesn't support their spiritual interests (in this case it's only her father, but his disapproval was intense).

As I say in the chapter Parents: Can't Live With Them, Can't Live Without Them, it's always good to have the support of your parents … but sometimes it can be a hard thing to achieve!

This is very unfortunate because Jessica is utterly talented and motivated — and gorgeous — and when I originally interviewed her, was a leading light in the growing world of Teen Witchcraft. We managed to get quite a lot discussed in our 48 minutes together before she had to jump in a cab and get back to where she was being picked up. Was she rebelling against her father's expectations? Yes, she was, but she is one of the most inspiring and delightful Witches, Teen or otherwise, I have met in a long time, and the time taken for this interview should prove valuable to every Teen Witch.

◇◇

Jessica, what inspired you to set up a Teen Witch/pagan network?

NightStar came about after a disturbing incident with my father. I had been starting to explore Witchcraft and one day he found out and trashed all my Witchy stuff. But probably the main inspiration would have to be the fact that there was nowhere for me to go in regards to following my path. At the time I was 14 and most established pagan organisations refuse to be associated with anyone under the age of 18. I, and some other teenagers in similar situations as mine, needed a place where we could talk, gain knowledge and learn in an environment where no one was going to ridicule us or throw derogatory comments our way.

How did you go about it?

Well, as I was a member of an organisation called NightMoon Pagan Network (now the sister ship to NightStar for people over 18) and as the founder, Adrian, and I are good friends, he told me that he would help me set it up. I wrote a letter to *Australian Witchcraft Magazine* telling them of my plight and situation and asked for anyone else who would like to be involved in organising a place where we could talk and be supportive of each other. I had a great response with many well wishings but no real assistance. So I searched the net and chat rooms, where I met Tim. Tim is my co-founder of the network and he helps to make sure it runs properly when I'm not around.

Adrian did all the web weaving and Crafted us a place like NightMoon but the only regulation to join was that you had to be under 18! I had to make all the basic rules of the network, such as equality to all members no matter what path they follow, because not all of our members are Wiccan. With anything you need to be able to control things happening in and around the network because you don't want members being silly and using other members' personal information, such as email addresses, in an unsuitable way.

After that we started to add things to the site's Book of Shadows, as each member has their own page on the site.

We set up an emailing list where members can talk and discuss anything of interest to them, mainly relating to the Craft. A discussion forum was also created, and we even made a section where there were some fun things like wallpaper for your computer's desktop and tarot and moon phase programs. We established a committee of people who were assigned specific duties such as media/relations officer and co-founders in order to operate the network smoothly. (Adrian helps watch over everything to make sure nothing goes wrong as we are associated with NightMoon.) After all this, all we had to do was wait for the member numbers to grow. And grow they have: in two years we now have over 800 members! It's fantastic to see that we are doing something that so many teens have a need for!

What service do you think your network best provides?

Our main aim was to provide a place where teens interested in the Craft could talk and discuss the things that really concerned them or just something that was on their minds. We provide a place that is free from any harassment of any sort where all members aged 12 to 18 can learn from each other and be supportive. It's great for people to know that they are not alone out there in this world and what they are interested in is in no way wrong, bad or anything else that it may have been labelled. It's also great to know that there are other people your age who are going through a hard time finding and searching for their spiritual and religious beliefs, and it feels so comforting to hear someone say 'I know what that feels like'. At NightStar the members are around for each other. When someone needs help everyone pitches in to help discover a solution and many people have made fantastic friends and even met up with them in real life. However, one of the best things that the network provides is a contact point, especially when you've been ostracised.

Are there any hidden dangers for Teen Witches on the internet?

With anything in today's world there are always dangers.

One of the things that we are really adamant about is giving out personal details to people, such as phone numbers and addresses. There is always a possibility that the person you have met is not truly who they say they are. Also, if the members do decide to meet up in person, we urge them to meet in a public place and take one or more people with them, just in case something unexpected happens.

You just never know. Just as you wouldn't meet someone in the street and tell them your address and phone number after only talking to them for a minute, you wouldn't do it online. Also, with many people trying to meet young people for all the wrong reasons (such as pornography), we ask the members if anything weird has been going on – such as requests for partners in sexual magic – to tell us. But the good thing is that members usually look out for each other in this way.

Jessica, tell me a little about yourself: what's school like and what interests and hobbies do you have?

Well, personally I have always gone to Catholic schools (shock horror!) and been brought up as a Catholic. I have grown up in Melbourne all my life. I'm interested in Wicca and Paganism of course, and your typical teenage girl things such as guys, clothes, music and hanging out with my girlfriends. I love soccer and horse-riding and I'm always reading, whether it be a book on Wicca or a novel! But don't get me wrong: I absolutely love going out to the movies or shopping or even clubbing with my friends. I don't want anyone to think that because I'm so involved in Witchcraft all I do is sit in a dark room doing spells; it's quite the opposite. I'm an outgoing person who loves nothing more than being outside in the sunshine close to nature!

Along with all this, I hold down three jobs whilst doing Year 12. So I'm a pretty busy person along with my Witchcraft, personal, school and family commitments.

Can you describe your parents' attitude to your interest in Wicca?

That would have to have been one of the hardest things I have had to face in my life. One time Dad came into my room whilst I was on the computer and saw some emails that I had received from a Witchcraft mailing list. He didn't give me a chance to explain and told me that I was a devil worshipper and that there was something wrong with me, and asked what I was learning at my Catholic school. Then he started to search my room. He delved into the drawer

that I kept all my tools and workings in, and that was the final straw I guess …
In the end everything was destroyed, including all my tools, spells and writings,
along with my Book of Shadows. All I could say was that he may take away my
material things but he could never steal from me my spirit. He searches my room
regularly and often wisecracks about my Witchcraft. He thinks I don't do it any
more and I hate keeping it from him, but I think he's being unreasonable and hard
on me about it. I don't impose my beliefs on other people, like some religions.
I keep it to myself and go about it quietly. Wicca has helped me find myself in a
way I didn't know existed and it makes me feel a part of something really unique
and worthwhilst. I guess it's just all these misconceptions that society has created,
which stem from mainstream religion's negative attitude towards Witchcraft, that
cause the trouble.

My mother is fantastic. She sometimes gets a little apprehensive because she
doesn't fully understand, but she supports me. I remember when Dad found
out, she asked if something had happened to me in church that made me turn
away from God I simply told her that I didn't agree with the Catholic Church's
teachings and restrictions, along with the many contradictions in the Bible. I feel
that, because mainstream religion is forced down young people's throats from
birth, it isn't always the right path for them to follow. In my case, I felt the church
was so ancient and set in its ways I just couldn't relate to or understand it. I don't
like the fact that in the church's teachings there's the one and only way. That's not
the way life is. But don't get me wrong: history is great and you need it to form a
foundation, but you also need to move with the times and changes.

What do your friends and schoolmates think of your interests?

Well, my close friends are absolutely fantastic! Another friend is also very supportive, because she too is interested in Witchcraft. They are all genuinely interested and supportive.

However, they don't like to ask too many questions or to impose in any way. I guess I'm lucky that my friends are like me in most ways. They don't like to be like everyone else but they equally only follow what feels right for them.

Some of them think that it's pretty cool to have a friend who is a Witch whilst other people who aren't as close to me think that it's either cool or a load of crap.

But it doesn't bother me much either way.

However, if they start to say ridiculous things then I speak out and usually win! My boyfriends have had a different approach. They like it to be proved to them in a physical way! They seem to be intrigued by having a girlfriend who is a Witch. Guys I've dated have wanted to do spells and rituals with me.

Do you try to keep your interest fairly private (especially at school) or are you open about it all?

I don't advertise it on a billboard or anything. If religion is the topic of conversation and someone asks me, then I will usually tell them what my beliefs are. However, if I don't feel I can trust them or they are immature, I won't say anything. I have, however, used my knowledge of Witchcraft at school, like writing essays in English class. I read and research a lot for my Craft so I tend to do well in this part of school.

But going to a private Catholic school, I don't exactly walk around with a sign saying 'Hey, I'm a Witch!' Sometimes you just have to be careful.

How do your teachers react, especially, for example, when you write a piece on Wicca for your English assignment? And how do you cope with compulsory Catholic religious training?

I have found that some teachers who I have submitted work to are genuinely interested in Witchcraft. A lot of them, believe it or not, think that it was an old wives' tale!

They often ask me questions about what I do, with the most common question being: 'Does it really work?' When I submitted a piece on positive and negative magick for an English journalistic piece, my teacher said it was great to read something that was different – and he is also my religion teacher!

Religion, however, in its entirety is a different story. I have to grin and bear it almost. I have no say in what school I go to; my parents decided that Catholic is the best and in their opinion it provides me with the best opportunity for the future. I have no real problem with that. I've accepted that, as part of going to my school, I have to sit through the torturous compulsory religion classes. It's not that bad sometimes but other times it is, especially when we were talking about a letter sent out by the archbishop of Melbourne who said that the media was turning away young people from their faith. That was really hard for me to stomach, and I had to sit there and listen and not start a debate on the real reasons why the church is losing followers! I usually tune out and just do other work or talk to my friends. When assignments come round, it's a bit harder but I manage.

Witchcraft is a demanding path. How do you cope with all your schoolwork and your part-time jobs?

Sometimes it's extremely hard to manage! With three jobs, a Year 12 workload, NightStar, family commitments and friends, it's just so hard to get everything done.

Sometimes I don't have time to do a full ritual on a special day, but I always make an effort to do something small like light a candle and chant in honour of the deities. I think one of the most important aspects is good old-time management and prioritising. When something means enough to you and you are serious about it, you will always make some time for it.

What do you like best about being a Teen Witch?

The best thing is the freedom. You are not told to do everything at an exact time and things are adaptable. Also, learning in a free environment and gaining knowledge that is so sacred and wonderful feels fantastic. Knowing you are also giving back to the earth in some ways is fantastic as well. Also, having the power to make things happen for yourself and not waiting around for fate is tremendous.

However, Witchcraft is not in any way a means for getting whatever you need when you think you need it. In Witchcraft you have to be able to give as well as receive. As soon as you start asking and asking you lose your connection with the Goddess and god – it's not worth the consequences.

It's not so much the teen aspect, but I guess that it is harder being so young because people don't take you seriously. I mean, I'm 17 and still people think that I'm a 10 year old playing fairy tales when I talk about Witchcraft sometimes.

What are the best and worst elements of the growing popularity of Teen Witchcraft and the way it's portrayed in popular media?

Media can be a great thing sometimes. Witchcraft is getting a fabulous amount of exposure and people are starting to realise that it is so much becoming a part of people's everyday lives and it's not devil worshipping! Teens are looking for something that does not force them to do things they do not want to do, and they are searching for that feeling of belonging. And the media coverage makes getting information easier. However, with popular media such as TV shows like [reboots of] *Chilling Adventures of Sabrina* and *Charmed*, you need to make sure that people know it's only entertainment value and you cannot, no matter how much of a fantastic Witch you are, point your finger and get a boyfriend. Witchcraft is realistic! I think the media needs to start researching factual Witchcraft because I certainly don't go fighting demons every day after school. I love *Charmed* and can sometimes pick up some truth in what the girls do; however, we have to remember that the fight for television ratings is high and the truth just doesn't cut it as far as shock value sometimes.

It's great that Witchcraft is rapidly becoming more acceptable and accessible. Before everything was done in secret and hidden away. It's just so out there now. Now more and more teens are grasping the great things that Witchcraft can offer and their initial interest is often fuelled by the media. However, the people who are genuinely interested in it will stick with it for the long run whereas those who are only dabblers will lose interest after a few months, because your spells don't work if you aren't sincere in your beliefs and intentions.

What's the most effective spell you've done?

To be honest, I don't actually do too many spells mainly because I don't have a lot of time and I don't feel I should ask for everything that I want. Most of it will come to me in good time if it was meant for me. However, sometimes things do need that extra little push!

During one of last year's blue moons I did a ritual with a good friend of mine, and that was a first because I usually prefer to work solitary. We used both our energies to wish for things that we would like to be directed our way for the coming year. That was pretty successful. I received everything that I indicated I would like: I found out who my true friends were, I went very well at school, I met that special guy and my family relations started to improve.

However, I wasn't very successful in deciding what to do with them when they came my way, so results like the guy didn't go exactly to plan. But that's another story!

Have you ever done any spells you now regret?

One time I wished to meet someone special who valued me for me and whom I could get along with. A terrific guy was sent to me and that was the problem: I was only 16 and he was 24. However, once he was sent to me I didn't use any magick to keep him. I left that up to the more natural forces of nature. To cut a long story short, I fell so deeply in love with him that when it came time to let him go I couldn't. I shared things with this person that I had never felt before. Sure, I am young and all but I know this was unique. Some people go their whole lives without ever finding anyone special. However, when this person met another person and they started going out I couldn't handle it. I did something selfish and I broke them up. It took three months to work but it did. I don't know what I planned to achieve but for some reason I had to do it. I feel bad that I did such a thing, but it was so important to me that I was willing to accept all karmic consequences of my actions and the threefold law. But believe me – I'm paying for it!

Do people approach you at school for spells and, if they do, what kind of spells do they ask for?

They sure do! The most common ones are to get great marks and to find a boyfriend or to get someone specific to fall in love with them. People seem to think that you can ask for anything and get it. Usually you can achieve what you want if you are sincere in your intentions. I don't like to do spells for people because it means that I am getting all the energy back if they are not exactly ethical.

If I think the person is deserving of what they want, I may help them by telling them what they can do or writing up a ritual for them. But I'm not the world's most experienced Witch – I've only been practising for three years – and I have so much more to learn before I take other people's fate into my hands.

What's the nicest thing anyone's said to you about being a Teen Witch?

I think the nicest thing is just to be truly accepting of my beliefs and my choices. See, a lot of people don't think I can be a Witch because I don't dress like a Goth or act weird. I'm pretty normal I guess, if there's such a thing. I don't think anyone has ever said anything that can be deemed genuinely nice, although my friends always say nice things. The nicest thing would probably be something as simple as a 'thank you' for help. Answering this question has made me realise that not many people say nice things about me being a Witch!

What's the worst?

I think the worst would have to be accusing me of being a devil worshipper, a follower of Satan, an absolute mental nut case – that sort of stuff. It doesn't really bother me any more because I'm used to it, but I shouldn't have to put up with it. You learn to ignore all these sorts of comments, mainly because you know yourself they aren't true.

What do you think the difference is between a Teen Witch and an adult Witch?

Well, it depends. Sometimes a Teen Witch can have more experience than an adult Witch if they have been practising for a longer period of time. However, an adult Witch usually has more maturity and can often practise without hindrance where most Teen Witches live with their parents, who sometimes don't approve, so it's hard! Adult Witches are usually more dedicated and have a deeper understanding of the Craft and its ways, because they have experienced more of life. However, some Teen Witches are so much like the adult Witches in their thoughts and actions because they, too, are here in this world and are going through things that change them. Some people grow up more quickly than others; you just have to be a little more patient with teens!

What sort of support do you think Witches should be giving Teen Witches?

I feel that adult Witches should be more tolerant and supportive of the younger members of the Craft. We are not all dabblers and a bunch of immature teenyboppers, as I've heard it put before. They should try and help teach the ways of the Craft, because you don't want things to be distorted and you don't want teens turning away from their paths because they feel rejected. Younger Witches need the emotional support and they need to feel accepted because in reality they are the future of the Craft.

However, I feel that older Witches are getting much more used to the idea of having younger, true followers around, and most of them feel that having new followers is a great thing for the Craft. Older Witches are the only ones we can truly learn from.

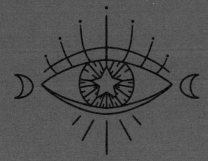

CHAPTER FOURTEEN

◇◇

POETRY, SPELLS, INSIGHTS

◇◇

The best way for me to find out how today's Teen Witches think was to invite them to contribute their insights, poems and favourite spells to be published in this book. Here are the results.

Thank you! And blessed be.

☉ BY ELISSA (LITHIAFAIRY, AGED 16)

Lunar Dance

She treads the starfield of eternal night,
And spreads her powdery moonrays as she goes.
Her silvered aura is pure and light,

Her eyes laugh, her skin is translucent white, she glows …

She carries her glowing orb as she walks,

To meet her equal, the sun god.

She shakes her hands across the sky,

Covering the deep velvet she just laid,

With dusty trails of moondust, shining bright.

She twirls and dances to the silent moonsong.

She spirals and swirls all night long.

She guides me in my dreams and through my rites,

She is the lunar mother, of dreams and of night.

Lunar mother, growing in your spiral dance,

Waxing, waning, full and dark.

Spellbinding majick, settles in a trance,

Of blue, silver, moonrays and stars …

Hecate's Rite

Hecate shrouds me in her dark veil,

Of mysteries, secrets, strength and love.

My darkness I've searched but to no avail,

My protection I wish to fall from above.

Hecate, my Goddess, hear my plight,

Through all darkness, I will be happy this night.

Drop your web and take the fear,

My troubles and woe will disappear.

Hecate, Kali, Lilith and all the crones,

Life, death, light and dark,

Avail me now and end my fear …

Ode to Artemis

Artemis flies her light across the sky,

Lighting the path of the unknown.

Glittering the sky with silvered sparkles,

And dusting the world below with blue powdered light.

She throws her orb across the velvet sky,

And it reaches me like a milky cloud.

Her power and majick entwines with mine,

To create a vortex of luminescent blue.

We propel the spell into the realms

And I feel the crescent light across my brow.

We whisper 'So mote it be … Our rite is done.'

And she flies back into the night …

☉ By Jacqui

Mountain View

The grass is green,

The sky is blue,

And everything looks like

It's all brand new.

From the mountain we can see

All around from tree to tree,

We can see above and below

And we can see the river flow.

On the road we do go fast,

And everything we see goes into the past,

The trees are high,

The grass is low,

And when I see it

My eyes glow. I wish I could see it every day,

But that's impossible,

There is no way.

☉ By Chitra (aged 16)

Miss Butterfly

Missy,

You're keeping a secret,

Holding it hidden,

Under your webbing.

Wanting to escape,

Run and not hide,

Fly and not fall,

Swim and not drown,

And find your way home.

The past seems like a dream,

A room filled with smoke,

The smell of disgust

Still lingers about.

What can you do,

To make the air fresh?

Look in your self,

The answer is there.

☉ BY ELLA (AGED 18)

A Protection Spell

Stand before any fire, look into the flames (or flame if you're using a candle) and visualise the fire bathing you with glowing, protective light. The fire creates a flaming, shimmering sphere around you. If you wish, say the following words:

Craft the spell in the fire;

Craft it well; weave it higher.

Weave it now of shining flame;

None shall come to hurt or maim.

None shall pass this fiery wall;

None shall pass, no, none at all.

Repeat when necessary.

Also, I have a wishing spell for you. You will need three bay leaves. When the moon is new, write your wish out on paper. Visualise your wish coming true as you do so. Fold the paper into thirds and place three bay leaves inside the paper and again visualise your wish coming true. Fold the paper into thirds again and hide it in a dark place. Keep visualising your wish coming true as you do this.

When it comes true, burn the paper as an offering.

☉ BY SLAYERBABE 182

Memory Spell – for finding lost things

Dear Fiona, I have a spell that worked for me, and it should help everyone else too.

Before going to sleep, take a bowl of fresh water and any small crystal into your bedroom. Sit with the water in front of you and the crystal in your hand and visualise the last place you saw the lost item.

Place the crystal in the bowl, and then place the bowl under your bed. Breathe calmly and say:

Spirits of the east and west,

Guide me in the realm of dreams,

Take me to a place of visions

And lead me to what has been lost.

Go to sleep. In the morning, take the crystal out of the water and carry it with you throughout the day to help jog your memory.

☉ BY MISS CHICKY

Spells and Legends

Hey Fiona, I have a little spell for your new book.

If your hairclip's come loose it means that someone you love is thinking about you.

If the clip comes out, take it and whisper your beloved's name three times. If you haven't seen them in a whilst and want them to get in touch, imagine their face and see yourself playing with their hair and lightly kissing their brow.

Put the clip back in your hair and you'll hear from them soon.

Here are some legends.

If you have the hiccups, it means someone you love misses you. Take a deep breath and say '[His/her name], I miss you too.' If it's the right person who is missing you, your hiccups will be gone!

If the clasp on your necklace falls to the front of your neck, someone you love is thinking of you. Take the clasp and kiss it, whispering their name and maybe a special message or wish, and place it behind your neck as usual. They will get your message.

If the left ear is burning, someone is speaking nicely or lovingly of you. If the right is burning, then nasty words of you are being spoken.

If your palms are itchy, it means good luck. The same if a spider is in your home or a bird poops on you.

These are off the top of my head:

Roses are red, pure and true,

Here is a message just for you:

When you're alone think of me only

'Cause with me by your side

You'll never be lonely.

I'm lost in a world, I'm lost in his eyes,

I'm lost in his smile, I'm lost without lies,

I'm lost in love.

True friends are like diamonds, precious and rare,

False ones are like autumn leaves found everywhere.

Depression is merely anger without enthusiasm.

☉ By Kym (AGED 17)

Healing Spell for a Loved One in Pain

Hi! I made up a really simple healing spell for my mother that was very effective. It is as follows.

Sit comfortably in a place where you won't be disturbed and meditate for a few minutes to clear your mind. Start to focus on the person you want to heal and the pain you want to stop; it could be physical or emotional. I did this when my mum sprained her ankle, so it was physical.

When you have a clear picture of the person and their pain, bring your arms out in front of you and slowly start to circle the palms of your hand around each other, like you're rolling an invisible ball. As you do this, envision a ball of bright blue light starting to form between your hands.

Keep doing this and thinking about your loved one until the ball is large and bright in your hands and you can almost feel it. Then, throw your hands up in the air, throwing the ball of blue light to the person. See it surround them and settle on the site of their pain and gently start to be absorbed and heal the pain. When the light begins to fade from your vision the spell should be working on them.

You have a choice about what you do after this. I went to bed and didn't tell anyone about it until I spoke to my mum again, which was about a week as she was on holidays.

She said she was better the second day she was away, which was the day after I did this spell.

☉ From Jessica

Dear Fiona, I have been into witchcraft for about two years. I am 12, 13 in three months. I have been writing some spells and I'd love to know what you think of them.

Beauty Spell

Beautiful in and

Beautiful out,

May I never be without.

Place all the glamour upon me

With shining hair,

Red rosy lips,

Perfect legs and

The right-sized tits.

May I be nice and kind

And my presence be seen by even the blind,

May I glow with love and kindness

Radiant in my blindness.

May I be loved for who I am, not what I wear and with who I hang,

Beautiful in and

Beautiful out,

May I never be without.

Provoke Water Power

Water power come to me, I need the power to set me free.

Balance the light with the dark,

Leave me with no obvious mark. I provoke the power buried deep inside,

May it never ever hide.

May the power be good and pure,

And of demons there shall be fewer.

Water I am yours,

Please open the doors.

Water you are mine,

This is a declaration to the divine.

Enter me so I can be

Flowing water is where I find peace.

Rough or calm,

Quiet or loud,

Water is my every thing.

So mote it be.

Travel Protection

Angels of the sky,

Spirits of the wind,

Protect me on my journey to other lands,

Guide me with your gentle hands. I place my trust in you, please say

you'll be true.

It's you I trust,

It's you I need,

Whilst I'm flying overseas.

So mote it be.

Rain Spell

Spirits' tears pierce the sky,

Spirits' tears cry, cry.

Open the skies to let rain through,

Clouds open, please do.

Rain fall and wetness go,

Rain fall flow, flow.

Think of the streams empty and low,

Think of the people who want water to flow.

Spirits' tears pierce the sky

Spirits' tears cry, cry.

☉ By Caitlin (AGED 13)

A Prayer to the Great Life Spirit

I'm a practising witch (with my mum). I would like to contribute the prayer that I read at my grandmother's funeral in January this year. It comes from a passage in one of the books in the series *The Witches of Eileanan* by Kate Forsyth. My mum and I found it really moving and very appropriate for a chant or blessing at any time.

Ea, ever-changing life and death, transform us in your sight, open your secrets, open the door. In you we shall be free of darkness without light, and in you we shall be free of light without darkness. For both shadow and radiance are yours, as both life and death are yours. For you are the rocks and trees and stars and the deep, deep swell of the sea, you are the spinner and the weaver and the cutter of the thread, you are birth and life and death, you are shadow and brightness, you are night and day, dusk and dawn, you are ever-changing life and death.

Blessed be!

☉ From Lidz (aged 18)

A Letter

Dear Fiona,

It's true that the world would be a dreary place without personal beliefs. I currently study at university and have spent a lot of time in the past year or so discovering my witchy half.

The point I would like to make is this: witchiness is present everywhere, even in my study of straight and sensible, and I think it's fantastic that people like yourself are able to come out and tell the world that these ideas are perfectly natural, especially us teenagers (who, let's face it, can be scared about all!). It is important to know that there are people who live very ordinary witchy lives rather than the stereotypical picture.

Also, many things such as the Gaia theory are very acceptable at university, and for those who don't know I would remind them that these kinds of things can be studied. It's not all maths and physics. I guess what I'm trying to say is that there is no need to choose between something like uni and witchiness – they can coexist.

No one told me that and I think it would really have helped me.

☉ By Jackie (aged 17)

My Goddess

The smile that spreads across my face with all the
Warmth and potency of the sun is induced by her.
All of the passion and intensity that burst from my heart.

That unique shimmer in my eyes.

They're all because of her.

The maiden, the mother, the crone.

She is my love, my light, my peace, my simplicity, destiny.

My one protector who is here with me for all of time. I am the radiant woman I am because of her.

She is the Goddess. My Goddess.

☉ By Holly (aged 10)

A Spell to Sleep

In lockdown I have discovered that lavender and orange essential oil make a wonderful smell combined! My friend was having trouble with her dreams like I used to and I found I didn't want her to have to deal with those scared dreams, so I gave her a pouch with the only things I had at hand: frankincense oil and some dried lavender that I soaked in a couple of drops of lavender oil. I also got a piece of paper that I wrote on 'May our minds be at peace', and folded that up with seven folds, secured with some headbands, all of the ingredients charged with good, peaceful energy. I told her to keep it under her pillow. We are both sleeping well now.

CHAPTER FIFTEEN

◇◇

Teen Witch Tips

◇◇

What to Wear?

Some of you may have heard the term 'skyclad'. If you're wondering what it means, it's 'clad by the sky' or, in other words, naked! As Witches we accept our bodies as perfect and sacred and it's often appropriate to do our rituals and spells with nothing between us and the sky.

Most solitary Witches work that way at least some of the time, and among Covens and other groups you'll find that some work robed (or otherwise clothed), some work skyclad and some just go with letting people make up their own minds about how they feel on the night. Having said that, you don't have to work skyclad to be an effective Witch, and if anyone ever tries to force you to get your gear off for ritual don't stick around! An all-skyclad group might only accept people who are cool about the idea, which is fair enough. If you're not happy working that way, though, just start looking elsewhere. Whilst the Craft teaches that 'naked is sacred', no Witch worth her or his salt (or water or oil or incense!) would ever think they were helping anyone by forcing them to do something against their own judgement.

If you're under 18 this is all abstract anyway, since most Covens don't accept members under that age. As Teen Witches, you'd probably want to wear something if you're working in a group. Maybe consider going skyclad just for solitary Circles or for when you hit the adult years. I have a couple of special garments that I save for Witchy work (sometimes it's just too cold for skyclad work!). Teen Witches don't need elaborate robes, though you can have them if you want. You also don't have to own a pentagram necklace, although heaps of Teen Witches do. Try to keep one special outfit that you wear only for your Witchy stuff. What's important in all this is that you feel sacred and special inside and out when you're practising Witchcraft.

A tip: if you are wearing regular gear and want to purify it for ritual, trace a pentagram of incense (sandalwood or frankincense blends are good) and walk through it wearing the gear you want to purify.

Something Simple

◇◇◇

Here's a ritual you can start and end the day with to remind yourself that you are a Teen Witch.

Stand somewhere where there is nothing between the top of your head and the sky. By this I mean it's preferable that you stand outside. If you can't, stick your head out the window!

Breathe in deeply and think for a minute what it means to you to be a Teen Witch; you may focus on the sense of empowerment and peace it gives you or the fun you have casting spells. Every time you do this you may focus on a different aspect. When you are ready, in your mind's eye see your crown chakra (the energy centre at the top of your head) open up and a stream of white light pour out into the sky. This is your offering to the Universe, and in doing this you are sharing your positive power with all things. When you are ready focus on the light pouring back into you, now equally charged by positive energies around you. As it pours in, focus again on your commitment to being the best you can be and a powerful Teen Witch.

When you are overflowing with white light, make the sign of the pentagram by touching first your third eye, then your right nipple, left shoulder, right shoulder, left nipple and then third eye again.

The ritual is complete!

Keeping On Track

◇◇◇

Sometimes there seems to be so much to remember — so many rituals to perform, so many sabbats and esbats to celebrate — that you're having a hard enough time keeping up with your schoolwork that you feel like chucking it all in and giving up on exploring the Craft. Don't panic: hold on!

Many, many times in the first few years I felt that the more I knew the more I didn't know. It would stress me out. Always try to keep in your mind that it's 100 per cent okay to take all the time you need in this very developmental stage of your Craft, but try to keep connected by doing something rather than giving everything up even if this means just reading a Craft novel by an author like Australian Kellie M Davies. Kellie's *The Clandestine Chronicles* series is amazingly inspiring and a great read as is (dare I say!) my own *Witch: A Summerland Mystery*.

Both are coming-of-age novels about girls and boys with magickal powers and can inspire real Teen Witches to dig deep and explore their unlimited potential.

Stay in touch with your inner Witchiness (picture it bubbling away like a cauldron inside you) and no doubt you'll be drawn to more formal practice again a little further down the track. Witchcraft is not about making your life harder – it's about making it easier and more enjoyable – so if it doesn't feel like it's flowing, just sit tight until it does again.

WHY AREN'T MY SPELLS WORKING?

If your spells aren't working ask yourself: are you doing the right spells?

Are you clear on your intent, obeying the Witches' Laws and not being manipulative? Sometimes spells will backfire or just not work if you are trying to interfere with the free will of others, or if you are working from a selfish perspective. Remember, too, that some spells do need to be repeated to get the job done.

If you're cutting wood with an axe, you often need to give a log a lot more than one single whack. Spells work just the same way: sometimes you hit the jackpot first time round; other times you need to keep on repeating the outpouring of energy in order to cut through obstacles. Just don't repeat the spell too often. Give it time to work. For a major goal in your life, casting the spell once or maybe twice (max) in a lunar month (on a new moon and full moon) is the most you should be doing. Other spells, like healings, seem to respond to a slow, steady outpouring of magic, like burning a candle for someone each night until improvement is felt.

HAVING A MAGICKAL PLAN

If you are sure that your purpose is honest and pure and your spells still aren't hitting their mark, go through this checklist:

1. Have a clear idea of what you're doing and what result you're hoping to achieve.

2. What are the likely outcomes, that is, how is it going to affect others,not only yourself?

3. Make sure you memorise your incantations and invocations well before you do the spell so that you don't have to keep referring back to a book, which will break your concentration and interfere with the powers you are conjuring.

4. When you are spell-casting remember to take your time, breathe and concentrate on your visualisation skills. Don't rush it! Focus and let the powers swirl around inside and outside you, fuelling your intent.

5. Remember to take action not only on the magickal, metaphysical plane but also the physical. For example, if you cast a spell to go well in your exams, you have to study too! The spell will help make your goals easier to achieve.

Dream Diary

◇◇

In addition to your Book of Shadows you may like to keep a dream diary. Some of my best spells and ritual ideas have come from my dreams, and as you get into the habit of writing down your dreams recalling them becomes easier.

Drinking a cup of mugwort tea before bed will help you more actively experience vivid dreams. If you can't get mugwort at a local health food store then you can look online or try infusing wattle seed as a substitute.

 ## Indigenous herbs

◇◇

A lot of traditional Witches' spells use European and American herbs, woods and oils because of the northern hemisphere origins of our Craft, but a lot of fantastic indigenous Australian plants work wonderfully for the southern-hemisphere Witch.

One teaspoon of ground, roasted wattle seed (available at bushfood supply stores) stirred with ¼ teaspoon of cinnamon makes a beautifully comforting tea to drink before bed, with the added benefit of stimulating a lucid dream state.

◇◇

If the start of your days are so hectic that writing your dreams down every morning would take up too much time and stress you out, perhaps choose one night a week to go on a magickal dream flight. Anoint a silver candle with some lavender oil and meditate on the flame as you drink your tea and mentally prepare for your night's journey. I have had some pretty intense dreams when doing this.

Once I dreamt I was in the kitchen of a country cottage with three other women. We were dressed in long, coarse, linen skirts and had white caps over our hair. It was early in the evening and we were making a cake together. We were related – mother, aunt, grandmother and me – and we were Witches. The cake we were making was an enchantment cake and whoever ate the first piece would become my husband. Together with four wooden ladles we stirred the eggs, cornflour, honey, caraway seeds, milk and crushed rose petals. Five drops of my blood were added (pricked from my thumb) and the four of us chanted a mumbled charm that I couldn't really understand as it seemed to be in another language.

Then the dream jumped ahead and it was night time.

The fire was glowing and the cake was on the table laid out on a piece of white cloth with a large knife next to it. Then three men entered the kitchen together. They were brothers and one of them was to be wed to me.

I was aware that the magickal cake would help me choose the right one. Whoever was attracted to cut and eat the cake first would be my husband.

On waking I checked out the magickal properties of the cake ingredients and my dream was spot on! They were all traditional ingredients used in love and enchantment spells. I was channelling my inner witch heritage in that dream.

CREATING MAGICK

An important part of being a Teen Witch is being creative – expressing your inner self through art. It could be through music (the voice of the soul), playing an instrument and/or singing, painting, photography, writing or even coming up with complex and beautiful mathematical formulae! Be aware that life is never boring for a Teen Witch; there is always something to do that taps into and expands magickal potential within and without. So if everyone has a date on Saturday night except you, rather than sitting at home being bored and depressed do something creative: decorate your Book of Shadows, write a song or do some Witchy research and create some spells. Notice I don't suggest joining Instagram. I honestly believe that taking a break from the digital virtual world is more magickal than messing around on your smart phone even if there is some beautiful inspiring stuff online. Try to balance your digital imprint with tangible hands on real-time natural magick.

Finally … Throwing your hands up in the air and saying 'life sucks' is not an option for a Teen Witch!

CHALLENGE YOURSELF

Part of being a Teen Witch is challenging yourself mentally, spiritually and physically. Don't be afraid to be different and seek out challenges that push you further. Set yourself difficult tasks knowing that you have the desire, drive and magick to achieve them. So whether it's taking that extra subject, trying sky diving or deciding that you want to write a book about your journey, just go for it! Use your Witchcraft to help you get there and to make you stronger but remember to focus on and enjoy the journey, not just arrive at the destination.

Be Quiet!

Remember one of the four magickal principles is 'to be silent'. If you are working spells, especially on yourself, don't tell anyone about it. Keep it quiet; that way you won't feel answerable to others' opinions of how your progress is going. It's like blowing up a balloon: you don't run around stretching the neck open to show everyone how much air is in it! Sometimes if people know you've got problems, their well-meaning concern or energy could just add fuel to your problem. Of course, if it's a situation like abuse or something that you know you shouldn't stay quiet about then you absolutely need to speak out and tell someone, but a lot of normal 'growing up' problems can be dealt with efficiently without attracting a lot of attention.

Be Realistic

Measure your successes on your own terms and don't compare your achievements or magickal advancements with those of others. As 'Desiderata' – a wonderfully insightful piece of writing – says: 'There will always be people greater and lesser than yourself.' So tread your path confidently and righteously, forging your own journey.

During the writing of this book I caught part of a television documentary on an extraordinary man who passed away in 1996. Sir Laurens van der Post was a white man born in 1906 in South Africa. For many years he lived among the Stone Age Kalahari bushmen, one of the oldest cultures on earth. He dedicated much of his life to teaching the West the importance of valuing the meaning and existence of indigenous cultures in the modern world. Even 60 years ago he was aware that the modern world was in danger of losing its spiritual identity to technology, racial and religious prejudice, empty consumerist values and a lack of understanding of the interconnectedness of all life.

Van der Post wrote 23 books and was an utterly fascinating man (check out all the websites on him!) The television special featured an interview with him just before he died, and one thing he said struck me as particularly profound. He was talking about his time with the Kalahari bushmen, who live a very physically demanding and harsh life especially when compared with the creature comforts and support systems of the West. One of the major insights he experienced was this: for an individual to have a sense of meaning and purpose in life is ultimate. When you have meaning it doesn't matter whether you're happy or not; you are at one with spirit. This struck me as particularly relevant for Witches, teens or otherwise. No matter how difficult life gets, how worn out emotionally and physically I feel, I know that there is a purpose and meaning to my life and that I am not a random accident. As a Witch I continually explore my relationship with the world through rituals, spells and just *being* a Witch, enjoying the outlook and perspective on life that being a Witch gives me.

After van der Post's death there was much speculation on the truth of his stories – with claims that he had fabricated his experiences in remote environments. Whatever the case he was a bonafide adventurer, a survivor of a Japanese prison camp in Java, and whether he stayed two weeks, two days or two years in a remote non-Western environment to share stories and experiences it doesn't really matter: his message is potent and relevant whether it's shared in the realm of fiction or non-fiction.

There are so many writers and so much wisdom in the world that is accessible through the internet, whether it's written word, YouTube channels and podcasts on the important of honouring indigenous wisdom, learning from it, treading lightly and respectfully and sustainably on the earth that a genuine Teen Witch seeking their truth will find themselves crossing paths with information and wisdom that is uniquely attuned to the star dust that vibrates within them and the world as it reveals itself around them. Trust your instincts and intuition, learn and put into practice what you learn.

Just a Thought!

One thing I have realised about modern Witchcraft is that, despite the huge amount of information about the traditional and right way to go about things, often the most meaningful and rewarding experiences come in those moments of absolute inspiration that do not follow any pre-determined method or pre-ordained procedure. The experience might be coloured by your knowledge of these, but it is not dictated by them.

This is an insight into the flexibility of Witchcraft: it's often the feeling and connection that matters most, not the procedure. For all the potential differences that this amount of flexibility allows, we have enough similarities to be considered unified. Our similarities are that we worship nature and recognise the Goddess and god within and without, although how we conceptualise them might vary from Witch to Witch. We also work magick: the art of changing consciousness and manifesting different realities at will.

There are wonderful new insights being reported on all the time in our Craft. We are a growing, evolving phenomenon.

Some Witches like to look to our nebulous past for guidance, others prefer to live in it, but ultimately our greatest strength is right now and our ability to evolve into an enlightened, empowered, healing future, and this is where the essential role of the Teen Witch is most excitingly anchored.

Another Thought

The world answers according to the questions you ask of it, and if you change the way you think you'll be surprised what happens around you in response to these changes.

It's hard to accept this sometimes even for Teen Witches with relatively short pasts and long futures, because humans hang on to the predictability of what we know from the past. In turbulent teen times we are especially just trying to stay afloat and hang on to the life raft of what we think we know.

However, part of being a Teen Witch is knowing that one of the most empowering things you can do is to accept responsibility for your thoughts and feelings and your reactions to others and events. Teen Witches need to look inside before they make a decision about the outside world, because usually the outside world will only be a problem when there is a problem within.

THE DAY AFTER

In the last stages of originally writing this book I got a major computer virus and all the files on my laptop seemed to be history. With the help of a technician I was able to go in quickly and save the work I'd done onto a floppy disk (yes: back when there were floppy discs and no cloud!); however, at the time there was no guarantee that the files were not corrupted. I was in a remote country location and I could not get to another computer to see if my book had been saved. So for a whilst there I thought I'd lost all my work and would have to start writing my book again from scratch, which was utterly devastating. (Yes, I was stupid and hadn't backed up any of my files! Major magickal lesson there: always have a second string to your bow.)

Eventually, I found that the files were safe and I had not lost the book, but my laptop was inoperable and it was going to have to be pen and paper for the next few days until I could get onto a computer again. The following is what I wrote upon awakening the day after one of the worst days in my life.

Well, it's the day after the annihilation of my laptop. All night I had nightmares about the long, difficult day. But guess what? The sun is shining this morning and there is steam coming off the lavender bushes that line the front porch. I am warm, pen in hand, enjoying a cup of coffee and the fresh winter's morning air. If I had the laptop I wouldn't be doing this. I would be inside hunched over the table, manically pounding out words.

Instead I sit, contemplating and watching low fluffy clouds scud across the top of the mountain, serenaded by the songs of different birds, and as I write I am enjoying watching the sharp shadow of my pen as it flits across the page. What happened yesterday was probably the worst thing possible, given my situation – killer deadlines and pressing television and radio commitments. But I've survived and in the wake of the turmoil of yesterday I feel calm and in some ways cleansed. Once again it's been proved that in the face of real adversity we find our greatest strengths. It is the Witch in me that helps me accept and understand what happened and the cyclical nature of it. Some of the trees around me are in the barren throes of winter, their gnarled branches stripped of leaves, forming a latticework of crone energy against the blue sky. But on this cold, crisp day already I can see little green buds forming on the spidery twigs – everything renews itself, the sun always rises … at the end is another beginning.

Once years ago a friend told me a very sad story of a 17-year-old guy who was in Year 12 and under a lot of pressure to do well in his exams. His computer crashed big time and he lost his CAT essay – it was 40 per cent of his mark, a major assessment. It wasn't backed up – it was gone. However, he didn't speak to his teachers, his parents or his friends. He felt so panicked and so isolated that he couldn't cope and he killed himself. This terribly tragic situation is unfortunately not an isolated event. There is so much pressure on teens and often the technology that is supposed to ease the stress of our lives only increases it. It's not only school work, it's not only extraordinary challenges like the global lockdown (happening at the time of writing this); it's also the pressure of social media, bullying, peer group competitiveness, and just the crazy pace of life in general with all its hyper connectivity – and everyone's three-second attention span, not allowing deep meaningful connection and communication.

A Teen Witch can look to nature in times of crisis, slow down and focus on breathing in the moment whilst comprehending the cyclical nature of life – things come and go and come again; begin, end and begin again. It's a necessary part of life's journey and we see *it played out over and over again around us: in the blooming and withering of flowers, in the ebb and flow of the sea.*

Sometimes, though, it can all just seem too much and this is where your Witchcraft can help. When I thought I had lost the files of the original edition of this book, I felt I was being sucked into a black hole and my life was just one big joke. I knew I had to do something, so I lit a charcoal disc and sprinkled a special 'inspiring and passionate' blend of incense on it: dragon's blood powder, cinnamon and myrrh. I whisked the smoke around with a blue feather that a rosella had kindly left in my path a couple of days before. I chanted Goddess names, 'Isis, Astarte, Diana, Hecate, Demeter, Kali, Inanna', and focused on releasing my problems and disappointments and allowing new healing energies and a sense of acceptance to breeze in. I quickly started feeling much better and much more prepared to move on and deal with the situation constructively and effectively.

If you see or sense someone is struggling, consider visiting: www.RUOK.org. au to learn gentle and effective ways to help people through deeply challenging times. A careful, healing conversation can make all the difference in helping someone know they are not alone and they can make it through an extremely challenging time.

The following is a vision quest ritual you can do to help cope when everything seems too much. It might be school, your parents, your friends, your siblings or just everything. It will help refresh you and cleanse your soul and give you rational insights into your current situation so that you can move on positively and with a fully charged heart.

⊕ Clear Vision Ritual

‹◇◇›

Best time: whenever you need it!

YOU WILL NEED:

- a pale blue candle
- clary sage oil (it is deeply euphoric oil and has many uses; lavender can be substituted)
- an aromatherapy oil burner
- a feather
- a piece of fabric that is brand new and large enough to wrap around you; gold cloth would be perfect, or perhaps a beautiful sarong (if you can't make anything new just make sure that it has been washed and ironed to establish a sense of the sacred)
- peppermint tea
- honey
- a stick/quill

DIRECTIONS

Cast Circle with the full ritual. Carve your name into the candle with the stick/quill and trace a pentagram next to it. As you do this, focus on how much you love your Witchcraft: how it helps give you a sense of meaning and how it puts you in touch with the beauty and bounty of life. In your sacred Circle things are always beautiful and well no matter what kind of turmoil is raging outside.

Lick your thumb and trace over your carving. Light the oil burner, and on top of the water disperse seven drops of the oil. When it starts to vapourise use the feather to waft the scent towards you, inhaling deeply. When you are ready, invoke the Goddess Rhiannon by draping your shoulders with the cloth and saying:

Rhiannon, come visit me

On your white and glorious steed.

Help ease my woes and carry me

To a space where I can rest easy.

In your mind's eye, see Rhiannon ride into your Circle on her beautiful white horse. She will invite you to join her, so mount the horse with her and let her take you on a journey.

Notice where you are going: look at the scenery, the people, the signs; listen to the sounds and smell the scents of your journey. Try to remember everything and anything she may say to you as all these will help your situation.

When you finally ride back into Circle and dismount thank Rhiannon by saying:

Rhiannon of the day and night,

Thank you for this glorious flight

And journey into dark and light;

I am now blessed with great insight.

Immediately write down everything in your Book of Shadows before you remove your cloak. Don't try to analyse anything; just jot it all down.

When you have finished, drink some of the peppermint tea with honey to refresh and centre yourself and eat a little food as you normally would as part of your Circle ceremony.

In the next few days read over the notes you made and start to analyse and understand the wisdom there and how it can help you.

Note: you can use your cloak to connect with Rhiannon again, and if you had any trouble seeing things clearly you will find holding an amethyst crystal as you journey will assist your inner vision.

CHAPTER SIXTEEN

◇◇

Magickal Meanings

◇◇

Following are all the different ingredients, objects, colours and phases of the moon and sun for spells and rituals mentioned in this book. The lists below are by no means everything that is available to the modern Teen Witch, especially when they can order anything online, but everything below is referenced in this book and will help you on the path. I've intentionally chosen oils and herbs that are easy enough to get and not crazy expensive — again to just help you get started and not put you off exploring.

Before you perform a spell or ritual it's important you refer to this section so that you have a good understanding about what you're doing and why!

Just about all the ingredients mentioned are easily obtainable in your local health food store, witchy supply store and online. Also, here's a suggestion: if you are ever curious as to what various herbs or trees look like in their natural growing state and don't know where to find them, go exploring in your local botanical garden. When I was first starting out on the path I would spend every weekend in the Sydney Royal Botanical Garden familiarising myself with various plants, trees and herbs. It's a gorgeous way to spend an afternoon and also helps improve your Witchcraft. Why not take a few fellow Teen Witches and a picnic lunch and make a day of it?

HERBS, FRUITS AND WOODS

ALMOND: good for prosperity and promoting opulence and fertility of ideas and dreams. A wand made from almond wood is very good for a Teen Witch as it works to boost growing skills.

APPLE: for good luck, wisdom and love (this fruit is considered sacred to the Greek Goddess of love, Aphrodite). When the apple is cut across to expose the pentacle arrangement of the seeds it is sacred for the celebration of Samhain or Halloween as it becomes a representation of the bridge of existence between life and death.

BAY LEAVES: can be used to attract love and can imbue an object or written desire with magickal potency and the ability to manifest. They can also be used to inspire truth and confidence in the spoken word.

BERRIES: strawberry, blackberry, cranberry and so on all represent fertility, positivity and potency.

BLACK PEPPER: can work to speed things up and bring ideas and plans to quicker fruition. Can also dispel negativity.

BORAGE BLOSSOM: encourages a strong and passionate sense of self and the ability to feel joy and love even in the most demanding of circumstances.

CELERY SEED: helps with concentration and can improve visualisation skills.

CHAMOMILE: healing, peace and love. Leave out in the sun to empower before a working. In ancient Egypt chamomile was dedicated to the sun god for its curing powers.

CINNAMON: can help to increase focus and mental powers, and it's also a bit of an aphrodisiac for cisgender boys! Can also bring good luck and fill a space with peaceful, content energy.

CLOVES: for the ability to compel others to accept your will.

CORNFLOUR: good as a base for magickal powders.

CUCUMBER: not only good for puffy eyes but can put you in touch with the subconscious and the wisdom we can reach through our intuition.

DILL SEED: to make yourself irresistible and also to anchor your personal powers.

DRAGON'S BLOOD POWDER: this is not really powdered blood of dragon (they're an endangered species after all, lol!) but the dark red resin of a tree. It's great to power up love spells or indeed any ritual energy.

EUCALYPTUS: cleansing, empowering, healing, purifiying.

FRANKINCENSE: one of the most essential ingredients of magick, as it's empowering, purifying, increases concentration, protective and helps to bridge the spiritual and the everyday.

GARLIC: one of the most purifying substances and very protective against negative energy, as well as being effective in completely banishing unwanted influences and presences.

GUM WOOD: all magick, instant transformation, protective.

HEART'S EASE (A TYPE OF VIOLET): promotes love and a full, happy heart.

HOPS: encourage restful sleep, and when burnt can cleanse a ritual space of unwanted energy.

IVY: for virtue and honesty.

JASMINE: great for girls as it is the essence of the sacred feminine aspect of the Universe; use it to honour the full moon. It's also excellent for promoting psychic ability.

LAVENDER: one of my favourites and an all-round staple for a magickal pantry. Increases magickal awareness, peace, is great for blessing, purifying, empowering, euphoria and can replace just about any other ingredient because of its incredibly pure vibrational qualities.

LEMON: for love and purification. Also good for focusing the intellect and to help with making choices.

MUGWORT: one of the best Witchy herbs! Useful for enhancing lucid dreaming and protection, especially when travelling either in this world or between in dreams and meditations. Also great for the consecration of Witches' tools (burn mugwort and pass the object through the smoke) and a general power booster, especially when doing rituals around the full moon.

NUTMEG: good for enhancing psychic ability and encouraging effective meditations.

OAK LEAVES: to the Druids, whose practices are a major inspiration to modern Wicca, the oak tree is one of the most sacred trees; using any part of the tree, whether it be the leaves or bark (dried and powdered as incense), emphasises and magnifies Witchy energy.

ORANGE BLOSSOM: for love.

ORRIS ROOT: for physical and spiritual protection and to promote love, honour, fidelity and companionship.

PARSLEY: use to honour the Goddess in her full moon and maternal aspect, as it helps to invoke her presence.

PATCHOULI: an aphrodisiac that honours the male and female creative forces and the cycles of life. It is also used to invoke the Greek Goddess Hecate.

PEPPERMINT: can speed up bringing things to fruition and can also encourage more colourful and lucid dreams and divination.

ROSE PETALS: for love, purity, friendship and protection.

ROSEMARY: stabilises and strengthens and can help increase memory, whether burnt as incense or essential oil or drunk as a tea. Rosemary is sacred to the dead and can be used to honour them. It is also good for protection and to purify spaces.

RUE: protection, benevolence and to release the past.

SAGE: purification, healing and cleansing, strength, mental health, wisdom and banishing any evil.

SANDALWOOD: to do work with confidence and ease.

SENNA PODS: promote compassion and a willingness to cooperate.

SIGIL: an inscribed or painted symbol that Witches consider to have magical power to attract, repel or bless.

ST JOHN'S WORT: for high-powered protection.

STRAWBERRY: for fun, light-heartedness and romance.

TARRAGON: for calmness and compassion, and to bond with the feminine aspect of the Universe.

TEA (BLACK): for clarity and strength.

THYME: removes negativity and is great for spring cleaning and bringing in new energies.

VERVAIN (ALSO CALLED VERBENA): improves psychic ability and can also increase confidence and a sense of inner well-being, especially when performing or doing the arts. It's great for protection and for love.

WATTLE SEEDS: enhance lucid dreaming, psychic abilities and intuition.

WILLOW: to move from one life to another, honouring another and protection.

YARROW: love and commitment.

Essential Oils

ALMOND: fertility of thoughts and ideas.

CINNAMON: good to balance masculine energies, a stimulant and also promotes a sense of inner peace and well-being.

CLARY SAGE: euphoric, healing, enhances intuitive abilities.

COCONUT: purifying, healing; can take the place of other oils.

EUCALYPTUS: healing, clarity, purifying.

FRANKINCENSE: purifying and protective.

LAVENDER: healing, anti-depressive, great all round magickal energy.

LEMON: nurturing, and honours the lunar essence.

NEROLI: balances feminine energies, minimises anxiety and promotes peace.

OLIVE: good for consecration (blessing) of objects, this oil was sacred to the ancient Greeks and used for their sacred temple lamps.

ROSE GERANIUM: calming, healing and loving.

ROSEMARY: protective, enhances mental powers like memory.

SUNFLOWER: brings happiness and can also be used to bless objects. Honours the solar essence.

YLANG YLANG: soothing, sensual, disperses frustrations and promotes confidence.

THE CELESTIAL BODIES

THE MOON

The different phases of the moon can influence spell-casting and ritual.

WAXING: a good time to do spells for abundance and to manifest new dreams, goals and desires. Energy is building and a forward propulsion is manifest.

FULL: energy is peaking and this is a good time to do spells of all sorts, as well as honouring and worshipping the Goddess and giving thanks for being alive.

WANING: a time for banishing unwanted energies or presences, and also a time to get rid of bad habits and to bind unpleasant influences.

DARK: a good time for introspective work like divination or just to take a rest from magick altogether.

THE SUN

DAWN: new beginnings, new goals, new dreams and also a time to restate intentions and recharge spells. If you have an amulet or talisman, leave it in the light of the dawning sun to recharge its potency.

NOON: a mega-potent time for charging up a spell, amulet or talisman, and also a great time for spells of abundance and empowerment and to give thanks for all the good and meaningful things in life.

DUSK: a good time for spells of closure and release, and also for moving on and establishing new patterns and ideas.

Days of the Week

◇◇

SUNDAY: Sunday corresponds to the sun, our closest star. This day is full of wonder and all sorts of magickal potential for success, wealth, and fame. Sundays are for personal achievements of any kind such as working towards a promotion at your job, seeking fame and wealth, or being acknowledged for a job well done. All of these goals fall under the golden influence of the sun. Some suggestions for Sunday enchantments would include:

- Sitting outside at sunrise and calling on a fire Goddess like Brigid for illumination and inspiration.
- Wearing gold jewellery or clothing that is gold or sunshine yellow to pull some colour magick into your life.
- Arranging a few sunflowers in a vase and empowering these flowers of the sun for fame and ambition.
- Gathering up the common marigold flower and scattering its petals about to encourage prosperity.
- Baking up a batch of cinnamon rolls for the family and enchanting them for health and success.
- Snacking on a solar fruit – the orange – and enjoying the magickal boost it brings to your life.

MONDAY: this day of the week is dedicated to the moon and all of her magic and mystery. Mondays are for women's mysteries, illusion, prophetic dreaming, emotions, travel and fertility. Some suggestions for Monday enchantments would include:

☛ Getting outside and looking for the moon in the heavens. Sit under the light and absorb a little glamour. Call on the moon Goddess Selene for practical help in magickal issues.

☛ Invoking the god Thoth for wisdom and insight.

☛ Empowering your silver jewellery under the light of the moon. Wear moonstone or pearl jewellery today to add a lunar and magickal shimmer to your outfit. Be mysterious and subtle and wear moon-associated colours such as white, silver and blue.

☛ Working spells for safe travel with a simple moonstone.

☛ Gathering bluebells, jasmine, gardenias or white roses to create a little garden witchery with the flowers that are associated with the moon.

☛ Reading and studying your tarot and/or oracle cards to increase your psychic powers.

☛ Eating a lunar fruit such as a melon to be healthy, serene and at peace.

☛ Brewing up a cup of chamomile or mint tea and enchanting it for sweet dreams and restful sleep.

TUESDAY: Tuesday is a Mars day, and just like the god of war this is the time to tap into magick to call for strength and courage. This day of the week is for rebels and warriors. If you are facing a challenge of any kind, need a boost to your courage or want to enhance your passions, Tuesday is the day of the week for you. Some suggestions for Tuesday enchantments would include:

☛ Wearing the fiery colours associated with this day: scarlet, red, black and orange. Don some of the more daring and bewitching colours of your wardrobe on Tuesdays and turn a few heads.

- Carrying a bloodstone in your pocket or wearing garnet-studded jewellery to reinforce your convictions.
- Working with protective and fire-associated plants such as snapdragon, thistle and holly to boost your shields and bravery.
- Burning spicy-scented, energy-enhancing candles to add a little magickal aromatherapy to your home.
- Cooking up a hearty meal featuring carrots, capsicum and garlic (all Mars foods and spices) to empower yourself for victory and success.

WEDNESDAY: Wednesdays are wild and wacky days. They are for communication, change, cunning and the arts. This is a Mercury day, and just as its patron god this day is full of contradictions, change and excitement. Some suggestions for Wednesday enchantments would include:

- Pulling a little Wednesday colour magic into your life by wearing purples or orange.
- Carrying a multipurpose agate with you and tapping into its various charms.
- Working with magickal plants such as the fern for protection. This plant will also boost the power of any other magickal plants with which it is arranged.
- Incorporating lavender into charms and spells for transformation.
- Using the charming scent of lily of the valley to improve your memory, or working with the aspen tree for communication.
- Calling on Athena, patron of arts and Crafts, for inspiration for a new project.

☛ Calling on Hermes on a Wednesday night to bring movement and good luck into your life.

THURSDAY: Thursday is a Jupiter day. Here is the day of the week for prosperity, abundance and good health. Thursday is 'Thor's day'. This Norse god gave the day his name and many of his attributes, including strength and abundance. Some suggestions for Thursday enchantments would include:

☛ Wearing a regal and royal shade of blue to see how it affects your mood and your magic. Other colours for the day include purple and green.

☛ Carrying a turquoise tumbled stone in your pocket to draw a little protective and healing energy your way.

☛ Incorporating green foliage into prosperity charms.

☛ Calling on Thor for abundance, or on the Roman god Jupiter for the ability to peacefully referee a fight.

☛ Adding a few oak leaves (or substitute with gum leaves) – which are sacred to these Thursday Gods – to your charms to see how much better your spell works out.

☛ Casting a charm with wheat stalks for prosperity, and calling on Juno Moneta to bring wealth into your life.

☛ Baking up some whole-wheat bread and blessing it for abundance. Be sure to thank the Gods for your family and your good health.

FRIDAY: Friday belongs to Venus, both the planet and its namesake Roman Goddess of love. This day is sacred to many other Gods and Goddesses of love such as Eros, Venus, Aphrodite and the Norse Goddess who gave the day its name: Freya. This day of the week is for magickal topics such as love, birth, fertility and romance. Colours for today include pink and aqua. Some suggestions for Friday enchantments would include:

☞ Carrying a rose quartz with you to send out some gentle and loving vibes to those crabby teachers and classmates.

☞ Working a little flower magic to enchant a single pink rose for friendship and inner beauty, and setting it on your school desk or placed in your hair (be careful of thorns; it's totally fine to break them off with a statement of 'love that inspires, not hurts').

☞ Burning rose-scented candles to encourage the same effect.

SATURDAY: this day of the week got its name from the god of karma and time, Saturn. This day is obviously associated with the planet Saturn and is our last day of the week. Traditionally Saturdays are great days for protection, banishing a negative situation and generally a good time to clean up any magickal messes that you have been trying to ignore. Some suggestions for Saturday enchantments would include:

☞ Wearing the colours of the day: black and deep purple. Here's your perfect excuse to be dramatic and witchy. Empower these dramatic pieces of your wardrobe for protection and strength by passing them through incense smoke of frankincense and patchouli.

☞ Burning black candles to absorb negativity and burning purple ones to increase your magickal wisdom and boost your spirituality.

☞ Adding a touch of garden witchery to your Saturday spells by working with the pansy (in black or purple, of course), the morning glory flowering vine or the cypress tree.

☛ Carrying an obsidian, hematite or jet tumbled stone in your pocket to reinforce your personal protection and to ward off bad vibes and sour feelings. You can also add these crystals to a candle spell on a Saturday night to really increase the punch of your spell-casting.

☛ Cleaning your bedroom or surprising your parents and cleaning the whole house whilst they are out … and magickally *cleansing* it whilst you are at it. Tap into those obstacle-removing vibes and smudge each room (fan incense) whilst saying, 'This home is blessed with positive communication, wisdom, happiness and love.'

☛ Trace a pentagram on the front and back door of your home (or just the door of your room as you think appropriate) and call on Hecate for protection and guidance.

A Teen Witch knows every day is a magickal day in all its lessons easy and hard. The way you perceive your days will give you the option every week to be grateful.

COLOURS

◇◇◇

BLACK: banishing, binding and can be used to access the subconscious.

BLUE: healing and happiness.

DARK BLUE: presence of mind.

GOLD: sun energy, empowerment and positivity.

GREEN: prosperity, employment, fertility, successful use of efforts and skill.

ORANGE: legal matters; also sun energy and pride.

PALE BLUE: calming.

PINK: love, self-confidence, luck.

PURPLE: power, success, enhancement of psychic powers.

RED: love, willpower, courage, ambition.

SILVER: represents the Goddess and lunar energy as well as purity, and can stimulate the intuition.

WHITE: can replace any other colour (except black). Represents purity and protection.

YELLOW: wisdom, stimulates the intellect and aids concentration.

OTHER STUFF

ASH: from anything burnt binds harmful energies and offers the potential of renewal.

BODY BITS: filings from nails, a lock of hair or drops of saliva bind a person's energy to the spell.

HONEY: to sweeten and empower.

ICE: slows or binds an action or energy.

MAGNET: draws and attracts a result or energy.

SOIL SCOOPED FROM THE IMPRINT OF A FOOTPRINT: captures a person's energy to bind it to a spell.

WHITE CORD THAT IS EXACTLY YOUR HEIGHT: captures and holds your energy and presence.

CANDLE MAGICK

◇◇

Among the easiest and most effective spells are those that are conjured by candle magick. The elements of fire and air come into play to encourage quick and effective results.

Choose a coloured candle corresponding to your desire or goal.

With a pointed stick or quill, carve in words or symbols of your desire or goal and then underneath carve the Witches' pentagram (the five-pointed star). Lick your thumb and trace over your carvings to seal your energy into the spell.

To charge up the spell, either with your spit or an essential oil relative to your needs anoint the pentagram you've carved into the candle with your thumb. Trace either widdershins (clockwise in the southern hemisphere or against the sun; anti-clockwise in the northern hemisphere) to take something away, or deosil (anti-clockwise in the southern hemisphere or with the sun; clockwise in the northern hemisphere) to bring it to you.

Light the candle and burn it as you gaze at the flame for at least five minutes, concentrating on your goal.

Note: when you are finished candle spell-casting always snuff the candles; don't blow them out unless the spell says to. Blowing them out blows away their energy.

CRYSTALS

◇◇

There are many different types of crystals, and a lot of them have similar properties and sometimes the choices are overwhelming! Here I have listed a few good ones specifically for Teen Witches. And please remember to be ethical and conscious in how many crystals you have, as the over-harvesting of them is slowly but surely erasing any magickal properties they have as they become smothered by exploitative consumer ideals. Consider fossicking for your own crystals or trading and swapping with other witches. Be mindful, ethical and conscious as you enjoy the blessings of crystals.

AMBER: not really a crystal at all but the fossilised resin of a tree, amber is great for grounding and focusing your energies.

AMETHYST: peace of mind and as a talisman for restful sleep and good dreams. Also amplifies growing psychic ability: very handy for a Teen Witch!

BLACK OBSIDIAN: good as a charm to ward away peer pressure.

CITRINE: mental powers (good to have around whilst studying).

CLEAR QUARTZ: good as an overall energy harmoniser and amplifier. Can give strength and courage aligned with masculine energies.

FLUORITE: another good one for mental powers, especially artistic expression.

MOONSTONE: great for girls, especially when worn around the time of your period/menstruation).

OPAL: can help release anger and resentment.

ROSE QUARTZ: the ultimate love amplifier.

TIGER'S EYE: courage and luck, as well as favourable results from a testing situation (whether a school exam or driver's licence test).

WHITE AGATE CRYSTAL: encourages good communication, purity and the promise of good things to come.

POWERFUL PRESENCES

The Goddess and god and other magickal beings below are all referred to in this book. There are many more, but I have suggested these as an initial way for you to become familiar with the process of invoking and connecting with the energies of these celestial and mythological beings.

There are also some suggested herbs, fruits and flowers that will help you commune with their essence. You can burn the herbs as incense, the fruits can be eaten and the flowers displayed.

THE LADY AND THE LORD

The Lady is the Goddess in her triple aspect of maiden, mother and crone, reflecting the cycles of life, creativity and destruction. She is all things, all faces of the Goddess, omnipresent and eternal.

The Lord is mostly related to by Witches as the horned god or god of the forests and animals (Pan). He interacts with the Goddess as her son, lover and consort and in the myth of the Wheel of the Year. Like the sun, he moves in cycles between his growing, light, overworld aspect (from Yule to Litha) and his dark, underworld presence (from Litha to Yule).

APHRODITE

Greek Goddess of love and the sea (called Venus by the Romans).
Sacred to Aphrodite: apple, parsley, rose.
Aphrodite is popularly depicted as rising out of the sea nestled like a pearl in a beautiful scallop shell. She is the patroness of lovers and is particularly good to

invoke for self-love and self-worth spells as her pure yet passionate presence is perfect to absorb when you are feeling down.

ARCHANGEL MICHAEL

A Judeo-Christian angelic force that I often call upon to help clear away negativity, blockages and sadness. He carries a huge sword that cuts through any psychic dross, and I always feel his presence as exciting and empowering yet also comforting, like a big brother!

ARTEMIS

Greek Goddess of the waxing moon (called Diana by the Romans).

Sacred to Artemis: almond blossoms or leaves from the tree, daisies, wormwood (its other name *Artemisia absynthium* is named for her).

Artemis is the Goddess of the crescent moon and is seen as the waxing or maiden face of the three faces of the moon. She hunts with a silver bow and arrow and is also an accomplished musician. She is virginal and very protective of her chastity, and is fierce and proud.

BAST

Egyptian sun Goddess.

Sacred to Bast: catnip, dragon's blood powder.

Bast is mostly recognised as the cat Goddess or as a cat-headed Goddess carrying her instrument: a sistrum (a sacred rattle), an ankh or the papyrus wand. In early Egyptian mythology she was seen as a fierce avenger and protector of the pharaoh. In later years she became associated with music, sensuality, fertility and arts. As such Bast's role started to change, and her status of protector was extended to women, children and families.

HECATE

Greek Goddess and patroness of Witches.

Sacred to Hecate: almond, garlic, myrrh, willow, patchouli.

Hecate is the Goddess of the dark and waning moon and is depicted as a crone of great age and wisdom. Her realm is the underworld, and she understands better than anyone the cycles of life and death. She also presides over crossroads, so these are a good place to leave offerings to her to gain her favour.

MERLYN

Magickal master of Arthurian legend and learning,

Knowledge and magickal wisdom.

Sacred to Merlyn: dill, marjoram, valerian, myrrh, amber, hazelwood.

Merlyn was magician, counsellor and entertainer to King Arthur and is considered a patron of male Witches. He also embodies the spirit of the Lord of the forests and woods.

RHIANNON

Welsh Goddess of birds and horses.

Sacred to Rhiannon: lily of the valley, carnations, honeysuckle, vervain.

Rhiannon is seen in her light and dark aspect as a Goddess who can travel between the overworld and the underworld (life and death). She rides a beautiful white mare (symbolic of faithfulness and endurance) and can talk to birds. There is the legend of the three blackbirds of Rhiannon, which sing so sweetly that their song puts the listener into a trance so they can access the worlds between the worlds.

SELENE
Greek Goddess of the full moon.
Sacred to Selene: myrrh, jasmine, vervain.
Selene is the Greek Goddess of the full moon and presides over the fertility and abundance of the land and sea. She is a great source of inspiration and empowerment representing the lush nurturing power of motherhood.

CHAPTER SEVENTEEN

<><><><><><><><><><><><><><><><><><><><><><><><><><><><><><><><><><><><><>

Witchy Words: a glossary

<><><><><><><><><><><><><><><><><><><><><><><><><><><><><><><><><><><><><>

ALTAR: a table or similar surface upon which the working tools of a Witch, representations of the Goddess and god and articles used in spellcraft are placed. A Witch's altar generally faces the earth quarter (due south in the southern hemisphere and north in the northern hemisphere). Altars may either be permanently set up or prepared only when required. In outdoor rituals, stones, tree stumps and so on are often used as makeshift altars.

ASTRAL REALM/ASTRAL PLANE: terms popularised by the spiritual/intellectual path of theosophy to describe the lower levels of existence. It is subtler than the physical plane but resembles it closely, all physical objects being believed to have astral equivalents. Whilst theosophy describes the various levels or planes very specifically, the term 'astral' is used less precisely in all paths of Witchcraft, including the religion of Wicca (and many other magickal traditions), to describe a variety of realms of being made of energies subtler than matter though still apparently retaining form. It is widely believed that changes made on the astral plane bring about changes in physical reality, this principle being used in many forms of magic (such as astral projection, in which the astral equivalent of the body of the Witch or magician is set free to explore and modify that plane).

ATHAME: representative of the god, it is a knife, traditionally double-edged and black-handled, used by a Witch to delineate sacred space, astrally inscribe pentagrams and other symbols and direct energy in consecrations (in spells, the charging of libations and liquids and so on). It also represents the power of air (or, less typically, fire) and a Witch's identity as a priest/ess of the Craft. The usual pronunciation is either 'ath-am-ay' or 'ath-aim-me'; however, since many Witches first learnt the word from books, virtually every other possible pronunciation is likely to be heard.

BIND: (1) To bind a spell is to complete its casting, releasing it to do its work independently of the weaver of the spell. The spell is bound to its desired result and should henceforth only be thought of in terms of its completion, not the manner in which it will work. Some spells incorporate the actual tying of a knot to bind the spell. (2) To bind an individual magickally is to use spellcraft to prevent them from behaving in a certain fashion. Some Witches never use such spells, feeling them to be overly manipulative, whilst others feel they have a duty to do all they can to prevent something (for example, a criminal can be stopped from repeating their crimes). A binding is very different from a curse since it only prevents specific behaviour rather than harming an individual. The caster of the spell can, therefore, safely accept the spell's 'return'.

BOOK OF SHADOWS: a book of spells, rituals and lore either assembled by the individual Witch according to their own tastes and requirements or deriving from one of several books of shadows compiled by Gerald Gardner and associates in the 1940s and 50s. The individually assembled Book of Shadows is the more widely used type now, and their contents may contain everything from magickal diaries, recipes and picture collections to transcriptions from grimoires and other magickal texts.

CELTIC: relating to a particular Indo-European race thriving in the pre-Roman era in Britain, France and other regions of Western Europe. The remaining strongholds of Celtic culture include Ireland, Scotland, Wales and Brittany. Wicca is strongly influenced by ancient and contemporary Celtic culture and magickal traditions but, contrary to many superficial books and articles on the subject, it isn't a Celtic religion or movement; it is, in fact, one of the most multicultural of all spiritual paths. Some traditions, however, do emphasise the Celtic aspects of the Craft, just as others might the Scandinavian, Italian or Jewish aspects.

CHAKRA: one of seven centres of spiritual energy positioned along the spine and skull of the human body that, when activated through meditation and visualisation, allow the flow of a current of energy, enhancing magickal and spiritual workings. An Eastern concept popularised in the West by theosophy and related organisations, chakra workings are now commonly used by Witches of many traditions.

CHALICE: a symbol of the Goddess, the bowl-shape representing the cauldron of creation, the great womb, from which life as we know it springs. In Witchcraft ritual it is a drinking vessel, generally handle-less and comprising a bowl, stem and base, used in Wicca to represent the element of water. The principal use of the chalice in adult Wiccan ritual is to contain wine (or mead, water, juice or whatever is preferred) to be blessed by the Goddess and god then drunk to take that blessing into the body.

Where more than one person is in the Circle the chalice is passed, with a kiss, around those assembled to deepen the bonds between them. A chalice may also be used in spellcraft to hold an item of jewellery or similar being consecrated.

CHARCOAL DISCS: small, flattened cylinders of compressed charcoal used to heat granulated incense. Best lit by holding them with tweezers over a naked flame. Once alight, a disk should be placed in a well-insulated container (a layer of sand is ideal) and a small amount of incense sprinkled on top of it. They are available at most new age and occult supply shops as well as online.

CHURCH: in a Wiccan context, generally a reference to the many forms of Christian church or, historically, either the Roman Catholic or a significantly powerful Protestant church. Though occasionally used disparagingly (generally by those viewing it as an historically oppressive, anti-Pagan force), the Christian church is afforded by most Witches the same respect they accord all religions. Wiccans and Witches in general have no grievance with any religious organisation or individuals except those who revile and seek to demonise the Craft or any other equally worthy faith.

CIRCLE: a space delineated and sanctified by a Witch or Witches for the purposes of protection or a ritual. A Witches' Circle may be visibly represented or simply astrally inscribed. The Circle is actually better visualised as a sphere than a boundary on the ground, and as a field of energy rather than a bubble (through which, presumably, one's head would poke out when near the edge!).

COLLECTIVE UNCONSCIOUS: a term from Jungian psychology descriptive of a deep stratum of shared knowledge and insight available to all members of the human race. This shared wealth of information is generally perceived to be encoded in symbols rather than verbal language. The concept was coined to provide a hypothetical explanation for the way in which distantly located cultures with no apparent means of communicating ideas and mythologies often seemed to generate very similar grammars of symbolism.

CORRESPONDENCES: in magickal theory, the kinship of certain sets of ideas or qualities. A keystone of contemporary magickal lore is the concept that a deeply encoded unity may be found in superficially different substances so that, for example, a particular colour, perfume, herb, element, magickal tool, planet, zodiacal constellation and day of the week share an inherent quality. Hence the colour red might be considered to relate to the planet Mars and the colour green to Venus; the scent of frankincense will relate to Jupiter and myrrh to Saturn and so on. In ritual, a particular energy can be magnified by concentrating as many different related substances and influences together as possible.

COVEN: a small group of three or more Witches who regularly join together for Circles. Though the term is often loosely used to describe any group practising the Craft, the Coven should ideally be united by a strong level of commitment to both Witchcraft and the group itself.

Bonds between Coven members should be those of very close friends or even family members, and groups of casual acquaintances getting together for an occasional sabbat or spell-casting are more properly referred to as groves or simply open Circles or working groups. The traditional ideal number of members is thought to be 13, although in practice this is more like a maximum number of members. Many of the most durable Covens only comprise three to six members.

CRAFT, THE: one of the terms used loosely to describe either Wicca (see below) or Witchcraft of all varieties. The term was used to describe Freemasonry long before Witchcraft adopted it, suggesting that it is one of many Masonic phrases adopted by Gerald Gardner in his reformulation of the Craft in the 1940s and 50s.

DEOSIL: movement in the direction of the sun, hence clockwise in the northern hemisphere (where the sun rises in the east and veers to the south, that is, the direction of the equator, before setting in the west) and anti-clockwise in the southern hemisphere. To relate to this, consider that if watches were invented in the southern hemisphere the hand would move backwards to what it does now. In Witches' ritual, sunwise motion tends to be used to draw power in and counter-sunwise movement to banish or cast energy out. See also Widdershins.

DRUIDIC: pertaining to the faith of the early Celtic priest- and Priestess-hood or their modern-day counterparts. In Britain, Druidery is the second-largest Pagan movement after the Craft, with which it shares many beliefs and practices.

ETHERIC PLANE: a term popularised through theosophy to describe the energy field interconnecting the physical and astral planes. The etheric is often referred to as 'life force' (and a host of other names) and is the most commonly perceived portion of the aura.

FAMILIAR: a spirit assistant to a Witch. A familiar may be either an elemental or a formerly human spirit, often taking the form of, or actually inhabiting the body of, an animal. It should be stressed, however, that not all Witches' pets are familiars. Witches enjoy the company of animals for their own sake as much as any intelligent member of the human race does!

GARLAND: a wreath of leaves or flowers or a combination of both, either worn as a crown or hung up as a decoration. Witches often use seasonal vegetation in garlands to emphasise the season they are currently celebrating.

GERALD GARDNER: an Englishman who in the late 30s and 40s popularised modern Wicca. He established the Gardnerian tradition of Witchcraft and is an important figure in the Craft. Before he claimed to be a Witch he had been involved in other spiritual paths like Co-Masonry and Rosicrucianism and had travelled extensively in the East learning of the indigenous spiritual practices of the people. All these influenced his teachings of Wicca. Read his book *Witchcraft Today*, written in 1954, to find out more.

GUARDIAN: generally short for 'guardian of the watchtower', one of many images used to personify the elemental powers of each of the four quarters (see 'Quarter'). Guardians may also be spirits, elemental or otherwise, called to protect a Witch, other individual or even a location from harm.

HEX/HEXING: a word derived from a German word for 'witch' describing the casting of a spell. Although the word itself has no connotation of either positive or negative spell-casting, in common usage the word is used synonymously with 'curse'.

INTUITION: a form of perception or thinking not apparently connected to rational structuring of thought. Witches tend to give this form of mental activity equal (or sometimes even superior) status to logical thought on the basis that the brain comprises two sides, each with its own mode of coming to conclusions.

INVOKE: to call a spirit or deity into oneself or one's Circle.

LADY: the feminine principle of divinity in the foundational core of modern Witchcraft that honours the procreative force as feminine and masculine. These forces can be channelled and experienced by all Witches no matter what gender they identify as.

LIBATIONS: in Witchcraft a beverage offering to the Goddess and god that is blessed within the Circle. In an outdoor ritual, the offering may be poured during the Circle; in indoor Circles, the offering is taken out after the closing of the ritual. Though libation literally means an offering of drink, Witches frequently extend the meaning to include the offering of whatever food was shared during the Circle as well.

LORD: the masculine principle of divinity in the foundational core of modern Witchcraft that honours the procreative force as feminine and masculine. These forces can be channelled and experienced by all Witches no matter what gender they identify as.

MAGICK: an archaic spelling of 'magic' popularised by Aleister Crowley largely to differentiate it from stage magic: the 'pulling a rabbit out of a hat' variety. The word has been repeatedly redefined by modern occultists and Witches but essentially refers to the manipulation of reality by apparently supernatural means by the will of an individual or group as well as the inherent magick of the Universe.

METAPHYSICAL: in general usage it is synonymous with the supernatural. Some Witches also interpret this to mean 'pertaining to matters not yet understood by science'.

MOJO BAG: a bag containing one or more magickal items, often a working spell that can be carried on a person or placed somewhere.

OCCULT/OCCULTIST: 'occult' is another term for that which is hidden, that is, that which is not yet understood by conventional wisdom. An occultist is, therefore, one who studies those subjects that exist within human experience but outside established understanding.

OUIJA BOARD: a board on which alphabetical (and related) characters are marked out and upon which an indicator (traditionally an inverted glass or a planchette – a small board on wheels) is held by the fingertips of two or more people in the hopes that disincarnate spirits will be able to communicate. Popularised by spiritualism, ouija boards are rarely used by Witches, who tend to feel that inviting any passing spirit into their bodies or homes is slightly more dangerous than leaving the front door open in a high-crime neighbourhood.

PATH: in this book 'path' refers to the practice of Witchcraft by an individual and emphasises the journey aspect of their practices.

PATRIARCHY: a social system in which males are dominant.

PENTACLE: a disc or stone inscribed with a pentagram and possibly other esoteric symbols representing the element of earth. The pentacle can be used to hold objects being consecrated to act as a shield against unwanted energy or to help ground energy. An alternative to the pentacle, as a Craft tool symbolising earth in some Wicca and Witchcraft, is a stone (often polished into a spherical shape). The word 'pentacle' is often also casually used to mean a pendant, ring or earring inscribed or moulded into the shape of a pentagram.

PENTAGRAM: a regular five-pointed star used as a symbol of blessing and power in many magickal traditions, including the Craft. The five points are often said to represent the four elements giving rise to the fifth: the element of spirit. For this reason the pentagram is generally shown with one point uppermost, representing the ascent of spirit through balanced matter, whilst the inverted pentagram is often seen as a symbol of the spirit in decline (hence its use in negative magic and satanism). However, in Gardnerian Craft, the inverted pentagram is used as a symbol of their second degree and in that context shouldn't be mistaken for a malevolent symbol.

PETITIONS: as referred to in this book, wishes and requests written on paper and thrown into fire or the air to bring in the power of these elements to make them come true.

POWER FINGER: the index finger of a Witch's dominant hand (that is, the one they write with or generally favour). The magickal tools of a Witch are ultimately just objects used to help fire up the imagination and so can be dispensed with for workings when necessary. In workings where an athame, sword or wand are unavailable or impractical a finger can be used to direct energy and is equally efficient.

QUARTER: within a Witch's Circle one of the cardinal points of the compass, each of which corresponds to one of the four elements. Correspondences will vary from tradition to tradition and place to place but the quartered circle is one of the most common features of ritual.

RUNES: alphabetical characters used by Germanic and Scandinavian people up till the Middle Ages. The original runes were associated with a number of magickal correspondences and have recently been revived as a tool for divination. A rune may also be a short poem used as a spell or invocation.

SATANISM: a form of inverted Christianity where the vices of the Christian faith are held to be virtues and vice versa. Despite some superficial similarity in magickal tools and trappings, there is no theological or philosophical connection between Wicca, a form of Pagan religion/spirituality, and satanism.

SIGIL: an inscribed or painted symbol Witches consider to have magickal power to attract, repel or bless.

SKYCLAD: a term borrowed from Jainism (a very disciplined religion of India) by Gerald Gardner to describe nakedness as a state of power and sacredness rather than vulnerability. Whilst some Witches work clothed in robes, costumes or even street clothes, the tradition of skyclad working remains popular since it emphasises several qualities necessary to the Craft: self-acceptance, individuality, freedom and mutual trust.

SOLITARY: a Witch who practises the Craft alone most of the time whether by choice or circumstance. Most Witches who are part of Covens or other working groups still work solitary at least some of the time. Whilst the influential Gardnerian Book of Shadows stated one couldn't be a 'Witch alone', contemporary thinking is of the opinion that a Witch needs to do just that, periodically, to avoid becoming dependent on group energy.

TAOISM: a Chinese religion/philosophy with a number of similarities to the Craft, notably an emphasis on spiritual polarity (in Taoism conceived of as yin and yang; in Wicca as the god and Goddess) and the interconnectedness of all things. Traditional Taoism also has a strong magickal element and recommends alignment with the natural flow of life's energy.

TEUTONIC: relating to either the Teuton tribes who lived in Jutland and southern France until falling to Rome or to Germanic people and culture in general.

THEOSOPHY: from the Greek *theos* (god, divinity) and *sophia* (wisdom), meaning divine wisdom. The Theosophical Society is a religious society founded in the late 1800s by a woman, Helena Petrovna Blavatsky (H.P. Blavatsky) and two men, H.S. Olcott and W.Q. Judge. They introduced Oriental philosophical and religious ideas to the West such as the concepts of reincarnation and karma. A primary idea is the essential oneness of all beings – all things are linked cosmically.

THIRD EYE: one of the chakras, positioned in the centre of the forehead and associated with the pineal gland. The chakra is related to the power of inner vision, both active visualisation and the ability to see between the worlds.

WAND: a length of wood, often decorated with carvings and tipped with crystals, used in Witchcraft to represent the element of fire (or, less typically, air). The wand was originally conceived as a symbol of authority in magick and is frequently described as being used in commanding spirits and the like. In the Craft it is more often used to direct energy either into an object or (in the case of healing energy, for example) out of the Circle and towards a spell's target. Since fire also relates to the will, the wand is often held aloft in the making of oaths or the proclaiming of an intention.

WESTERN MAGICK: the magical practices associated with the Western mystery tradition, an array of systems given the collective name to differentiate them from Indian and Far Eastern esoteric magical practices. Many influential occult organisations such as the Theosophical Society have had eras in which they championed Eastern traditions but showed little interest in ancient European esoteric traditions. Whilst much of value was imported to Europe by these organisations, many occultists felt their own cultures were being dangerously neglected, hence the emphasis on the West.

WICCA: a contemporary form of Pagan Witchcraft owing much to the mid-20th-century work of Gerald Gardner. Whilst Gardner represented Wicca as being a magical tradition existing for centuries in much the form described in his books, it's now clear that he was much more like the innovative, creative Wiccans of today, formulating his own vision of Witchcraft from a wide range of influences. Wicca wasn't Gardner's invention any more than rock and roll was Elvis Presley's. Both, however, were enormously influential in changing and popularising their chosen fields. Using the word 'Wicca' in this sense is useful in differentiating modern Pagan Witchcraft from the many other species of Witchery around the world.

WIDDERSHINS: movement in the opposite direction to that of the sun, hence anti-clockwise in the northern hemisphere and clockwise in the southern hemisphere. See also Deosil.

WITCH: you! A seeker of knowledge, a healer, a dreamer, a magick maker – blessings as you journey on your path.

Appendix

<><><><><><><><><><><><><><><><><><><><><><><><><><><><><><><><><><><><><><><><><>

IN YOUR OWN WORDS

Whilst originally preparing for this book, I invited Teen Witches to email me with any queries they might like to have published and answered. For this reworked edition, the Teen Witches PMd me on Facebook. What struck me was the similarities of the questions between those from the first edition and from Teen Witches today. As evolved and sophisticated in the world as we are now young witches have the same concerns and queries. Below are questions from the original version and some more recent.

2004 | AMELIA, AGED 14

I have attended circle with my mother and enjoyed it. i am also interested in jesus and the bible. how does it all seem relative as the teachings are so different – or are they?

love amelia

2019 | TOM, AGED 17

I resonate strongly with the teachings of Jesus – and Buddah ... teachers of peace and tolerance. I have been taught that Jesus and Buddah even knew each other over different lifetimes. At the same time I am really drawn to the natural magic of witchcraft and of personal empowerment to be able to make a positive difference in the world. Could I study witchcraft also?

Thanks

As I wrote in my first book, *Witch: A Personal Journey* (30 years ago), despite being brought up in a strict and rigid Catholic environment myself I went on to say that 'If he [Jesus] was around today, with his values of tolerance, acceptance, respect for nature and fellow people, he'd probably be a Witch!' I dig Jesus!

And as Tom points out in his email, Jesus shares a message and way of living that is expounded by other mystics of spiritual enlightenment who have positively guided many different cultures and peoples, like Buddha.

One of the main differences between the Craft (and many other spiritual paths) and mainstream forms of Christianity is how we see the nature of religion. I think mainstream churches look at religion as if it were science: a system with theories that are either right or wrong; if their religion is right, anyone else's must be wrong. The Witch sees religion as being more like culture or language. If an Aboriginal dancer moves completely differently from a classical ballerina, we don't say that the Aboriginal person is moving incorrectly. If a French person calls her house '*ma maison*', we don't say that she's using the wrong words. And similarly, if a Buddhist seeks spiritual union through one method or philosophy, a Jew another way and a Muslim another, we don't claim that one is doing it the right way and the others are messing it all up (or that all three are barking up the wrong trees and only Witches are going about it the right way).

Witches feel that it's important to learn about lots of spiritual practices so that they can let themselves be drawn to the one that best suits them. The best for me was Witchcraft, since it makes the most sense to me personally.

Read the Bible if you're drawn to it, and see what you think. I found, despite some good stuff, that it was too often contradictory, disempowering, convoluted, confusing and depressing – but you might find otherwise! A lot of people find a lot of inspiring stuff in the Bible. Remember as you read it that, really, it's a collection of works written over a long time and edited and translated over and over again, and that to really come to terms with the book is the study of a lifetime, not something you'd gain from a single reading of a particular version. There's been oceans of blood spilt over the centuries through people believing that they were experts on the subject when they were really only beginners. I have to say that I don't relate to Jesus as he's described in the Bible as well as I do to his presentation in alternative writings about him, like the book *Jesus the Man* by Australian biblical scholar Barbara Thiering.

GOD'S VOICE FROM THE NAKED WITCH

Reprinted from *The Naked Witch*, about an experience I had during the filming of the TV show *Mad Mad House* in 2004:

I was breathing deeply and in a meditative, calm state as I mused over what had been happening in the house. There was a lot of squabbling going on. The guests' opinions on world religions had been stirred into debate and questions of right and wrong, true and false, had been raised. Suddenly a hawk flew into my vision and landed in front of me on the stone wall – barely two feet away. And then it spoke to me. 'Fiona, look at all the trees in the Garden.' The hawk had a masculine voice. It sounded like the Christian Father God (as I had imagined he would in my Catholic childhood). I turned my head to look at all the trees – a swathe of green, brown and grey tones surrounding me. 'Do you see that the trees are different and yet all the same? An oak tree, a jacaranda tree – all different yet all united.' I nodded. The hawk continued. 'A tree's survival depends on its diversity. If every tree was the same, it would die.' I nodded again that I understood. 'So, it is with my love,' said the hawk. 'My survival depends on the diversity of my love. Every spiritual path is an instrument, and when these instruments are played together they become a symphony – a symphony of the soul – and that is my voice. The voice of God.' A wave of comprehension washed over me. God's voice depended on the diversity of its expression.

2004 | KRYSTAL, AGED 15

What about nightmares? i mean i would love to read about nightmares, i get them all the time and i would like to know what other witches get them as well blessed be shahla (my name).

I'm sure lots of Witches get nightmares – I certainly did in my teen years, though they have lessened now as an adult.

Nightmares are generally a symbol of growth and change within the individual, where your subconscious is shaking off the past or dealing with present hang-ups by releasing them as dreams. Unless your sleep's being seriously disrupted by nightmares, it's best to let them run their course rather than trying to use spells to suppress them. If you block the dreams, the emotions they release will only have to find another outlet. Oh, and contrary to what our TV Witch equivalents experience so often, our nightmares are very rarely prophetic, or indicative of us slipping off into some strange demonic world! And when a challenge presents in a dream state, you could consider it an opportunity to hone your 'slaying' skills. Challenges in life are not presented to show us how weak we are … but how strong we can be. So consider exploring your nightmares as opportunities to reveal your hidden strengths. Keep a dream diary next to your bed and, upon waking, write what you remember.

If it was a scary dream, write your power solution. I am very sure if you have the nightmare again you will conquer or rise above the thing you fear.

2019 | MELISSA, AGED 15

Hi Fiona

My mom is a Witch and we were brought up practising simple rituals and celebrating the eight sabbats. Not once has the word Satan been used in our home – but at school recently I got given a hard time for worshipping Satan. The guy who was hassling me is a jerk, but it was kind of stressful for me because he got really aggressive with his opinions. I eventually was able to get away from him, but he was in my face for ages. If he hassles me again, what do I say?

Twenty years ago when this book was first written, Witches were often judged as Satan worshippers. But now there is a huge wave of enlightened information out there – not in the least because of the internet. And people know Satan is a Christian concept and has nothing to do with modern Witchcraft. And yet, as Melissa mentions very recently, she was harassed at school. Melissa should feel comfortable to speak to her principal and parents, and the bully has to be disciplined. Wicca/Witchcraft is recognised as a world religion now and afforded all the rights and privileges as the major religions. And Melissa could also have compassion for the bully because he is acting upon ignorance and fear. But she is right to not engage with him – we Witches do not proselytise and try to convert people to 'our ways' as we know there's plenty of room in the spiritual world for people to walk their own paths. But we have a right to stand up for ourselves when we are judged and abused. The challenging thing as a teen and a victim of bullying, which is essentially what this situation is, is that we have to go to trustworthy adults and have them discipline the bully – without wasting our time and energy or potentially putting us in a more vulnerable situation by engaging. As Gandhi said, 'Be the light you want to see in the world.' Be magickal, be compassionate and be free.

Some fundamentalist followers of other religions seem to get some sort of odd excitement from the notion that there are evil Witches in the world, but I can't see the attraction myself. It's an archetype that might have seemed thrilling once, but real power doesn't come from the ability to harm others and inspire fear. Real power is most magnificent when its healing, helping and transforming lives and our planet for the better in these challenged times.

2004 | LISA, AGED 14

Fiona,

If possible, in your new book could you include a self initiation spell for some of us who are solitary witches? Also a list of how to meet others of like mind would be helpful in your new book, as I find it is pretty difficult to meet others who are also interested in the Craft.

2019 | CAITLYN, AGED 14

Fiona, I know a lot of solitary witches, but they are all online and I'm wondering if you have any tips for going to actual physical group gatherings or creating real life groups.

As evidenced by Lisa's letter in 2004 and Caitlyn's in 2019, there are so many more solitary Witches now thanks to the internet – and especially social media channels like Instagram. But meeting up in person can still present challenges. No longer is there the stigma associated with solitary Witches – it's very accepted now that you don't need to be initiated into a Coven to be considered a real Witch. The self-dedication ritual on page 33 of this book can guide you through a spiritual dedication to your path.

As far as meeting in person, use the internet as a tool and remember that you don't have to put the pressure on to create a Coven or do elaborate rituals together. It can be magickal to meet up and grab a coffee, with some witchy books on your iPad, to discuss with each other; or you could catch a magickal movie or take a walk in a natural environment. If you are an urban Teen Witch consider visiting a botanical garden or garden store and look at the herbs and medicinal plants section and immerse yourself in the natural world. Communicating is so easy now, yet we often perceive it as being hard to meet up in real life. But it's not hard because we can't get to a meeting point, or because there are no opportunities – it's because we tend to spend most of our time with our heads down, looking at our smart devices or looking at ourselves in selfies, and we miss seeing and connecting with the people around us. It's ironic that Gen Zers' hyper-connective world leads to more isolation and introversion than ever before. At its core, Witchcraft is a nature-worshipping spiritual path and we are of the natural world, too. Make a date IRL, leave the smart devices at home and go and do some magick together under the stars and the moon.

2019 | CATHERINE-SILVERDRAGON, AGED 16

Those who are High Priestesses and High Priests – are they required to have followed the path and studied it for a particular amount of time, and who decides whether they may become a High Priestess/Priest?

Thanks

When contemplating the requirements and possible rules to being recognised as a High Priestess/Priest, the thing to bear in mind here is that, along with thousands of very individualistic, solitary and eclectic Witches, there are also lots of Wiccan traditions, clans and tribes out there.

Among these there's a whole range of different styles of working magic, different titles and degrees and different initiatory requirements. You can read up on some examples of these in various books (for example, Brian Cain's *Initiation into Witchcraft*, Warlock Press, 2019, is an excellent place to start), and these days online searching 'Covens near me' brings up many results. And Facebook groups like https://www.facebook.com/groups/australianwitchcraft provide wonderful ways to connect with communities and groups. But getting back to the point, if you ever choose to join a formal group (usually called a Coven or a Grove), you'll still need to learn that group's particular system.

Usually a High Priestess or High Priest (or HPS and HP for short) is part of a Coven and it is their Coven that bestows this acknowledgement. They are often gender-specific, being a female and male partnership representing the union of egg and sperm and their role in procreation and perpetuation of our species, and may be the permanent principal organisers of the group. In other groups the positions are temporary, being titles given to the Witches who are running a particular ritual rather than running the whole Coven. In this case, the positions will be given to different qualified people at different times, to avoid the group becoming too hierarchical. Some Covens also acknowledge HPS and HP being embodied by people who identify as female and male ... and yet have different reproductive organs, thus representing symbolically the procreative forces as related to human reproduction.

Solitaries are not generally considered High Priest/esses, though they may hold that rank if they were once part of a Coven. I am not an initiated High Priestess, though I have the knowledge and experience that would qualify me as one if I were part of a Coven. Several Witch friends of various traditions have told me that they'd happily grant me an honorary HPS status at some of their Circles on the basis that they consider I know my stuff well enough to do the job, even though I'm not of their tradition. This sort of professional courtesy is quite common among Witches and shared workings happen much the same way as a marriage between a Jew and Christian might be jointly officiated by both a Rabbi and a Priest or Minister.

It is not the ultimate goal or seal of approval for a Witch to be called High Priest/ess. The ultimate goal is to never stop learning and evolving as an adept Witch.

2019 | DOROTA, AGED 17

Hi Fiona!

My name's Dorota, and I'm 17. I've read your books and I think they're great. Your way of expressing your passion for witchcraft and all things related is fantastic and it's really easy to relate to.

I've been sort of practising wicca for a couple years now, and one thing that keeps on cropping up and still kind of confuses me is that it's so hard to practise something which is so pro-life and promysticism, whilst a lot of people these days seem to be wanting to reduce human contact and seem to have less respect for human life.

How do you cope?

Thanx. Blessed be.

I know what you mean! As a nature-worshipping Witch it can be very confronting when you realise the extent of ecological and social strife this planet is in. You can only live your life the best way you can in acting locally as you think globally. Magickally, do healing spells for the planet; practically, tread lightly and consciously on the earth and perhaps get active in environmental support and action groups.

Perform nature-worshipping rituals of gratitude with your magickal friends – the earth senses when she is adored by us, and it is healing on many levels for the planet and the humans involved in the ritual.

Shop, consume and dispose in an environmentally aware way – and even better, try not to shop and consume as much as you are encouraged to. Being in touch with nature does not happen by buying a t-shirt that says 'tree hugger' – it's better just to hug the tree.

And do at least three nice things for people every day, out of the blue. As the bumper sticker says: 'Practise random acts of kindness and senseless beauty'.

Don't feel swamped by the problems in the world – more than ever, teens are shouldering the burden of mistakes that previous generations have made. The sense of responsibility can be even heavier for a Teen Witch. Once you've started getting positive responses to your spells and seen tangible results from your practical actions (because every real Teen Witch is also an environmentalist at heart), you can easily feel that it's up to you to get the whole planet back on track. There's just so much one little Witch can do to help a planet currently largely run by short-sighted, selfish corporations; so keep doing what you can, but don't try to carry the whole weight of the world on your back. Tiny adjustments add up to big changes over time and I have great confidence that inspired thinking and behaving by many humans – especially Gen Zers – is making the difference to ultimately arrest the problems, and for us as a species to maintain a relevant place in the bio-scheme of things on our beautiful planet.

2004 | HELENA, AGED 14

Dear Fiona,

This is a question I would be interested to see you answer in your new book. I have bought your previous books and I found them very interesting and enlightening. I know many Teen Witches have the same problem as me. I'm 14 and I have been studying and practising Wicca for 2 years now. I have tried a few spells (sometimes with friends) and did a lot of meditation exercises and recently started celebrating the Sabbats. Even though I do all this, I still feel like there is something missing in Wicca for me.

My motivation and enthusiasm is unpredictable and erratic. I was wondering if you have ideas or suggestions for me to keep up the practising and regulate it? I feel that this is truly my religious path but it gets hard to sit down and do something seriously whilst I am swamped with my schoolwork and social life. Sometimes it seems as though I am missing the point on Wicca completely. Can you please help me?

Thank you very much! =)

Blessed Be

As Witches, the one thing we need to be constantly aware of is the flowing of the tides of life and seasons. Some of our inner seasons will align themselves to those in the natural world, but there are also subtler tides and energies that we need to be conscious of.

So, as I mention in my introduction, the way in which you express your Craft will ebb and flow in varying intensity throughout your life as you explore the path created by others and go on to forge your own. Don't feel you have to celebrate every esbat or even every sabbat in a full-on elaborate way. I always recognise and celebrate the sabbats, but sometimes it might just mean lighting a candle and meditating for a little whilst on the meaning of the event and how the wheel is turning in my own life. All through this book there are quick, easy little things you can do to keep you on the path, even if it seems that you're only moving a millimetre at a time for a little whilst.

Why not do some spells to help you cope with your schoolwork and social life, throw in a ritual of gratitude for the fact that you are a Witch and don't be afraid to take your time with your magick – you've got your whole life ahead of you! It's also worth considering that being a Witch is just that, 'being' … not necessarily doing all the time. As you grow and evolve as a Witch you will notice that everything you are is inherently magickal – you will experience yourself and your place in the Universe differently to when you started on the path and were finding your way. Being a Witch is something in your soul, so relax and trust the process and your efforts. Whatever they are.

2019 | TARA, AGED 16

Dear Fiona, I and a few friends have been interested in Wicca for the last six years. I would just like to know how long it takes before you can call yourself a witch?

That's a trickier question to answer than it might sound.

In the more formal traditions of the Craft, the title of Witch is one you gain at your initiation. For solitary followers of the Craft, it's really something you need to feel for yourself. Of course, since the Craft is so flexible there's nothing to stop someone calling themselves a Witch after performing one spell or reading a single book on the subject. Whether that sort of 'instant Witch' would be acknowledged as such by other, possibly more conscientious, Witches is another matter. In general, whilst people in the same tradition use another person's knowledge of that group's magick as a guide to whether they're genuinely a Witch, most people in the Craft just seem to go on a gut feeling. There's just a particular energy that we recognise in each other.

As to where this energy comes from – well, some are born Witches, some are made Witches and some have Witchiness thrust upon them! Most of us who've been in the Craft for some time have met people who are just absolute natural Witches … although they mightn't be initiated, well-read on the Craft or even aware of the fact themselves. And we've met one or two people who've gone through all the right training, reading, exercises and initiations and just don't seem to have the spark at all.

If you know other long-term Witches you can probably tell if they have the spark and whether it's something you can recognise in yourself as well. If not – well, clearly the first person you'll have to examine for the spark is yourself.

Beyond that, I think when you have a clear understanding that a Witch works to honour, protect and heal nature, recognises the Goddess and God (or Lady and Lord) as symbols of the Divine, lives by the three laws of Witchcraft (and possibly the fourth Moral Law I now offer; see page 16) and seeks to expand their knowledge of the Craft by reading books, researching and sharing on the internet, casting spells and practising rituals of gratitude (and maybe we can even include positive magickal presence on social media), then you'd be pretty safe in considering yourself a Witch! Whether you've been doing this for six years or six weeks, the most important thing is your recognition of the magick you contain within you.

When you are ready, you could consider a self-dedication ritual (see page 33). Also see the chapter 'What is a Real Witch?'

2004 | GWEN, AGED 17

Fiona,

I'm a 17 year old female from brisbane who lives in a sharehouse with four other people. I sometimes find it difficult to do rituals and other witchy stuff because the others ask questions. I've tried to explain to them (the two housemates who don't understand) why i need to be left alone at these times but they just don't get it – they interrupt me all the time! I find it hard trying to fit rituals into the timeslots in which those two aren't home but it's really hard. I don't have enough room in my room to do rituals and stuff and I can't go to parks etc around here either because the council hire security guards to keep 'weirdos' out. any suggestions?

Witchcraft is about being resourceful and understanding that, more often than not, it's not the big showy rituals and spell-castings that give you the most magickal feeling and the deepest sense of what it is to be a Witch; it's the little things. The stillness in the air just before the sun rises as you light a candle in honour of its growing presence is magickal. Burning beautiful incense and meditating on sending love to those who need it as you hold a crystal and stare at a candle flame is magickal. These are small, easy, unobtrusive things you can do. You don't need to be calling out to the Goddess and waving your athame around all the time!

When I was on tour with Def FX (my old band) I had to share a room with one of the boys. At these times my mobile altar was a crystal, a feather, a tea light candle (rarely lit because hotels had smoke detectors), a glass of water and a beautiful Goddess card drawn by Elizabeth Kyle, a wonderfully talented and magickally inspired New Zealand artist. I would just set this up on the night-stand next to my bed and throw it all back in my bag the next day as we moved on to another town. I would do my Witchy ritual work as I sang on stage, conjuring up energy as well as channelling it and sending it around as a healing and empowering force.

Use your intuition and find new ways to practise your Craft rather than giving up and doing nothing at all. When you can, practise the formal disciplines but take the pressure off yourself and do a 'Keep Out of My Space' spell to keep your friends out of your hair!

⊕ KEEP OUT OF MY SPACE SPELL

- Sprinkle a line of sea salt across your doorway as you chant 'Leave me be' – simple as that. You will be surprised by how well it works!
- Until then, a really good exercise (one I recommend all Witches learn how to do) is to visualise in complete detail every step of yourself performing a full Circle casting.
- Developing this skill will repay the effort at times in your life when you need to cast a Circle (sacred space) but can't do the whole thing physically... because, for example, you can't get privacy!

2004 | CARA (A.K.A. MAGICKAL_PRINCESS), AGED 17

Hi Fiona,

I'm a HUGE fan of yours! I just wanted to take this opportunity to say that you are a true inspiration to me. When I was diagnosed with cancer in November 1998 you helped me get through so much with your books. Through your introduction to Witchcraft I was able to find spiritual fulfilment in a time when I was experiencing a great lack of faith and reasons for living and I am eternally grateful for that. I have a *few questions that I would love for you to answer for me:*

1. I know that when casting circle it is important to cut a gateway if you are going to leave the circle during the ritual but what if animals are in the room? My dog is with me most of the time and I don't like her being kept out of my room. What can I do about this, especially if she wanders in and out?

2. My brother has asked me to be his sponsor at his Confirmation (he attends a local Catholic school where it is compulsory). This is not important to him and he has always been interested in Wicca since seeing my books around. I have told him that he is too young to make any decisions about his faith yet (he is 12) but I would like to possibly tie in some Wiccan practices on his Confirmation day either before or after the mass. I know that may sound strange but I have heard of Christian Wiccans and wondered if you had any ideas?

Well, thanks again and sorry about the long email. Fiona – keep on doing what you do because you make a lot of people happy and never forget that.

****Blessed Be****

Blessed be, Cara!

As far as your dog wandering in and out it can weaken a Circle a little, and if he's not your familiar and finds magickal energies conjured in Circle a little intense, it's not surprising he needs to leave.

An animal wandering in and out creates less of a problem than a human, so don't worry about it too much. But if you feel your Circle is 'seeping' energy then use your gut instinct to go to where the 'leak' is and seal it by channelling blue light from your athame or power finger.

About your brother's confirmation – I was confirmed and it didn't have an adverse effect on my magickal life, so it doesn't have to affect his interest in

Witchcraft negatively and, yes, there are some Christians who are open to the practices of Witches (and, though being a Christian Wiccan sounds like quite a juggling act, certain Witches do, for instance, invoke the energies of Jesus and Mary into their Circles along with other manifestations of divine male and female power). Perhaps, at the end of the day, you could both do a little dedication to the Goddess. In being confirmed he is being presented to the aspect of Christian deity, the Holy Spirit of God, so you could balance it by honouring the Witches' female deity by lighting a silver candle (hopefully under a full moon, if by some lucky chance his confirmation is on the same day!). Have him make an offering to the Goddess – perhaps cut a little of his hair and bury it under a flowering plant (jasmine, gardenia or white rose would be great), take a sip of some juice (preferably apple – a sacred fruit) and then pour a little on the ground as he says, 'Great Goddess, I give thanks for the bounty and blessings of my life in your eyes.'

Teen Witch Familiars

QUESTION: *you have a beloved animal significant other. How do you know this animal is your familiar and not just a pet?*

ANSWER: they have an affinity for ritual – sitting quietly whilst you meditate in front of a candle. When you cast Circle they sit inside it with you, peacefully, and don't move around. They appear to you in dreams with messages for you. They sense when you are sad and challenged and will sit with you and offer healing energy. They will sit gazing into your eyes for long periods of time. You innately know they are your familiar – trust your gut on this.

WAYS TO ENHANCE YOUR RELATIONSHIP WITH YOUR FAMILIAR: CRYSTAL COLLARS

Your dog, cat or pig familiar, and any other significant other who wears a collar, will likely enjoy a crystal-studded collar with the backing of each crystal left open (just as human crystal magickally purposed jewellery is constructed) so that the beneficial energies of the crystal can be instantly aligned with the energies of your familiar. You can also hang a crystal from their collar for similar effect. Choose a crystal that you feel personally aligned to and wear one also to further enhance your magickal bond with your familiar.

ENCHANTED CATNIP GARDENS FOR CATS

Cats are the most familiar familiar for Witches!

Lay smooth crystals into a spiral in the dirt or in a box and plant or place a pot of fresh growing catnip in the centre. Your cat familiar will love rubbing their face in the catnip and their physical form will be energised by the crystals as they writhe in nip ecstasy.

YOUR FAMILIAR'S ROLE IN RITUAL

For a long time I had two snakes – a five-foot-long coastal carpet python named Sebastian … who was a loveable thing but not my familiar, and Lulu, a small desert python who was my familiar. I would save Lulu's skin when she shed, and use it in rituals. Consider working with the shed body bits of your familiar to give your spells and rituals extra power. The skin of a snake, the fur of a dog or cat, the hoof filings of a pig or horse or feathers from your bird familiar can be placed in amulets and pouches, sprinkled around or placed under candles or buried in dirt to purify and release for energies to be reborn positively. Consider how your familiar offers appropriate body bits and use them in your spells and rituals, with gratitude.

QUESTION: *if your significant animal other is clearly not a familiar, how can you make your regular pet's life magickal? (By the way, the following is also great to do with your familiar and will only enhance your established magickal bond.)*

ANSWER: gently massage your significant animal other, visualising pure blue or white glowing light moving from your hands into them whilst you align with them energetically. Hold them during your meditations and align your breathing with theirs to automatically enhance your magickal potential together. Feed your pets and familiars pure quality foods, not cheap commercial pet food that has colouring, sugar and additives. And most importantly, love them unconditionally like they love you.

2019| CARLA RAELENE, AGE 16

Dear Fiona,

How do you usually tell if someone is your soul mate? What are the signs? Do you know much about this kind of thing ...?

Love and Light, xxoo

One thing I've learned in the 20 years since originally writing this book is that it is possible to have more than one soul mate ... and preferable, too, as we humans live very long physical lives now, and whilst it is possible to have a deep soul love connection with one person, it's also totally possible to have more than one.

As to the signs that someone is your soul mate ... well, you might just have a strong gut instinct when you look into their eyes. There may be eerie similarities in your backgrounds, extremely similar taste in things, and then there is that ability to read the other's mind and finish each other's sentences. In these hyper-connected times, an individual will 'know' 100 times more people than they would have just 10 years ago by virtue of the internet, online dating and social media. It's worth considering, too, that even the closest friends can drift away sometimes. Ultimately, I think every human has lots of soul mates, lots of people to bond with, share energy with, learn from and love.

2004 | CASSANDRA, AGED 11

Dear Fiona,

My name is Cassandra, I'm 11 years old and I have recently become interested in Witchcraft, particularly spells, the tools of Witchcraft, and their unique properties. Here are some questions I thought might be good to include in your new book.

Is Wicca and Witchcraft the same thing?

Could you tell me something about Pagan and Satanic practices and how they differ from Witchcraft? Where are the best places for performing spells and rituals? And do you need to open and close a circle when doing spells?

Thank you for taking the time to read my questions. I hope they will be useful for your book.

Witchcraft is a spiritual path and Wicca is the religion of Witchcraft, like Catholicism is a religion that is part of the path of Christianity.

Within Wicca there are traditions … like Alexandrian, Gardnerian and Dianic. These traditions were forged by individuals who created methods, teachings and disciplines to unify people and practices to explore the path of Witchcraft together.

As such, all the traditions and disciplines are part of the same whole, but there are just different ways of viewing, exploring and contributing to this whole.

Witches don't have to be religious and practise Wicca. I am spiritual, not religious, and as such I am not Wiccan – although I know a lot about the religion. I am a Witch walking her path in a spiritual way.

Wicca

◇◇◇

The US government first officially recognised Wicca as a religion in 1985. In a court case involving a prisoner (*Dettmer v Landon*) the federal government argued that the doctrine of the Church of Wicca was not a religion because it is a 'conglomeration' of 'various aspects of the occult, such as faith healing, self-hypnosis, tarot card reading, and spell casting, none of which would be considered religious practices standing alone'. The court noted that the government was essentially arguing 'that because it finds witchcraft to be illogical and internally inconsistent, witchcraft cannot be a religion'. The appeals court ruled that 'the Church of Wicca occupies a place in the lives of its members parallel to that of more conventional religions. Consequently, its doctrine must be considered a religion.'

The origins of the word 'Pagan' are from the fourth century AD and originally meant 'heathen' and described a person who did not follow the world's major religions. It was, therefore, a derogatory term. In addition, the Christians who coined the term observed the Romans worshipping multiple Gods (practising Polytheism). So, Pagans were also

considered Polytheistic. More recently, Pagans have been described as people who honour nature as sacred … so that could mean every Witch is a Pagan. But not all Witches recognise multiple Gods and Goddesses (some, for example, specifically only recognise The Lady and The Lord), so it can all start to get somewhat convoluted calling all Witches Pagan! The truth lies somewhere in the middle. The reinterpretation of meaning in our magickal community is exciting to me because it indicates growth, evolution and expansion. In fact, the Oxford Dictionary's latest definition of Paganism is: 'Belonging or relating to a modern religion that includes beliefs and activities that are not from any of the main religions of the world, for example the worship of nature.'

From *Patheos.com*, an excellent online resource for the magickal community: 'Paganism today is constantly evolving and growing. Wicca has evolved into

myriad strains, and the broader Pagan movement has built upon and expanded beyond Wicca and Witchcraft. Several Druid traditions are thriving, and the old ceremonial magick lodges like the Golden Dawn and Ordo Templi Orientis have seen a resurgence since their original heydays. The revival of ancient paganism has spurred incredible growth in the Heathen, Hellenic, Celtic Reconstructionism and religion Romana communities. Unbroken traditions of indigenous religions such as Vodou, Santeria, and African Traditional

Religions have a voice in the world religious community like never before.'

It's a fascinating time to be Pagan.

Satanic practices evolved as mostly a knee-jerk reaction to Christianity and are not based on real Witchcraft. Most recognisably, the Church of Satan was formed in 1966 by Anton LaVey and received notoriety but did not establish itself as a sustainable, bonafide religion. More recently in 2013, the Satanic Temple was formed as an official house of worship. In May 2019 it received tax-exempt status from the United States Internal Revenue Service. But they are not a part of Modern Witchcraft and do not practise Witchcraft. Interestingly, they are atheists and do not believe in Satan as an entity.

The best places for performing spells or rituals is out in nature, but any space can be cleansed and consecrated to work in – that's what a Circle-casting ritual does. As I write in the chapter 'Circle Casting and the Tools of Witchcraft' there are different methods for casting Circle, and I have also suggested a couple of less-complicated options for Teen Witches. Not every spell and ritual requires you to cast Circle, though it's often preferable because it helps to intensify energies and make workings more effective.

What's the difference between religion and spirituality?

RELIGION: this is a specific set of organised beliefs and practices, usually shared by a community or group.

SPIRITUALITY: this is more of an individual practice and has to do with having a sense of peace and purpose.

2019| LEIJA, AGED 16

Dear Fiona

How do I find a Coven to join?

   And what should I look for when doing so (ie: should I be careful)?

   Lejla

I recommend reaching out to online magickal communities congregating on social media, like Facebook, more so than hashtagging on Instagram. Engaging in meaningful dialogue, and not just posting aesthetically pleasing photos, will help a lot in making connections that can lead to growing your magickal family. If anyone demands lots of money or tells you that you have to do things that you know in your heart are questionable or wrong – or if your gut just tells you something is 'off' – then that is not a Coven or group you want to be a part of.

2004| SAM, AGED 14

Dear Fiona,

Do I have to join a Coven in order to be a real Witch?

Dear Sam,

   No, you don't have to join a Coven – though if you do join a traditional Coven you will likely learn a lot of interesting things. But you can be a Witch by reading, researching and practising on your own and with other Witches. You could also consider forming your own Coven with a group of Witch friends who don't practise a formal tradition but who you are likely to work and grow magickally with. Teen Witch Coven meetings could be as simple as having a potluck meal together, doing each other's astrology charts and reading oracle cards together.

2019 | RAIN, AGED 14

Dear Fiona!!

U're definitely my fav witch :) i have just discovered the Craft for half a year, and only own 2 books, which are yours! You have given me so much inspiration and insight. I just want to say thank you so much! i also have a query that i've been wondering about for a whilst. i am Chinese and immigrated to Australia a few years ago. i have been wondering if it would be OK to write Chinese in my BOS or use Chinese in invocations, etc. i've been doing it, but not so sure about if it's appropriate to do that.

Love you, and thanx 4 ur time :)

Rain

It's absolutely fine! Your Book of Shadows (BOS) is your personal record of your magickal work and journey as a Witch. How you want to express yourself in it is up to you. I love that you express your cultural heritage on your path! Whilst much of the Witchcraft we know (and especially it's religion, Wicca) is heavily influenced by ancient Celtic, Nordic and classical religious beliefs, the Craft is a truly multicultural spiritual path and is enriched by the culture of every person drawn to its ways. In recent decades, the Craft has been blessed by wider teachings from Aboriginal, Native American, Slavic and African cultures, to name just a few, and there are now so many Jewish Wiccans that they coined the word 'Jewitch' to describe themselves!

Personally, I would love to hear Witchy invocations and chants in Chinese!

2019 | KAODORITE (MEANS 'DANCER OF THE FIRE' IN JAPANESE), AGED 17

Dear Fiona, I have a question for your book:

Sometimes when I was just beginning (and even now, when I've been pagan for years) I started to believe that you're just making it all up, that magick didn't exist and the Lady and Lord weren't within me.

When I start to doubt like that, it sometimes takes me a really long time before I feel the magickal charge again. Did you ever doubt yourself and your path like that, and if you did, how do you handle it?

By the way – thank you for this book on behalf of everyone who is going through now what I did when I was younger and trying to find my path whilst everyone told me that I wasn't old enough to believe in anything. I'll still appreciate it because I haven't completely grown out of my indecision and doubt.

I often fell in and out of the Craft when I first started, especially if something went really bad. This was before I had fully comprehended the cyclical nature of living and the light and dark aspects of the path. I thought Witchcraft was like a big band-aid that would cover up all the hard stuff and give me easy answers. But the best thing about it is that it's not like this! In my adult life, after I became a commercial pilot, I felt I had to hang my broomstick up for a plane because I was worried I would not be taken seriously by my peers. But it was soon revealed to me that I have always been, and always will be, a Witch. My professional career is just that – my career – and I am legally afforded the rights to align myself with the spiritual path of my choice. My last boss said, 'I don't care what you call yourself as long as you can fly the airplane safely.'

Every moment of every day I sense inside and around me a Higher Power of my understanding and the Divine miracle that life on our planet and beyond is … and that all humans are a part of that. As a mature adult I try to stay out of the way and be a channel for this Divine force rather than letting my ego get involved and trying to micro-manage the world. But when you are a teenager and setting your personal boundaries and learning about parameters, then you will try to direct this energy. That is the way things are meant to be as we come to know ourselves.

When my magickal charge is low, I take time out and bond with nature (check out the chapter 'It's Only Natural'). I also devoutly practise yoga as a spiritual discipline — not a workout — and a way to connect and amplify my Craft as a Witch.

You are young and you're going to find the Craft will get easier and harder in ways you can't anticipate in the coming years. Hang in there, and don't be rigid with your beliefs and expectations. Allow them to shift and evolve and reflect your growth as a human and Witch.

In 2019 I wrote my manifesto *The Art of Witch* (Rockpool Publishing). It addresses a lot of what I'm saying here and your concerns. Although it's written for a mature human with some life experience under their belt, sometimes age really is just a number. So this book could be helpful for you also.

2019 | KRISTEN, AGED 17

Fiona, I would like to ask your advice in how to handle a problem as you may have come across something similar before. My long time boyfriend is a Christian and believes that witches worship the devil and he really hates it when I look at anything in a shop which has something to do with Witchcraft. How can I make him feel better about Witchcraft?

Kristen

Give him this book to read! Or perhaps my first book: *Witch: A Personal Journey*, in which I interview real Satanists and show how they have nothing to do with Witchcraft. As I have said many a time to my parents – especially the first time they hassled me about my Craft – 'You have more to do with Satan than I do, you're Christian. I don't believe in Satan. He's a part of your religion, not mine!'

You could tell him that Paganism (which modern Witchcraft has its roots in) has older origins than Christianity, and a lot of the Pagan Gods and Goddesses, as well as Pagan holy days and festivals, were absorbed into the Christian tradition and just given different names.

You might also remind him that more people than ever have suffered and died in the name of the Christian God than in the name of the Witches' Goddess, and that even Pope John Paul II at the time of writing the first version of this book apologised for the abominations of the Witch hunts of the Dark Ages. Recently, environmentalist Pope Francis referred to his 'God' as the 'ultimate source of life' and then went on to proclaim that 'the earth is a source of life for the entire human family' and as such 'some people worship in nature'. In saying this he gave Witches and indigenous religions the thumbs up.

But perhaps instead of simply trying to out-argue your boyfriend, you'd do better to point out that Witches strongly adhere to the notion that there's enough room in the world for everyone's beliefs and you'll let him get on with his if he lets you get on with yours. Really, the only aspect of certain forms of Christianity that Witches take exception to is their contempt for the deeply held beliefs of others.

That's not to say that all Christians advocate narrow-mindedness; many do take the words of their gentle, compassionate founder to heart, and there's a new type of Christian who not only tolerates but welcomes Witches in the world.

In the end, the best (though by no means the easiest!) way to deal with ignorance and prejudice is with knowledge and love.

2020 | HOLLY, AGED 10

Fiona, you are my inspiration just when i have only read 2 of your books: witch — a summerland mystery, and witch — a magickal journey. I love them and think they are both so well written. I especially like a bit of mystery. I feel a bit weird because i have only recently discovered witchcraft and i am only 10. At school, only my friend Rosie deeply knows about it and my friend Daisy a little less. Some of the people in my class saw what i was reading - witch a magickal journey and spells for teenage witches by Marina Baker. I know the second book isn't by you, nor am i a teenager. I hope you don't take it personally. In witch a magickal journey, i skipped the two chapters labeled magickal sex and magickal drugs - my mum is a chiropractor! But anyway, some of the people in my class have made fun of me a bit. I would do a spell but i am worried it will backfire plus i do not have an athame because my mum thinks i am not old enough. I just need a witches help. Please will you help me?

Also it was amazing when I read in your first book that you went to that naked Coven thing whilst you were on holiday with strangers! I am just inspired by your trust and affinity with people, and i think it is amazing that you have a snake called Lulu! I used to have a friend called Lulu, but she moved away, taking one of my favourite angel necklaces with her! I still wonder if my familiar is my dog Sadie, but then you said that thing that pets could just just be pets. And i am sad to say that i don't think Sadie will still be living when i am older. I hope she comes back as a whale or something that i can call on if i am sad. Thank you for being part of finding who i am. I really feel connected to witchcraft, and your book was the first one i saw when i looked!

Oh, and is there a spell for healing someones spine? my mum has hurt her back. She is a wonderful chiropractor but she cannot give an adjustment to herself! She has to wait until this Wednesday, but even i can't wait that long! I can't even give her a hug without it hurting! Thank you.

love from Holly xoxo :):):)

Hello Holly,

Thank you for writing to me and I'm thrilled to be a light on your path.

I appreciate you having a 'maturity compass' regarding a couple of the chapters in *Witch: A Magickal Journey*. Yes, it is a book for a more mature Witch in physical years.

I'm so happy you are feeling fulfilled as you set out on your life's magickal path.

To answer your questions: regarding people making fun of you . . . just have compassion for their fear and lack of education on the subject. Your magick is between you and the Universe, so you don't need anyone's approval. Just ignore the people who tease you – it's important in life to stick with the people (Witches and non-Witches) who make you smile, not frown!

You don't need an athame at this point: because of its symbolism it would be more appropriate to have one after you have crossed the magick bridge of puberty. So not for another few years.

I suggest you use a wooden wand instead of an athame – or even your pointed finger can work to channel energy. You can make a wand yourself by finding a strong straight stick, sanding it smooth and carving or writing your initials onto it. Maybe bind a crystal to it, or decorate it in any natural magick way you like.

Rather than a spell right now, perform a ritual of gratitude for all the good things in your life. That positive energy will put a shield around you and deflect any negativity.

⊕ Ritual of Gratitude

- Write a list of all the things that you are grateful for.
- Kiss the list three times.
- Place the list under a white candle that has your initials carved into it.
- Light the candle on a full moon and let it burn for at least one hour.
- Snuff the candle and then roll the list up and place it under your pillow for seven nights.
- There will be no more negativity projected at you.

It's so interesting you had a friend and she took your necklace . . . she needed the guidance more than you did. As witches we know that when things move on — whether that be people, things . . . anything, really – it's an opportunity to understand that its role is finished in our lives and it's needed elsewhere. There is always something positive that comes from even the most difficult experiences in life . . . everything is ultimately transformed to love because that is what the Universe is made of.

If you would like to offer healing energy to your mum, I recommend this ritual: light a white or blue candle that has both your initials carved into it. Have your mother sit in a comfortable chair. Sit next to her and place your left hand (your lunar healing hand) over the area that is painful for her (she can also lay down if this is more comfortable for her). Ask her for permission to offer healing energy.

This is important, for any spell or ritual offered directly to another should have their consent when possible for best effect.

For five to 10 minutes hold your hand gently a few centimetres over the painful area and focus your mind and heart so they are connected on the love you have for your mum and your true desire for her to be pain free, comfortable and happy. See that energy shine out of your hand into your mum. Relax and do your best to stay focused. Don't force it.

The Universe will help you.

When you are ready to finish, press your hand firmly but gently on her back to seal the healing ritual and slowly get up and together blow out the candle flame to blow away any pain or residual energy. The element of fire (which is the candle) transforms and heals, too.

I hope you both enjoy doing this together. I recommend doing this once a day for seven days, or as long as you both like or until your mum's back is feeling a lot better.

2020 | ARDEN, AGED 18

Here's a question...what counts as an altar? I feel like I already have had an altar but idk. Got a little corner in my room with my incense, tarot cards, a pedestal with candles on it, gypsy witch cards, and some crystals, and a mineral stone from my birthplace. I like to meditate and face the corner idk why I just do. But idk if it's an altar HAHA

Dear Arden

That counts as an altar!!! As far as elemental alignment:

INCENSE: AIR

CANDLES: FIRE

CRYSTALS AND MINERAL STONE: EARTH

CARDS: SPIRIT

So all that is missing is water . . . what could you add to represent water?

Dear Fiona

I live on a boat and am surrounded by water, so I could use a piece of sea glass that is the color of the ocean!

Love Arden

www.fionahorne.com

Visit my website for easy links to get my other books, regular updates on what I've been getting up to, and where I may be making personal appearances –
I would love to meet you!

All my socials – Instagram, Facebook, Tumblr and Twitter – are also linked on my website, and there are links to all my TV appearances over the years and music and media . . . lots of stuff!